Books by Robert Claiborne

Loose Cannons and Red Herrings: A Book of Lost Metaphors (1988)

Saying What You Mean: A Commonsense Guide to American Usage (1986)

Our Marvelous Native Tongue: The Life and Times of the English Language (1983)

Mysteries of the Past, with Lionel Casson and Brian Fagen (1977)

The Summer Stargazer: Astronomy for Absolute Beginners (1975)

The Birth of Writing (1975)

God or Beast: Evolution and Human Nature (1974)

The First Americans (1973)

On Every Side the Sea (1971)

Climate, Man and History (1970)

Drugs (1969)

Time (1967)

Texts

Cell Membranes, with Gerald Weissmann, M.D. (1975)

Medical Genetics, with Victor McKusick, M.D. (1973)

The Roots of English

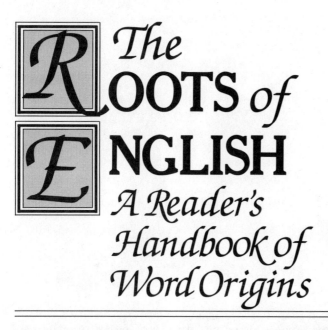

The Roots of English

A Reader's Handbook of Word Origins

ROBERT CLAIBORNE

Times BOOKS

Copyright © 1989 by Robert Claiborne
All rights reserved under International and Pan-American Copyright
Conventions. Published in the United States by Times Books, a
division of Random House, Inc., New York, and simultaneously in
Canada by Random House of Canada Limited, Toronto.

Library of Congress Cataloging-in-Publication Data

Claiborne, Robert.
The roots of English.

Includes index.
1. English language—Roots—Dictionaries. 2. English
language—Etymology—Dictionaries. 3. English language—
Word formation—Dictionaries. I. Title.
PE1580.C56   1989   422'.03   88-40498
ISBN 0-8129-1716-2

Designed by Leon Bolognese

Manufactured in the United States of America

First Edition

*To the millions of men and women,
known and unknown, who over the long
centuries have made English the
marvelous communicative instrument it is.*

ACKNOWLEDGMENTS

Peggy Dye did most of the work of transferring the "basic" material—the roots and the words derived from them—onto disk, thereby saving me several weeks of "hard labor."

CONTENTS

The Roots of English

INTRODUCTION

Ye knowe ek that in forme of speche is chaunge
Within a thousand yeer, and wordes tho
That hadden prys now wonder nyce and straunge
Us thinketh hem, and yet they spake hem so.

You know that even forms of speech can change
Within a thousand years, and words we know
Were useful once, seem to us wondrous strange—
Foolish or forced—and yet men spoke them so.
—CHAUCER

THE ENGLISH LANGUAGE HAS FAR MORE WORDS THAN ANY other tongue on earth. Our most comprehensive lexicon, the *Oxford English Dictionary*, lists no fewer than 600,000 words used in English writing since the twelfth century, of which perhaps 450,000 are still in current use. French speakers must make do with less than a third of that number, and Russians with only a quarter.

Anyone at all interested in our extraordinary native tongue must at some point have wondered where on earth all these words came from. The answer is: almost everywhere. "Alcohol" and "alkali" are from Arabic; "amok," from Malay; "bizarre," from the mysterious Basque tongue of northern Spain. "Coach" comes from a Hungarian town; "parka," from the Samoyedes of the northern Urals; "skunk" and "chile" from the Native Americans; and "taboo" from Tahitian. "Okay" was brought into English by slaves from West Africa; "corral," by Mexican cattlemen— who learned it from Portuguese sailors, who learned it from the Hottentot herders of southern Africa.

But though English has plundered the whole earth for words, such exotic birds of passage account for only a small fraction of its oversize lexicon. The overwhelming majority of our words come from three root sources.

The first is the extinct tongue called Primitive Germanic, ancestor not only of English but of modern German, Dutch, Yiddish, and the Scandinavian tongues. The thousands of Germanic words in English include most of its "basic" vocabulary: names for most parts of the body (arm, head, brain, eye), family terms (father, mother, brother, sister), scores of everyday verbs (have, be, come, go, look, know), and every one of our pronouns (I, you, he, she, this, that, which). Also Germanic are nearly all our prepositions (to, for, in, etc.) and conjunctions (and, but, if, etc.)—the inconspicuous but utterly essential linguistic "particles" without which nobody could construct an English sentence.

The second root source of our words is Latin—the language of the western Roman Empire—and its descendants, French, Italian, and Spanish. Collectively, Latin and the Romance tongues have contributed more than half our words, some of them literary or scholarly but many both plain and simple—as are the two adjectives I've just used ("plain" is from Latin; "simple," from French).

The third root of English, less important than the other two but still substantial, is Greek, a version of which was spoken all around the eastern Mediterranean in Roman times. Greek words have reached English both indirectly, through Latin (to which it contributed hundreds of terms), and directly—notably, from English-speaking physicians and scientists, who have drawn heavily on Greek roots to construct their specialized vocabularies.

Even more remarkable is that all three of these root sources—Germanic, Latin, and Greek—can be traced back to a single "taproot": the ancient tongue known as Indo-European. This language, like Primitive Germanic, is lost—that is, it was never written down. But over the past two centuries, scholars, by comparing and analyzing similar words in its daughter tongues, have reconstructed much of its vocabulary and syntax. Indo-European has contributed, through one route or another, at least 80 percent of our English words.

But how do we know this? On what evidence can we say—as scholars do say—that a single tongue, which no living person has ever heard or read, is the source of nearly all our English words? In a word, through similarities.

If you have even a slight acquaintance with other languages, you know that some of them resemble each other— and that some of the resemblances are more marked than others. Nearly all of us, for example, have been exposed, through books, films, and TV, to both British and American English, and have learned that they differ in some ways, though they are alike in many more. History tells us why: both come from the same source—the seventeenth-century English that British settlers brought to the east coast of North America.

Likewise, if you have even a smattering of both French and Spanish (or French and Italian, or Italian and Spanish), you must have noticed that they are not only alike but more alike than either is like English. Again, the reason is their common source: the Vulgar (popular) Latin that Roman soldiers, traders, and colonists carried from Italy into much of western Europe around the beginning of the Christian Era.

These linguistic relationships are obvious because we can look up the answers in the back of the (history) book. For more remote relationships, such as exist among English, Latin, and Greek, we lack any such crib sheet: it took a man endowed with both scholarship and imagination to perceive them and to deduce their origin.

The begetter of this great leap forward in linguistics was a British man of letters, Sir William Jones, who in the late eighteenth century served as a judge in British India. Jones was interested in Indian languages—notably, the most ancient of them, Sanskrit, in which the earliest surviving Indian documents were written.

Like many other educated Englishmen of his time, Jones knew both Latin and Greek, and as his studies in Sanskrit progressed, he was startled to discover similarities between it and the two classical tongues. Sanskrit *trayas* (three) resembled Latin *tres* and Greek *trias*, Sanskrit *sarpa* (snake) was clearly akin to Latin *serpens*, Sanskrit *devas* (god) was close to Latin *divus* (divine), and so with hundreds of other words.

In 1786 he presented his conclusions to a meeting of the Asiatick Society of Calcutta, in a paper that can fairly be said to mark the beginning of modern historical linguistics. Sanskrit, he declared, bears to both Greek and Latin "a stronger affinity, both in the roots of verbs and in the forms of grammar, than could possibly have been produced by accident; so strong, indeed, that no philologer could examine them all three, without believing them to have sprung from some common source which, perhaps, no longer exists." He found similar though less marked affinities between Sanskrit and the Celtic and Germanic tongues.

Jones's brilliant conjecture has been confirmed and documented by two centuries of scholarly research. We now know that his "common source"—which, indeed, no longer exists—was the ancestor not merely of Latin, Greek, and English but also of the Baltic and Slavonic tongues, the Iranian languages of western Asia, and, through Sanskrit, of nearly all the languages used in the central and northern parts of the Indian subcontinent. Altogether, its daughter tongues are spoken by about half the human race. The "common source" itself is variously known as Common Indo-European, Parent Indo-European, or simply Indo-European.

Indo-European was never written down. Yet scholars, by comparing "cognates"—words of similar sound and sense—in some of the older Indo-European tongues (they include Sanskrit, Hittite, Old Latin, Gothic, and Old English), have reconstructed much of its grammar and some two thousand of the fundamental word-roots from which its vocabulary was derived. It is these ancient Indo-European roots, proliferating over the centuries into tens of thousands of limbs, branches, and twigs, that are the ultimate roots of English (and, of course, of all the other modern Indo-European tongues). They, and the English words descended from them, are the subject of this book.

The Indo-Europeans and Their Language

Before examining these ultimate roots, however, let us take a look at the people who used them.* Though we don't—can't—know for sure when or where the Indo-Europeans lived, we can make some pretty good guesses: if you know the words a people used, you know what they talked about—meaning that you have a pretty good idea of what they saw (in particular, their physical environment) and what they did (their way of life).

The "environmental" terms in Indo-European (notably, its names for trees) tell us that its speakers lived somewhere in inland eastern Europe. The most likely region (though some disagree) is the valley of the middle Danube, where the

*Since I have discussed the Indo-Europeans at some length in an earlier book, *Our Marvelous Native Tongue: The Life and Times of the English Language* (New York: Times Books, 1983), the following account will be rather summary.

so-called Danubian or Linear Pottery culture flourished in the centuries just after 6000 B.C.

The archaeological remains of the Danubians and the linguistic "remains" of the Indo-Europeans agree in telling us that these people were farmers; indeed, they were the first farmers in that part of the world. Farming—agriculture and stock raising—was "invented" around 8000 B.C., in the subtropical lands of the Near East, and spread fairly quickly around the eastern Mediterranean. But it was the Danubians who adapted this "new" technology to the rather different climatic conditions north of the Mediterranean basin.

The Danubian–Indo-European farmers raised wheat, barley, and perhaps rye, along with legumes—fava (broad) beans, peas, and perhaps lentils. They herded cattle, sheep, goats, and swine, and gathered wild apples and cherries, along with honey from wild bees, some of which they fermented into mead. They lived in houses framed with timber, walled with mud-plastered wattle, and roofed with thatch.

They were also among the first—perhaps the very first—farmers to use the plow: that is, to apply animal power to raising food; thanks in part to this technologic revolution, their agriculture was notably productive for its time. More food meant more people, who, inevitably, spread out over the centuries.

By around 3500 B.C., groups of Indo-European migrants had taken over nearly all of northwestern Europe except the Scandinavian peninsula. Conquest of the more densely populated Mediterranean lands took longer, but by 2000 B.C. most of Greece was "Indo-Europeanized," and not long afterward the same fate befell Italy. Meanwhile, other groups of emigrants had pushed far across the Russian steppes into central Asia, while others had wandered southeast into Asia Minor, Iran, and India, which they reached around 1500 B.C.

The migrants, of course, took their language with them. What sort of language was it?

The most succinct thing we can say about it is that it was very unlike English, in both sounds (phonetics) and syntax. Phonetically, it lacked our consonants F, V, and the two we spell TH (as in "THin" and "THis"). Conversely, at least half a dozen of its consonants are strange to us—notably, the "aspirates" BH, DH, and GH (pronounced roughly like B, D, and G followed by a puff of breath), and the even more obscure "laryngeals." These, say the experts, had an H-like sound, but could also serve as vowels—and if you find this confusing, so do I!

Indo-European syntax also differed radically from ours, notably in its heavy use of inflection: changing the ending of a word, or its vowel(s), to indicate its relationship to other words in the sentence. Readers who've studied Latin will recognize this device immediately: thus Latin *homo* (man) must be the subject of a verb; *hominem*, a verb's direct object, and *homini*, its indirect object, while *hominis* shows that the man possessed some other noun in the sentence.

Other inflections modified the meaning of the word, rather than showing its relationship to other words, as with English "sing" (present) and "sang" (past); the same device could shift a word from one grammatical category to another, as with our "sing" (verb) and "song" (noun). Other changes were produced by suffixes, which could change verbs to nouns, active voice to passive voice, and so on. (One of the few English examples of such a suffix is "-ly," which converts adjectives into adverbs—for example, quick-ly.)

By these and other devices the two thousand or so basic Indo-European roots that have been reconstructed (plus, no doubt, others now completely lost) begot at least ten times that number of actual words, just as English "mother" has also given us "to mother," "motherly," "motherhood," and "mothering." Even the most "primitive" peoples today have vocabularies of around twenty thousand words, and there is no reason to suppose that the Indo-European lexicon was any less copious.

As the Indo-Europeans spread beyond their original homeland, their tongue split into dialects (as with American and British English), which eventually evolved into separate languages (as with the Romance tongues). Moreover, as happens with all languages, their words changed in both sound and sense, often to the point where the relationships among their descendants can be established only by very sophisticated analysis.

The analysis rests on a fundamental principle of historical linguistics: when the sounds of a language change, they almost never do so at random, but systematically. That is (to simplify somewhat), a given change will affect not just some words in a language but nearly all words where that sound occurs.

It is the systematic nature of sound changes that enables us to establish relationships among otherwise dissimilar words in different tongues. On the face of it, "foot" seems unrelated to the "pod-" in "podiatrist," though we know that a podiatrist treats foot ailments. But when we find dozens of similar pairs, such as "fire" and "pyr-" (as in "pyromaniac") and "five" and "penta-" (as in "pentagon"), the relationship becomes clear: in each case, initial F in one word equals initial P in the other. From other evidence, we can deduce that P was the original sound, which in the Germanic branch of Indo-European changed to F.

Changes in meaning are sometimes harder to elucidate—in part because we often can't be sure what the original Indo-European word meant. See, for example, the root **AIW-** in the Dictionary of Roots, which, judging from the meanings of its descendants, may have meant youth, vital force, life, long life, even eternity—or any of the above.

In short, relating the ultimate Indo-European roots of English to modern English words is often a matter for experts—and, for nonexperts, requires a certain faith that the experts know what they're talking about. Usually they do, but (as we'll see later on) there are not a few cases where they themselves concede they're not sure—and others where I think they should have said so but didn't.

Now let us take a closer look at the three great streams that have brought ancestral Indo-European into English.

The Germanic Connection

The Germanic strain in English accounts for only a minor part of our vocabulary; nonetheless, English is classified as a Germanic tongue, and for good reason. First, our Germanic words, though only a minority in our dictionaries, paradoxically make up a majority of the words we speak or write. A computerized study carried out some years ago revealed that of the hundred English words we use most often, every one was Germanic, while of the second hundred, eighty-three were Germanic.

If you need further evidence—the preceding paragraph contains eighty words; sixty of them are Germanic.

Moreover, if we compare the grammars of English and (say) modern German, we find that though they differ in many ways they are still more alike than the grammars of Indo-European but non-Germanic languages such as French or Spanish. For example, both English and German words are typically accented on the first syllable, rather than the last (French) or next-to-last (Spanish). Again, we say sing/sang/sung, and the Germans, *singen/sang/gesungen*; the French say *chanter/chantai/chanté* (all, by the way, pronounced identically), and Hispanics, *cantar/canté/cantado*.

As I've already noted, the Germanic words in English include many of our simplest, most everyday words, including nearly all our particles. The Germanic connection has supplied only a relatively small part of the "body" of English, but that part includes something absolutely essential: the skeleton that holds it together.

The primitive Germans (not to be confused with the modern Germans, who are only one group of their linguistic descendants) began as a tribe of Indo-Europeans who moved north from their ancestral homeland some time after 6000 B.C. By around 5300 B.C., their cultural and physical descendants were well established in parts of what are now southern Poland and East Germany. After more centuries, *their* cultural descendants (or some of them) had reached a new frontier: the Baltic Sea.

Neither these "proto-Germans" nor, probably, their Indo-European ancestors knew anything of the sea, and their new, maritime environment confronted them with numbers of things they'd never seen before. They thereupon did what people in foreign lands usually do under such circumstances: asked the natives "What do you call that?"—and added the new word (probably mispronounced) to their vocabulary. These additions included the ancestors of such English words as "herring," "sturgeon," "seal," "eider," "auk," and "ship"—and, not least, the name of the sea itself (see **SAIWAZ** in the Dictionary of Roots).

Along with new animals they found new technologies. Like their ancestors along the Danube, they had watercraft of some sort, but these were almost certainly no more than dugout canoes. The peoples along the Baltic shore had larger craft that they called *skipam* (whence "ship")—or anyway, that's how the newcomers pronounced it.*

---

*Words or roots preceded by an asterisk, such as *skipam*, are semiconjectural. That is, they are not based on written documents but have been "reconstructed" by comparing words descended from them.

The proto-Germans kept on moving, and shortly after 4000 B.C. reached what would be their homeland for nearly four thousand years thereafter: modern Denmark and north-west Germany. But this area was already populated fairly densely by people who knew something of farming; for reasons I've given elsewhere, I call them the Folk.

Whether the Germanic conquest of the Folk was peaceful or violent we have no way of knowing. What seems certain is that the two peoples fairly quickly became one, marrying each other's sons and daughters—and borrowing each other's words. And not just names for new things—exotic animals and technologies—but simple, everyday terms, the kind that are normally among the most "conservative" (rarely replaced) in any language.

These included the ancestors of "wife," "bride," and "child"—plus a word for "boy" (*knapon*) that eventually ended up as English "knave." (If you have male children, you can perhaps guess how this shift in meaning came about.) No less conservative are names for parts of the body, yet the "Folkish" contribution to Germanic includes the sources of "hand," "shoulder," "leg," "bone," and "womb."

Other borrowings from Folkish include the originals of "rise," "leap," "near," "like," "all," "sick," and dozens more. Whenever you see in the Dictionary an entry classed as Germanic (for example, **Germanic HUSAM**) you're probably looking at what was once a Folkish word.

The borrowed words in the Proto-Germanic vocabulary are interesting but not very surprising—no more so than American terms such as "canyon," "ranch," and "stampede," whose originals were borrowed by English-speaking settlers in the Old Southwest from its Mexican residents. Far more remarkable—indeed, totally inexplicable—are a series of phonetic changes that radically modified the original sounds of Indo-European.

Indo-European employed some eighteen consonants, if we exclude W and Y—which, as in English, could serve as either consonants or vowels—and the mysterious laryngeals. By the time Proto-Germanic had become Primitive Germanic, no less than half the eighteen had changed.

First, P, T, and K evolved into F, TH, and H. We can see the effect of these changes clearly when we compare English words of Germanic origin with similar ones derived from Latin, in which the changes did not occur. Thus Germanic "FaTHeRly" is equivalent to Latin "PaTeRnal," and English "HoRN" is close to Latin "CoRNet." For further examples, consult the Dictionary of Roots under these letters.

(An important point to keep in mind is that to make sense of these and the many other phonetic changes that have occurred since Indo-European times, you must focus on the consonants, not the vowels. The latter, for some reason, are much less "stable" than the former; for example, the phonetic differences among modern varieties of English— e.g., Cockney, Scots, New England, Deep South, Australian—involve the vowels almost exclusively.)

Generations or centuries later—nobody has any notion when—another consonant shift occurred among the ancestral Germans: Indo-European B, D, and G evolved into P, T, and K, thereby "replacing" the consonants lost in the earlier shift. Again we can trace the changes by comparing modern words of Germanic and Latin origin (technically, such pairs are called "doublets"), as with "CoRN" and "GRaiN"— which is what "corn" still means in Britain—and "TooTH" and "DenTist."

Still later, these "lost" consonants, too, were replaced, when the Indo-European aspirates BH, DH, and GH became B, D, and G. Here, unfortunately, we have no convenient doublets to illustrate the changes, since the aspirates also changed in Latin (as in most other Indo-European tongues), albeit in different ways.

These phonetic changes, which collectively are known as the Great Consonant Shift, radically altered the sounds of Proto-Germanic into what we can now call Primitive Germanic or simply Germanic. When they occurred, or how rapidly, we have no way of knowing—nor has anyone ever explained convincingly why they occurred at all. Indeed, phonetic changes that have occurred even within the past few centuries are no less mysterious.

(To help you keep track of these sound changes, I've tabulated them, along with other changes that occurred—or, more often, didn't—in Greek and Latin, on pages 35–39.)

Around the beginning of the Christian Era, the primitive Germans began to expand to the south, east, and west. Why this happened is uncertain; an improvement in climate (and therefore in food supplies) may have had something to do with it. So far as the English language is concerned, the important thing is that the expansion brought the Germans into contact—sometimes collision—with people speaking a very different (though still Indo-European) language: the Romans. What this contact did to Primitive Germanic we'll see later.

A few centuries later, the decline of Roman power allowed a group of Germanic tribes living along the North Sea coast to migrate into the island of Britain, then inhabited by peoples speaking Celtic languages akin to modern Welsh and Breton. The newcomers spoke a tongue they called English but which we call Old English—the direct ancestor of the English we speak today.

More Germanic Connections

The Germanic connection did not end with the migration of the English into Britain. Within a few centuries, another Germanic people invaded the island: the piratical Northmen (or Norsemen), speaking the tongue we call Old Norse (it is the ancestor of modern Swedish, Danish, Norwegian, and Icelandic).

The Norsemen conquered large parts of northern and central Britain, but within a few generations evolved from bloodthirsty pirates into peaceful settlers who intermarried with their English neighbors, much as the proto-Germans and the Folk had done several thousand years earlier. But the Norse settlers, being much outnumbered by the English, rapidly learned the language—though (as you'd expect) with a considerable infusion of their own Norse words. And hundreds of these eventually passed into the vocabulary of their adopted tongue.

Still other Germanic streams flowed into English in medieval and early modern times, but through trade and warfare rather than conquest. Most English trade was with the North Sea coastal lands whence the English themselves had come, whose inhabitants spoke (and still speak) tongues not unlike English: Dutch and Low German, often lumped together as Low Dutch.

The North Sea trade centered on wool and textiles, which were mostly carried in Dutch and German ships. Later contacts were military as well as mercantile: the English were first allied with the Dutch against Spain and later fought three brief wars against them for control of North Sea shipping.

The Low Dutch words borrowed into English are exactly the kinds you'd expect under the circumstances: terms from clothmaking and the wool trade, such as the originals of "spool," "selvage," "bale," and "pack"; merchants' terms such as "freight," "wagon," and "dollar"; sailors' lingo such as "bowsprit," "sloop," "smuggle," and "skipper"; a scattering of military terms such as "holster" and "onslaught"— and a few words beloved of both soldiers and sailors: the originals of "crap," "bugger," and "fuck." *Low* Dutch indeed!

In the eighteenth century, a few more Dutch words passed into American English, from Dutch settlers in New York and the Hudson Valley; they include the originals of "spook," "snoop," "scow," and "boss." Several of these eventually passed into British English as well; indeed, "boss" has even been borrowed into Russian!

The other main Germanic tongue, known as High German, has contributed only a few terms to English, most of them reflecting German preeminence in mining and metalworking during late medieval and early modern times—for example, the originals of "quartz," "nickel," and "cobalt." But Yiddish, an offshoot of High German, has moved into English during this century, contributing "kibitzer," "schlemiel," "chutzpah," and half a dozen other terms that are becoming increasingly current in both the United States and Britain.

The Germanic connection, then, has not only endowed English with its "basic" vocabulary and syntax but has also contributed (via Old Norse) such everyday words as "sky," "take," "husband," and "sister"; trade and technical terms (via Low Dutch and High German) in fields ranging from clothmaking to geology; and (via Yiddish) some of our most vivid modern slang.

Worth emphasizing is that the Germanic element in English is not and never was "pure"—a fact worth bearing in mind when you hear people complain that English is being "corrupted" by borrowings and other new words. Several times in the past, some scholars and literary folk have called for a return to "pure Anglo-Saxon"—a view mocked by Lewis Carroll when he jibed at "Anglo-Saxon attitudes" in *Through the Looking-Glass*.

But Anglo-Saxon—what we now call Old English—was, as we've seen, already "corrupted" by borrowings from Folkish (and, no doubt, other lost aboriginal tongues), plus—as we'll see in a moment—a small but significant collection of words from Latin. Somewhere on earth, perhaps, there exists a really pure language, derived entirely from its own ancestral roots with no exotic intrusions. But English isn't it.

The Latin Connection

Something like four thousand years ago—the best guess is between 2000 and 1500 B.C.—another group of Indo-Europeans migrated out of eastern or central Europe, making their way southwest into the Italian peninsula. As they spread out over the new lands, their version of Indo-European split into dialects and eventually into distinct languages, all of them long extinct except one: Latin. But this one, by the chances of history, became the language of the largest empire that the ancient world had ever seen—and perhaps the most successful that has ever existed.

Long before the Romans built their empire, however, they had borrowed words from the native inhabitants of Italy—notably, the names of two important crops unknown north of the Alps, the vine and olive, along with the wine and oil they yielded and the ass on whose back both wine and oil were carried to market.

Latin also borrowed from a later group of immigrants, the Etruscans, who arrived around 1200 B.C. from Asia Minor. These, thanks partly to their mastery of the new technology of ironworking, quickly made themselves masters of central and northern Italy, including even Rome itself, which at one period was ruled by Etruscan kings—the "royal house of Tarquin" in Macauley's famous verses, "Horatius at the Bridge."

The Etruscan language is one of the great unsolved linguistic puzzles. A few Etruscan inscriptions have survived, and can even be "read" phonetically—but nobody can understand them, since Etruscan is related to no known language. Thus we can seldom be sure which of the exotic (non-Indo-European) words in the Latin vocabulary were borrowed from Etruscan; some likely candidates are the root **MERK-**, the ultimate source of English "merchant" and "commerce," and **FERRUM** (iron), which has contributed a number of scientific terms, including the chemical symbol (Fe) for that metal.

As the Romans gradually made themselves masters, first of Italy and eventually of the entire Mediterranean region, their language continued to absorb foreign terms—notably, from the Indo-European tongues of the Celts (Gauls), who occupied the Po Valley of northern Italy and most of Europe west of the Rhine, and of the Greeks, spoken over most of the eastern Mediterranean and in "Great Greece"—Greek colonies in Sicily and southern Italy (more on this later).

At the same time, Latin evolved into two quite different versions: the formal or literary Latin that some of us studied in school, and Vulgar [popular] Latin, spoken by the *vulgus* (common people). It was the latter that was carried by Roman soldiers, traders, officials, and settlers over much of western and parts of eastern Europe, and that in due course evolved into the modern Romance languages.

In the nature of things, Vulgar Latin was a highly informal tongue, whose vocabulary was enriched by slang terms and by borrowings from native peoples such as the Gauls. Later, during the Roman decline and fall, it picked up more terms from the Germanic tribes who infiltrated and eventually took over most of Rome's western territories.

The first Latin contributions to English date from around the beginning of the Christian Era, with the first Roman-Germanic contacts along the Rhine frontier. The words the Germans borrowed—mainly from Vulgar Latin—were almost entirely new words for new things, the same process that contributed the exotic "maritime" words that their ancestors had borrowed earlier along the Baltic.

That is, the new words came almost entirely from the fields of trade, warfare (Germans both served in the Roman armies and fought against them), cookery and food crops, and building, in all of which the Romans knew a great many things new to the Germans. Commercial borrowings include the originals of "wine," "cheese," and "oil," the main Roman exports to the Germanic lands, as well as the sources of "pound" (weight), "copper," and "cheap."

Cookery and food crops contributed the originals of "kitchen," "dish," "cup," "pan," and "chicken," along with "butter," "mint" and "parsley," "cherry," "plum," and "chestnut." From the military came the sources of "pit" (originally, a deep hole, often with a sharpened stake at the bottom, dug to hamper enemy movements), "street" (originally, one of the paved roads that gave the Roman armies mobility), as well as "mile" and "wall" (originally, a military fortification). The building trades, finally, contributed what would eventually become "tile" and "chalk" (originally, the lime used to make mortar).

The next Latin connection came through Christianity—at first, from Vulgar Latin (the first Christians were overwhelmingly common folk); later through Church Latin. This was a somewhat modified version of literary Latin, brought to England by missionaries beginning around A.D. 700. It was through these routes that we got "church," "priest," "bishop," "monk," "nun," and—inevitably—"cross."

The Church also brought new crops—whence "radish," "beet," and "cucumber"—and new technologies, preserved in such words as "sickle," "mattock," and, above all, the (water) "mill," which set off a real technologic revolution in England, as it did in most of western Europe. The

Church's care for the sick and unfortunate brought in such terms as "alms," "fever," "sponge," and "plaster"; its predominant role in education (the pre-Christian English were essentially illiterate) contributed "paper," "verse," "school," and the "master" who ran it.

The French Connection

Thus far, the Latin contribution to what would one day be modern English had come in a few sparse showers; the conquest of England by the French-speaking Normans in 1066 set off a downpour. The conquerors, though originally Norse settlers in northern France, spoke a dialect of what we call Old French, a descendant of Vulgar Latin whose vocabulary had been enriched by words borrowed from the Franks and other Germanic peoples who had swept over the western Roman Empire.

(This fact, too, is worth keeping in mind when you read the fulminations of some French academics against "Franglais"—French supposedly corrupted by borrowings from English. In fact, French was long ago "corrupted," by borrowings first from Gaulish and Germanic, and later from Italian, Spanish, and Arabic. Ironically, many of the modern "corruptions" are English words previously borrowed from—French.)

The earliest French infusions into English were mostly the kinds of words that common folk naturally pick up from their rulers: terms of government, the law, warfare, and the Church, all of which were dominated by the new Norman elite. Other borrowings were words for the food and clothing of the upper classes—much fancier than those enjoyed by the native English.

Within a couple of centuries, however, the descendants of the conquerors had become assimilated, speaking English nearly all the time. But it was a "new" English, which had absorbed not hundreds but thousands of French words: some ten thousand between A.D. 1100 and 1500. And the borrowings have continued ever since, albeit at a more leisurely pace; beginning around 1500, they were joined by words from two other Romance languages, Italian and Spanish.

The sixteenth-century influx of Romance words was condemned by some critics as "oversea language"—but their countrymen kept on borrowing, as English-speaking people around the world have done ever since. Witness such twentieth-century "oversea" terms as French "fuselage," "ambiance," and the quiche that real men don't eat—along with the (Italian) spaghetti and pizza and the (Spanish-American) chile and tacos that they do.

Latin did more than enrich English indirectly, through its Romance descendants: during the Middle Ages it became a powerful influence in its own right. It was the language of the Church and of scholars (nearly all of them clerics), some of whom undertook to translate Latin books into English. They found, however, that (as one of them put it) "there ys many wordes in Latin that we have no propre English accordynge thereto." Accordingly, they pressed Latin words into service to fill the gaps; thus the fourteenth-century English translation of the Latin Bible, by John Wycliffe and his associates, brought more than a thousand Latin words into English.

The invention of printing increased the demand for translations: the "reading public" for English books was much bigger than for Latin ones. The natural result was more hundreds of Latin borrowings, plus a sizable number from Greek. And the rise of modern science, whose English-speaking practitioners chose to coin nearly all their special vocabulary from Latin and Greek roots, multiplied the hundreds into tens of thousands.

Most of these scientific coinages simply supplied new names for new things and concepts, and are therefore used only by the specialists who deal with those things. But many of the other Latin and Romance borrowings didn't supply needed words, but rather enriched English with words it *didn't* need. As the sixteenth-century educator Richard Mulcaster noted, English has acquired new words not simply from "necessitie in new matters," but "to garnish itself."

The "garnishing" process has given us many hundred clusters of synonyms or near synonyms: words meaning almost the same thing, but with subtly different overtones and quite different sounds. As a result, English has something no other tongue possesses: a large "double" and even triple vocabulary, in which a Germanic term is paralleled by a French one and often a Latin one as well. Sometimes the French word is more "literary" than the English one, but not always—witness the homely pair "pail" (English) and "bucket" (French). Almost always, however, the Latin word is more scholarly—or, sometimes, pretentious.

Thus along with Germanic "rise" we have French "mount" and Latin "ascend"; some other linguistic triplets are kingly/royal/regal, ask/question/interrogate, fast/firm/secure, goodness/virtue/probity, holy/sacred/consecrated, and work/labor/exertion. (The same thing happened, though on a much smaller scale, with the assimilation of Norse words mentioned earlier. Thus "hide" is from Old English, "skin" from Norse, and so with carve/cut, ill/sick, want/wish, and craft/skill.)

All this borrowing, in the words of the sixteenth-century writer George Pettie, served "to inrich our tongue and make it copious." It is above all this willingness to borrow from other peoples—a loan that, unlike a financial one, leaves the lender no poorer—that has indeed "inriched" English far above any other language, making it the most copious in the world.

The Greek Connection

About the same time as the Italic Indo-Europeans were migrating into Italy, some of their cousins were pushing south into Greece, where they encountered, and eventually conquered, the relatively sophisticated people we call the Minoans (what they called themselves is unknown). The conquerors were simple folk, perhaps nomadic herders; the Minoans were farmers, craftspeople, and merchants, living in towns and trading with Egypt and the Near East; moreover, some of them could write, though we can't read their "Linear A" script.

The Greeks naturally borrowed words from their new neighbors: terms for new plants and their products, such as the vine and olive, mint, and coriander; for the resinous terebinth tree, whose name is the source of "turpentine," and many others. You'll find some of them listed in the Dictionary—for example, **Greek ANGELOS**.

After many travails, including a "dark age" lasting several centuries, the Greeks began building the remarkable culture that is one of the foundations of our own. Greek colonies, extending from the Black Sea as far west as Massilia (Marseilles), spread that culture, and the Greek language, far beyond its original home; so, on an even larger scale, did the conquests of Alexander the Great.

Well before the Christian Era, Greek had become a lingua franca or trade language all around the eastern Mediterranean; in the process it changed, much as Roman expansion had changed Latin, into the *koine dialektos* or "common tongue." The *koine*, as the language of the Gospels and the early Church, contributed the Greek originals of "church," "priest," "bishop," "monk," and "nun."

Much more extensive was the influence of "standard" or literary Greek. The Romans, though they conquered Greece (along with the other eastern Mediterranean lands), found Greek achievements in literature, philosophy, and science impressive—as we still do. Upperclass Romans learned Greek as routinely as, much later, the upperclass English learned Latin.

Through this process, formal Latin absorbed hundreds of Greek words, many of which eventually entered English by the same processes as other Latin words; some examples include "atmosphere," "climax," and "parasite." But beginning in the sixteenth century, when some of the English began learning Greek as well as Latin, Greek words passed into English directly. As you'd expect, nearly all of them were rather high-flown terms, as "catastrophe" and "ostracize" still are, but some eventually passed into the everyday vocabulary of English—"anonymous" and "tonic," for instance.

How Roots Branch

At a guess, the Germanic, Latin, and Greek connections together have contributed close to 90 percent of the English tongue's oversized vocabulary. And some 90 percent of that 90 percent—altogether, perhaps 300,000 words—can be traced back to one of the basic Indo-European roots listed in the Dictionary that follows this Introduction. But—given that there are only about two thousand known Indo-European roots, how did this very modest number proliferate so remarkably?

First, we should bear in mind that while there were probably no more than a few thousand Indo-European roots (even allowing for those that have simply disappeared over the past seven thousand years), there were—as I've already noted—a great many more Indo-European words than roots.

These were formed by modifying the basic root in various ways—sometimes by changing or even omitting the vowel (nearly all the roots were monosyllables), sometimes by adding one or more suffixes.

For some roots, the experts have reconstructed twenty or thirty such variants, with different meanings—some of them only remotely related to the "basic" sense. Other Indo-European words were compounds, formed in the same way as recent English coinages such as "space shuttle" and "user-friendly."

Words and roots, in short, proliferate by a sort of linguistic free association, in which one idea suggests others more or less akin to it; the Dictionary itself will supply scores of examples. Sometimes the connection in meaning is obvious; sometimes there is no traceable connection at all—that is, we must be dealing with two or more distinct roots of identical sound but quite different sense, comparable to "so," "sew," and "sow" in modern English.

In other cases the connection is tenuous, yet suggestive enough so that we try to guess how it may have come about—a chancy matter, since we're trying to reconstruct the mental processes of people dead for thousands of years. But we persist—among other reasons, because we know that words can shift their senses in highly improbable ways in a mere few centuries. Notable examples include "nice," which in the thirteenth century meant "stupid" but by the eighteenth had come to mean "agreeable," and "silly," which originally meant "happy"! With attested historical examples like these, it's dangerous to be dogmatic about what might or might not have happened in prehistoric times.

The evolutionary processes by which one word gave birth to many in Indo-European continued in its various daughter languages. Latin in particular developed its own set of suffixes for forming new words, and also an exceptionally rich collection of prefixes, which Indo-European had employed very sparsely.

Another way in which words multiply is through metaphor—the transfer of (usually) concrete terms to things or concepts thought to resemble them. Sometimes the word itself remains unchanged, as with the actual foot we walk on and the figurative foot of a hill, but over the long run the two terms are likely to acquire different sounds, as with "heart" and "creed" (what you believe in your heart)—both from Indo-European **KERD-**.

Since I've described many of these metaphorical formations elsewhere,* I haven't taken the space to elaborate on them in the Dictionary; instead, I've referred you to my previous work, which will give you a much fuller account.

In these ways, a single Indo-European root can engender twenty or more words. Bear in mind, moreover, that just as not all known Indo-European roots, or (even less) all variants of each root are represented in (say) Latin, so not all the Latin derivatives of the root passed into English.

Using the Dictionary of Roots

To make the best use of the Dictionary of Roots, you need to be clear on what it is—and also what it's not. First, as I've already noted, it's in no sense a comprehensive dictionary of Indo-European roots but rather one of Indo-European roots *in English*. And only some of those: I've excluded roots whose only English descendants are scholarly, rare, or archaic. Altogether, the Dictionary includes about a third of the known roots.

In partial compensation, I've added a modest selection of non-Indo-European words or roots that have contributed to

Loose Cannons and Red Herrings: A Book of Lost Metaphors (New York: Norton, 1988).

our everyday vocabulary. These entries are enclosed in [brackets], and the word or root itself is preceded by its known source; see, for example, [**Latin BASSUS**] and [**Germanic BUSK-**]. Some of these entries doubtless represent borrowings from lost languages such as Folkish, as I've already described; others may well have been simply made up, as words occasionally are (such commonplace words as "dog," "pour," and "job" probably fall into this group).

But there are many other things I've had to omit to keep this book to a reasonable size and avoid taxing your patience. I've given only the basic form of each root, not the many variants that specialists have reconstructed, which are of interest mainly to—specialists; I've also omitted most of the intermediate steps between a root and its modern descendants, which would show much more clearly how one evolved into the other.

These unavoidable omissions mean that you must be prepared to take a lot on faith—particularly when it comes to phonetic changes. As Chaucer pointed out six centuries ago, in the verse that heads this Introduction, the forms of speech can (and do) change. If you compare his verse with my fairly literal translation, you'll get some notion of how much they can change in only six hundred years—and the changes from Indo-European to modern English spanned not six hundred but more than six thousand years. As I've already noted, the connections between roots and their descendants will be clearest if you focus on the consonants, not the vowels. For example, vowel changes have turned the root **AL-** into "el," "ol," "ul," and "il," with only the L surviving from the original. Even so, you'll sometimes find yourself wondering how anyone can possibly say that such-and-such a word derives from a given root: neither their sounds nor their meanings are at all alike.

Thus SQUAT shows no relationship in either sound or sense to its root source, **AG-**, to drive. Yet they *are* related, as you can see when you trace the connection in detail: **AG-**, drive, became Latin *actus*, driven or forced; which begot Latin *coactus*, forced together; which became Vulgar Latin **excoactire*, to force together; whence Old French *esquatir*, crouch; whence SQUAT—which, when you think about it, amounts to "forcing" your body together.

But to give this sort of detailed pedigree for the hundreds of words with elaborate pedigrees of this sort would require a book many times the size of this one. Which means that much of the time you'll just have to take my—and the experts'—word that the connections I've cited are real ones.

More: for some words there is *no* pedigree that credibly links the sense of the word to the sense of its root. That is, its sound tells us that a connection probably exists, yet the meaning doesn't reflect that connection. For some words of this sort I've tried to guess what the connection might be; in other cases, I've ducked the issue by labeling the derivative word "idiomatic," leaving readers to do their own guessing. I've used the same term to label words whose connection with their ancestors, though certain, is too intricate to recount in a brief work like this one: "nice" and "silly" are examples.

In some cases, I myself find the experts less than convincing—and say so. Sometimes, I think, they've tried too hard, deriving from a single root words so diverse in sense that no plausible connection among them seems at all likely. In some of these cases, we may well be dealing with a number of roots having similar sounds but quite different senses—though I myself don't have the expertise to speculate on what those roots might be.

In other cases, I suspect we're dealing with a borrowed, exotic word that the borrowers mangled into the semblance of a familiar, native one. This process, called "folk etymology," is not uncommon in linguistics: it was responsible (to take just one example) for transforming Spanish *cucaracha* into "cockroach," whose meaning has no connection whatever with the barnyard cock or the finny roach of European ponds and streams. (For an example of what I—but not the experts—see as folk etymology, rather than a connection in meaning, see DOLPHIN under the root **GWELBH-**.)

In short, to spare the reader's patience—not to mention his wallet or her pocketbook—I've done a lot of simplification, which some scholars will undoubtedly call oversimplification. I've tried to sketch, briefly and sometimes crudely, the "association of ideas" that transformed one root, or word, into another (more often, half a dozen or a dozen others), but for the details you'll have to seek out far more compendious volumes. Some of these are cited in the section headed "A Note on Sources," which follows.

Should you consult these books, you'll also find that I've "distorted" the history of a few words—notably, some borrowed from Latin—by omitting what might seem to be vital facts: the *earliest* senses of the words in English. I've done this, quite deliberately, where these early uses obscure the connection between the Latin original and the modern word. And I've done it, I think, for legitimate historical reasons.

Medieval borrowings from Latin were overwhelmingly from the Church Latin used in ecclesiastical documents and theological treatises. As I've already noted, this was not altogether the same language as the Classical Latin that Cicero and Horace had used a thousand years earlier, and the senses of some borrowed words reflected that fact. Later, during the sixteenth and seventeenth centuries, when scholars began studying Classical literature, they found that Horace, Cicero, and the rest had used some words in quite different senses than had medieval churchmen—and changed the senses of the related English words to correspond with the "new" (actually, much older) meanings.

Also for reasons of space, I've almost never given more than one meaning for a particular English word, though any dictionary will tell you that most of them have several and some have dozens. Meanings change and proliferate over the centuries, and to give a full account of these changes would require an encyclopedia. If this book leads you to dig deeper into the subject of word origins and meanings, no one will be more pleased than I.

For the same reason, I've included only one form of each English word—unless (as sometimes happens) different forms mean distinctly different things. Thus I've included both ACT and ACTIVE, but omitted "acted," "activate," "activity," and so on. If you're literate enough to be reading this, you'll know without being told that they're related to ACT or ACTIVE, and can make a pretty good guess as to how.

Perhaps the most useful way of making sense out of the Dictionary is to think of each entry as a family of words. As with human families, some are very small, with only a single descendant in modern English; others are enormous. And— also as in human families—in some the members show a strong family resemblance; in others, you'd have to trace out the full pedigree to convince yourself that they're all really kin.

Each entry follows this general plan:

First, naturally, comes the root; next, those of its Latin, Greek, and Germanic descendants (if any) that retained the original meaning *and* are represented in Modern English; then the meaning itself. A simple example is

ABEL-, Gc APPLE.

This tells you that the root meant what the modern English word still means—"apple"—and also, incidently, that the root has no other descendants in everyday English. For more complicated examples, see **AKWA-** and **AG-**.

From these and other examples you will see that I've focused on meaning rather than phonetics. That is, where a given root, or (say) its Latin derivatives, had a number of different meanings, I've tried to group the English derivatives by meaning, even though they may derive from several different Latin words. Meaning, after all, is what words are about, and in writing this book I've tried to keep that fact in mind.

Before leaving the subject of roots, I should mention one peculiarity of Indo-European spelling (by modern scholars, of course; the language itself was never written). Some experts show the mysterious "laryngeal" consonants by an inverted lowercase E, called the "schwa" (ə), others, by lowercase H; since my computer doesn't have a schwa, I've used h. For simplicity, think of it as being pronounced UH, like the A in "CubA."

When it comes to Latin derivatives, you'll usually find two forms of the word—for example, *agere*, *act-* (to drive, act, etc.). If you know Latin, you know why; if not—many Latin nouns and verbs had two different (though similar) roots, both of which have contributed words to English. Thus in the above example, *agere* has given us such words as NAVIGATE, from *navis agere*—to "drive" a ship; *act-*, words such as ACT and ACTIVE.

Should you be curious about what Latin words sounded like, give the vowels their modern Italian values: AH, EH, EE, O, OO. Consonants take their English values—with one partial exception. Latin V originally stood for both U and W—for example, *avgere*, increase, pronounced "owgere" (with a hard G), and *vinum*, pronounced "weenum." In late

Roman times, however, the W sound was transformed into a V. For this reason, I've spelled some Latin words with U, some with V, depending on which spelling makes the connection between Latin and English clearest—for example, *uinum* and WINE, but *via* and VOYAGE.

We find a similar spelling problem in rendering Greek words: the Greek letter upsilon (**Y**) stood for a vowel between OO and Y, like the U in French *dur* or German *Führer*. So I've transliterated it sometimes as U, sometimes as Y, depending on which most clearly shows the relationship to its English descendant.

After this rather lengthy preface, here are the two ways of using the Dictionary. If you're interested in word families as such, simply reading the entries will give you all the commoner English words in each family. If, on the other hand, you're curious about the pedigree of a particular word, look it up in the Word Index starting on page 269, which will tell you which family it belongs to; thus the index entry "ACT **AG-**" tells you that the English word belongs to the **AG-** family.

If you don't find a word in the Index, it's either one I omitted, for the reasons given above, or it's not a member of any family but is, as the dictionaries say, "of obscure/unknown origin." If you want to find out more about these oddball terms, consult the sources listed below.

A Note on Sources

In compiling this Dictionary, I've relied mostly on two sources. The first is *The American Heritage Dictionary of Indo-European Roots*, published by Houghton Mifflin in 1986, and hereafter referred to as *AHD*; an earlier version will be found at the back of the original *American Heritage Dictionary*, published in 1969. The second is the *Oxford*

Etymological Dictionary, published in 1966 by Oxford University Press, and referred to as *OEtD*.

It happens that these two books complement each other rather neatly. *AHD*, as you'd expect from its title, focuses on the Indo-European end of things, and therefore includes many roots, and *many* variant roots, that I've omitted. Taken straight, it will tell you much more than you really want to know about Indo-European—and less than you want to know about how the roots evolved into English words. A more serious criticism, in my judgment, is that it sometimes tries too hard: some of its derivations seem to me farfetched, at best, and a few are plain ridiculous (for an example of the latter, see the note at **FERRUM**).

The *OEtD*, on the other hand, scants the Indo-European end of the story; often it gives no Indo-European root at all, even though a plausible one is known. In exchange, however, it gives you a much fuller picture of the word's subsequent history—for example, how **AG-** evolved into SQUAT.

It also gives you thumbnail histories of how the words have changed in meaning *after* being incorporated into English, many of which are fascinating stories in themselves. For a really comprehensive account of such changes, however, you'll have to go back to the prime source—the *Oxford English Dictionary* (*OED*) itself.

Unless you're lucky enough to own the compact edition of that enormous work, this will mean a trip to your local library—but it will be worth it! The *OED* is the greatest dictionary in any language, *hors concours* (if you'll pardon my French), and anyone interested in words who hasn't at least looked into it is like—well, a theater buff who's never seen a Shakespeare play.

Good luck—and good hunting!

Consonant Changes in Some Indo-European Languages

This table summarizes how the consonants of Indo-European (I-E) changed in Common Germanic (CG), Latin (L), and Greek (Gk)—the three languages that are the direct or indirect sources of most of our English words. The changes are very consistent for consonants at the beginning of a word, less so for those in the middle or at the end. (Vowel changes—even less consistent—have been omitted.)

Note, however, that in a few cases a sound changed differently in the same language. For example, BH in Indo-European usually became F in Latin—but sometimes B. Similarly, GW in Indo-European became B, D, or G in Greek.

The changes are sometimes obscured by spelling conventions. For example, in Latin both W and U were spelled V (see note 3 below). In all cases, the table gives the actual sound first, followed by the spelling, if it differs. (For both Indo-European and Common Germanic the spelling is that of modern scholars; neither language was ever written down.)

I-E	CG	L	Gk
B	P	B	B
BH	B	F (sometimes B)	F (spelled PH)[1]
D	T	D	D
DH	D	F (sometimes D)	TH[1]
G	K[2]	G	G
GH	G	H	KH[1]
GW	KW or K	GW (spelled GV) or W/V[3]	B, D, or G
GWH	G or B	F	TH, KH, or F (spelled PH)[1]

I-E	CG	L	Gk
K	H	K (spelled C)[4]	K
KW	HW[5]	KW (spelled QU)	P, T, or K
L		unchanged in all	
M		unchanged in all	
N		unchanged in all	
P	F	P	P
R		unchanged in all	
S	S[6]	S	H
T	TH	T	T
W	W	W/V or U (spelled V)[3]	(lost)[7]
Y	Y (spelled J)	Y (spelled I/J)	H or Z

1. Greek PH, TH, and KH are English transliterations of the Greek letters phi (ϕ), theta (θ), and chi (χ), the last pronounced something like the CH in Scottish "loch" or Yiddish "chutzpah."

2. Common Germanic K was spelled C in Old English; in many words its sound shifted to CH, and is now so spelled.

3. Latin V originally stood for both U and W (see page 00 above); later the W sound became V.

4. In Latin the pronunciation of K (spelled C) later shifted to CH or S before I or E, as in modern Italian and French respectively.

5. Spelled WH in modern English.

6. Indo-European SK was unchanged in Common Germanic (and remained so in Old Norse), but became SH in the western Germanic tongues, including Old English.

7. Indo-European W is found in the very early Greek of the Linear B documents, and occasionally in Homer; in Classical Greek it simply vanished.

Abbreviations and Definitions

>	became, evolved into
<	from
*	reconstructed form (not attested in writing)
=	means/meant/meaning
?	perhaps
??	just possibly
BLM	*Loose Cannons and Red Herrings: A Book of Lost Metaphors* (New York, Norton 1988)
Fr	French (from circa A.D. 1500—see OF)
Gc	Germanic, Germanic-derived
Gk	Greek, Greek-derived
h (in roots)	Indo-European laryngeal consonant/vowel
L	Latin, Latin-derived
MedL	Medieval Latin (Church and scholarly Latin circa A.D. 700–1500)
OE	Old English (ca. A.D. 700–1100)
OED	*Oxford English Dictionary*
OEtD	*Oxford Etymological Dictionary*
OF	Old French (circa A.D. 800–1500)
OMNT	*Our Marvelous Native Tongue: The Life and Times of the English Language* (New York: Times Books, 1983)
ON	Old Norse (circa A.D. 900–1200)
VL	Vulgar (popular) Latin

Roots or words in **BOLDFACE CAPITALS** are primary Indo-European roots (e.g., **ABEL-**) or, in a few cases, non-Indo-European terms from Common Germanic, Latin, Greek, etc., that have left descendants in English. (*All* Indo-European and Common Germanic terms are reconstructed, whether or not preceded by an asterisk; the Latin and Greek terms are, of course, documented.)

Roots in **boldface lowercase** (most of them printed in the margin) are cross-references to roots elsewhere in the Dictionary. For example, the reference to **nau-2,** under **AG-,** tells you that it's the source of the NAV- in NAVIGATE, with **AG-** supplying the -IGATE.

Derived English words are printed in SMALL CAPITALS (e.g., APPLE).

Words or roots in *italics* are from languages other than English, known (e.g., Latin) or reconstructed (e.g., Common Germanic).

The DICTIONARY of ROOTS

ABEL-, Gc APPLE.

AD-, Gc AT, L AD-, A-, to, near.

AG-, L *agere*, *act-*, Gk *agein*, to drive (originally, animals). But the root sense has been almost lost except figuratively, as in L *navigare* (< *navem agere*), to NAVIGATE or "drive" a ship, and in L *coagere*, *coact-*, to drive or force together—what happens when certain components of the blood COAGULATE into a clot. A more intricate evolution (see Introduction) produced SQUAT ("force one's body together"). See **nau-2**

The L verb had many other senses—notably ACT, whence ACTION, the AGENT acting for someone else, the AGILE person who is skillfully ACTIVE, the AGENDA of things to be acted on at a meeting, and TRANSACTION—an action going "across" from one person to another. A third sense, to bring ("drive" something to a particular place or person) produced *exactus*, brought to perfection—the EXACT state desired. From the same original root is L *agitare*, *agitat-*, to "drive" (move) something to and fro—AGITATE it. Gk *agein* meant "lead" as well as "drive," whence the *demagogos* who led the common people but now the DEMAGOGUE who allegedly misleads them. The *strategos* led an army and devised its STRATEGY. An *agon* was a contest in which one "drove" onself—perhaps to AGONY; an ANTAGONIST ("anti-agonist") is the opponent in the contest. In Gaulish, finally, the root acquired the sense See **da-** See **ster-2**

See
(a)mbhi-

"send," whence (via L) the AMBASSADOR who is "sent around" by his/her government.

AG-ES-, fault, guilt, ? the source of Gc ACHE (? originally = feel mental pain—"heartache"—from guilt).

AGH-1, be depressed or afraid, whence Gc AWE—originally = dread (even today, awe often involves a bit of fear). If you're Gc AILing, you'll probably be depressed, and perhaps frightened as well.

AGH-2, Gc DAY, whence TODAY ("at [this] day"), DAY-BREAK, and DAWN. A less obvious descendant is DAISY—the "day's eye" (see *BLM*). But nobody knows how the D got into the act; some think the words came from a different root,* *dheigwh-*, to warm (not included).

See **kwel-1**

AGRO-, L *ager*, *agri-*, field, whence AGRICULTURE ("field cultivation"), as against horticulture (small-scale, "garden cultivation"). From Gc we get the ACRE we still use to measure fields.

AGWESI, Gc AX.

■ The puzzle here is why so common a tool had so elaborate a name (normally, the commoner the word, the shorter). A likely reason is that in many Indo-European cultures the ax was not just a tool but a symbol of patriarchal authority (compare **bharda-**); often men were buried with their battle-axes. Eventually the ax ceased to be a symbol and became merely a tool—and its name shrank accordingly.

[Germanic AIRO, OAR (compare **erh-1**).]

■ Perhaps an early borrowing from Finnish, in which the modern word is the same, but the borrowing may have gone the other way—or both the Germans and the Finns may have borrowed the word from some aboriginal Baltic tribe.

AIS-, to wish or desire, whence Gc ASK—express one's desire for something.

AIW-, a root of blurred meaning; the possibilities (not necessarily mutually exclusive) include vital force, youth, life, long life, even L ETERNITY. From Gc we get EVER (at any or all times, "eternally")—whence FOREVER and EVERY—and its opposite, NEVER (at no time). From L we get AGE (the length of one's life), MEDIEVAL (in the Middle Ages), and PRIMEVAL (in the first age)., aeon

See **medhyo**
See **per-1**

AK-, KA-, L *acer*, *acri-*, sharp, whence ACRID (sharp-smelling), ACID (sharp-tasting), and the sharp, ACERBIC remark. Also from L are VINEGAR, "acid wine," and EAGER—sharply intent on doing something.

See **w(o)in-**

From Gc we get the sharp EDGE of something and to EGG someone on—"sharpen" their eagerness or aggressiveness. Another root sense, a (sharp) stone tool, begot, improbably, Gc HAMMER—once made of stone, but hardly sharp. A possible Gc descendant may have evolved from the "sharp" (peaked) roof of a house, whence the HEAVENS—the "roof" of the world.

In Gk, as in L, the notion of "sharp" > "acid," whence eventually OXYGEN—literally, "acid-former"; two centuries ago, chemists believed that all acids contained oxygen (in modern German, it's called *Sauerstoff*, "sour stuff"). But in Gk "sharp" also > "point," whence ACNE—the pointed pimples that afflict teenagers. The highest point of something is its tip or top, whence the ACROBAT who stepped on tiptoe along a stretched rope (see *BLM*). The

See **gen(h)-**

See **gwa-**

Acropolis of Athens was the "high city"—the cliff-girdled citadel around which the ancient town grew up.

AKS-, L *axis*, pivot or AXIS—e.g., the one the earth turns on; the Gc AXLE is what a wheel turns on.

AKWA-, L *aqua*, water, gave us the AQUARIUM where AQUATIC animals are kept, the AQUEDUCT that transports water, and even SEWER—originally, a pipe that drained water from a fish pond (see *OEtD*). A Gc word meaning "thing on the water" eventually > the I- in ISLAND— originally spelled "iland."

See **deuk-**

See **lendh-2**

AL-1, L *ultra*, beyond, > ULTRA-, as in the ultraviolet rays beyond the violet (end of the spectrum). ULTERIOR meant "more beyond" (an ulterior motive is "beyond" the obvious or admitted one) and ULTIMATE, "most beyond." Through Gc we get ELSE (something else is something "beyond").

From the same root are two L words meaning "the other" (something "beyond" another thing); both have left many descendants. From *alter*, we get ALTER (give something other qualities), ALTERNATE (first one thing, then another), ALTERNATIVE (another possibility), and ALTRUISM (concern for others). ADULTERY is what some of us do with people other than our spouses, and to ADULTERATE is to add other (inferior) ingredients.

From the other L "other," *alius*, come ALIAS (another name), ALIEN (from another country—or planet), and ALIBI—originally = in another place (when a crime was committed), but now any tale that supposedly establishes one's innocence. Finally, from Gk *allos*, other, we get the PARALLEL lines that lie alongside each other but never meet.

AL-2, L *ambulare*, to wander, whence the ALLEY in which people sometimes wander, and EXILE, a wanderer out of his or her own country.

See **(a)mbhi**

AL-3, to grow, nourish, > Gc OLD—originally, having lived ("grown") a certain time, as in "How old are you?" An obvious Gc relative is ELDER; less obvious is ALDERMAN, now a minor municipal politician, but once an elder of the tribe whom the king or chieftain consulted on policy.

See **man-1**

From a L verb = grow up we get both the ADOLESCENT who's still doing it and the full-grown ADULT. A more remote L relative is *altus*, high—what something becomes if it keeps growing—whence ALTITUDE and ALTO, originally, the highest male voice (now, a counter-tenor) but today a low female one of about the same range. To EXALT something is to raise it high, while to ENHANCE it is to figuratively heighten or increase it.

Celtic // alp alb ?

[**Germanic ALLAZ,** ALL, whence ALSO—originally = ALTOGETHER SO.]

ALU-, a root of blurred meaning, found in words involving magic and magical or religious possession—and therefore intoxication. Someone who Gk HALLUCINATES seems possessed; so, sometimes, does someone who's had too much Gc ALE.

■ Ale was a Germanic favorite (as is its modern equivalent, beer, in every country speaking a Gc tongue); according to the Roman historian Tacitus—who doesn't seem to have cared for the stuff—it was sometimes consumed for days and nights together.

(A)MBHI, around, > Gc BY—if you're standing by something, you're around it—whence the BE- in such words as "beside" (by the side of) and "because" (by cause of).

(AM)BHO, L *ambi-*, Gk *amphi-*, Gc BOTH. The L prefix
See **deks-**   turns up in AMBIDEXTROUS, dexterous with both hands;
See   the Gk one, in AMPHIBIOUS, able to live both on land and
gwei(h)-   in water.

AMMA-, L *amma*, mother—and one with many children.
They include L *amita*, AUNT (sometimes a "deputy"
mother) and *amare*, to love (what most mothers do to
their kids), whence the AMATEUR who does something for
love, not money, ENAMORED (in love), and the PARAMOUR
one loves alongside one's lawful spouse. From L *amicus*,
the friend you love in a different way, come AMICABLE and
its opposite, the INIMICAL "un-friend" or ENEMY.

[**Latin AMPLUS,** wide, AMPLE, whence AMPLIFY—make
something "wider" (bigger).]

AN-1, Gc ON.

AN-2, this, that, > Gc OTHER—originally = that one of
two.

ANh-, to breathe, > L *anima*, breath, soul, spirit. (Many
cultures link "breath" and "spirit," believing that the
spirit leaves the body with the last breath.) An ANIMAL is
a living, breathing creature; someone or something that's
ANIMATED is "alive"—lively. The related *animus*, mind,
See **meg-**   gives us the "great-souled" or high-minded MAGNANI-
MOUS person; an ill-minded one is full of ANIMOSITY.

[**Greek ANGELOS,** messenger—what an ANGEL originally was: a messenger from God to man. Or to woman,
like the angel who brought a very important and personal
message to the Virgin Mary. An EVANGELIST was originally

48

one of the authors of the "good news (message)"—trans-lated into Old English as *god spel*, gospel.]

ANGH-, tight, painfully tight, painful, whence L ANXIOUS ("uptight") and ANGUISH. Gc ANGER originally = pain or trouble—which anger may well bring. Finally, Gk *ank-hone*, a strangling (from something tight around the neck), gave doctors a name for the strangling chest pain of ANGINA.

ANG-, ANK-, to bend, whence Gc ANKLE, the bend be-tween leg and foot, and the ANGLER who uses a bent hook. Gk ANCHOR is another kind of hook, and L ANGLE is the "bend" between two lines that we study in geometry.

ANO-, L *anus*, ring—but later also ANUS, the tight ring of muscle that closes off our intestinal tract.

ANT-, front, forehead, and many figurative senses: in front of, before, opposite, opposed to ("head to head"). The "opposite" sense has given us Gc ALONG (opposite = alongside of), and UN- ("unhappy" is the opposite of "happy"). L *ante*, before (previous to), gave us the ANTE we throw into the pot before the deal in draw poker, and ANCIENT—something from a long time before. Gk *anti*, opposed, opposite, > the ANTI- we know best (antidemo-cratic, anticommunist, even antidisestablishmentarian-ism), as well as the ANTARCTIC that lies opposite the arctic.   See **rtko-**

See **del-1**

AP-, to take, reach, > the L ADEPT person who's reached a certain level of skill—and the INEPT one who hasn't. A more distant L relative is *apere*, *apt-*, to attach or fasten, ? implying a rope that "reached" and "took" something; whence APT, "properly fastened," hence, well-suited ("an apt quotation") or well ADAPTED. A married COUPLE is fastened or linked together; when they COPULATE they're linked even closer.

(A)PO-, away (L AB-), Gc OFF, whence OF, AFTER, the EBB-tide when the water goes away, and AWKWARD, from an Old Norse word meaning "turned backward" (away). We find the same general sense in L POST-, behind, afterward, the source of PREPOSTEROUS ("turned backward"—see *BLM*).

From the same root comes L *ponere, posit-,* to place or put (? "leave behind"), the source of many English words including the POSTURE or POSITION we put ourselves in and the POST where soldiers are put and where we put our letters (but wooden post is from **sta-**).

See **paus-**

COMPOUNDS (things put together) include COMPOSE, as when a composer puts together notes; DEPOSIT ("put down," as money in the bank), and DISPOSE ("put away," as in the garbage). PROPOSE = put forward, as an idea; IMPOSE = "put (something) on" (someone), OPPOSE = "put (oneself) against," and a PREPOSITION is placed before a noun.

APSA-, Gc ASPEN.

AR-, to fit together. Depending on which expert you believe, **ORDH-**, **RE-**, and **RI-** either are or aren't members of the same family; what's certain is that their descendants are very diverse indeed.

The **ar-** version gave us the Gc ARM that fits together with the torso, plus a whole series of L terms. *Arma*, tool (for fitting things together), > the tools of war, ARMS and ARMO(U)R, whence ARMY, ARMADA, and DISARM; less obviously related are ALARM, originally = To arms! (see *BLM*),

and ARMADILLO—the creature that Spanish explorers in the New World christened "little armored man." L *ars*, *art*- was the skill or ART of the ARTISAN (later, the ARTIST) who fits things together, while *inertus* meant unskilled, hence inactive—INERT.

The joints of our limbs, fingers, and toes are fitted together, whence L *articulus*, "little joint"—originally, actual joints; later, the "joints" (component parts) of something. We still speak of the ARTICLES of a contract or the U.S. Constitution, but the word has acquired many other senses only remotely akin to the original.

The **re-** or **ri-** version > Gc *redan*, advise (? "help someone fit things together"), which > interpret (something mysterious), such as a RIDDLE, which > READ—interpret the (originally) mysterious symbols of writing. In L, the same root > a verb meaning reckon or think ("fit things together"), which eventually > the RATE at which we reckon something. A related L noun meant judgment or REASONing—which, hopefully, is RATIONAL. And a soldier's RATIONS are the provisions the brass hats reckon will keep him going.

L derivatives of the **ordh-** variant relate to weaving (? "fitting together" threads into cloth); thus *ordo*, *ordin*- originally = a row of threads placed in ORDER on a loom. When we COORDINATE things, we place them in order together, while a SUBORDINATE is under the orders of someone. ORDINARY comes from a related adjective meaning orderly, usual (when people or things follow their usual course, they're likely to be orderly). Probably also related to the "weaving" sense is *ornare*, to furnish or deck (? with clothing), whence the ORNAMENTS with which people ADORN themselves or their homes.

Gk members of the tribe mostly derive from the **ar-** variant, in its original, "fit together," sense. Thus *aristos*, the best (most fitting), gave us ARISTOCRACY, rule by (supposedly) the best people. *Arthron*, the joint that fits together, gave us the joint pain of ARTHRITIS; another word for joint gave us the HARMONY of well-fitted musical notes—or people, for that matter. Gk *arithmos*, number, may derive from either the "fitting" or the "ordering" sense—numbers both set things in order and "fit" them together—whence ARITHMETIC, "measuring with numbers."

See **kar-1**

See **me-2**

■ I've chosen to treat all these words as derivatives of a single root, since with a bit of pulling and hauling they can all be related to the original "fit together" sense; the "one root or several" question is really an argument for specialists—who don't agree.

AREK-, to hold, contain, guard. L *coercere*, restrain ("hold back") > COERCE; a remote relative, *exercere*, to keep busy (originally ? to drive—"coerce"—cattle) > EXERCISE. (Surprisingly, EXERT comes from a quite different root, **ser-3**.)

ARG-, to shine, white; also, silver—the white, shining metal. The "shining" sense > brilliance, then clarity, whence L *arguere*, to make things clear—what (sometimes) happens when we ARGUE. When a lawyer argues a case, he's supposedly making it—or his version of it— clear.

ARh-, to plow; L ARABLE land is "plowable"—cultivable.

■ This is the only surviving English word that reflects the Indo-Europeans' use of the plow (see Introduction); English "ëar" (< Gc) is obsolete. For "plow" itself, see **plog(w)az**.

[**Greek ARKHEIN,** to begin, > take the lead, which > rule (rulers—sometimes—take the lead, though not always in the right direction). The "begin" sense > AN-CIENT ("from the beginning"), ARCHAEOLOGY (the study of ancient things), and the ARCHIVES where ancient documents are stored, frequently enshrining ARCHAIC laws. The "rule" sense produced the MONARCHY ruled by one person and the ARCHITECT who is the "ruler" of construction—a master builder.]

See **leg-1**

See **men-4**
See **teks-**

ARKU-, bow and/or Gc ARROW, > L *arcus*, bow—whence the ARCHER who used it and the bow-shaped ARC of a circle and ARCH of a bridge or building.

AS(G)-, L *ardere*, to burn, > both ARSON and the ARDENT lover, burning with passion; L *aridus*, parched (by fire), > ARID. A related Gk word = dry begot the AZALEA—supposedly because it flourishes in dry soil, though all the azaleas I've ever seen prefer moist, often shady places. From Gc we get only the ASH left by burning.

[**Latin ASINUS,** ASS, whose legendary stupidity was ASI-NINE. The L word also begot (via Gc and Dutch) the painter's EASEL—which, like the ass, patiently bears its burden.]

■ The ultimate source of the word is probably Sumerian *anshu*; the Sumerians or some related Mesopotamian people first domesticated the ass ca. 4000 B.C.

AT-, to go, also "a period gone through"—or so the experts tell us—whence L *annus* (< *atnos*), year, whence AN-

NUAL, ANNUITY (originally, a sum paid yearly), and ANNI-

See **wer-3**

VERSARY—"when the year turns." A MILLENNIUM is a thou-

See **ghesio**

sand years, while PERENNIAL plants come up year after year.

ATER-, fire. The L *atrium* was the open inner courtyard of a Roman mansion—originally, the site of the family fire; the modern ATRIUM is the (usually covered) court-yard of a trendy hotel or apartment building. Things scorched by fire turn black, whence L *atrox*, "black-look-ing," frightful, ATROCIOUS.

■ This and other figurative senses of "black" have noth-ing to do with anyone's skin color; a "black-looking" per-son has a face like a black storm cloud.

AU-, to perceive, > L *audire*, *audit-*, to hear (one way of perceiving), whence AUDIBLE, AUDIENCE, and the AUDITO-RIUM where you hear a lecture or concert. A related verb is *obedire*, "hear toward," OBEY—what soldiers do when a superior snaps "Now hear this!" Gk *aisthanisai*, to feel (another kind of perceiving), gives us the AESTHETIC feel-ing we're supposed to get from a work of art, and the ANESTHETIC that makes us, or part of us, "unfeeling."

AUG-, L *augere*, *auct-*, to increase or AUGMENT, begot the AUCTION with its increasing bids. The L verb also acquired an idiomatic sense, "originate," whence the AUTHOR who originates something and the AUTHORITY that allows someone to do so. Through Gc we have the obsolete

See **no-men-**

"eke" (in addition, also), whence NICKNAME (originally, "ekename")—an additional name.

AUKW-, cooking pot, > Gc OVEN.

AULO-, hole, cavity. Gk *aulos* was a hollow tube—specifically, a flute, whence the *khoraules*, a flute player who accompanied a dance. Eventually, via L and OF, this > CAROL—originally, a song accompanying a dance, then just a song. Gk HYDRAULIC takes us back to the hollow tube or pipe, since it refers to running water through pipes—something both Greeks and Romans (who borrowed the word from them) did to supply their cities with water.

See **gher-1**

See **wed-1**

[**Latin AURUM,** gold (?? from **aus-1**) begot a number of scientific and technical terms such as "auriferous," gold-bearing. Most of us know it only from the ORIOLE. (American orioles come in many colors, but the European bird—not closely related—is indeed golden hued.)]

AUS-1, to shine, whence Gc EAST (where the dawn light shines from), and also **Austron*, the Gc goddess of dawn; she was worshiped at the spring equinox—now the EASTER season. (The first Christian missionaries in England shrewdly combined their celebration of the Resurrection with the older, pagan festival.)

From L *aurora*, both dawn and the goddess, we get the AURORA BOREALIS, "dawn of the North" (Boreas personified the north wind) that sometimes lights the northern night sky, and its southern equivalent, the aurora australis, which few but antarctic explorers have seen.

AUS-2, to draw water, > L *exhaust-*, water drawn out—EXHAUSTed—as you are if your energy has been "drawn out."

AWI-, L *avis*, bird, whence the AVIARY where birds are kept and the AVIATOR who emulates them. **OWYO-,** Gc EGG, may be a separate root, but "bird" and "egg" seem obvious relatives. Its L equivalent, *ovum*, > the female animal's OVARY, which produces "egg" cells, and OVAL (egg-shaped).

AWO-, "adult male relative other than the father," > L UNCLE.

AYER-, day, morning, whence Gc EARLY.

AYES-, copper (or ?? bronze). L *aes*, *aera*, copper coin(s), > counters used in calculating, then the epoch or ERA from which dates are calculated. The figurative use dates from Roman times.

■ The "bronze" sense is possible only if you date the Indo-Europeans much later than I do; seven (or even six) thousand years ago, bronze was unknown anywhere.

BABA-, like **amma**, is a "nursery" word; its senses included Gc BABY and the BABBLE it emits. L *balbus*, stuttering or stammering, gave us BOOBY—which means both a fool and, more recently, a genus of "foolish" seabirds akin to the gannets. Gk *barbaros* originally meant "babbler"— someone who speaks incomprehensibly, whence the later sense of "foreign" and even "rude"—BARBARIAN.

■ The Greeks applied *barbaros* to anyone who didn't speak Greek (rather like the modern French attitude to-

ward people who don't speak French), including their
Persian enemies, whom they called *barbaroi* in (usually)
both senses. When you're fighting against someone,
they're uncivilized by definition.

BAK-, L *baculum*, walking stick, whence BACTERIA—originally, stick- or rod-shaped microbes but now almost any
kind; BACILLUS ("little rod") comes from the same source.
In Gc the walking stick shrank to a PEG.

[Germanic BAKAM, BACK, whence the BACON made
from the backs and sides of pigs.]

BAMB-, a word imitating dull or rumbling sounds. Gk
bombos, booming, ultimately > BOMB; L *bombus*, a deep,
hollow sound, eventually > BOUND (leap), but the sense
evolution is intricate: a deep sound resounds or echos and
an echo REBOUNDS—"leaps back" to its source.

[Latin BASSUS, low—whence the BASE ("low" or "lowborn") person, the low-voiced BASS singer, and the low-
slung BASSET hound. If you ABASE yourself, you "lower"
yourself (to someone); if you DEBASE something or someone, you lower its or their quality or morals.]

■ The Romans also used the word as a family name, equivalent to English Short or Little.

[Latin BAT-, to yawn, begot the openmouthed BAYing of
hounds and the gaping BAY window, whose walls are
slanted—"BEVELed." ABASHed people are figuratively
standing with their mouths agape.]

[Latin BATTUERE, to beat (which, surprisingly, comes
from a completely different root—see **bhau-**). If you beat

someone or something violently, you BATTER them or it; from the same source comes the batter we beat up in the kitchen, the BAT with which we "beat" balls, and the BATTLE in which two armies beat up on each other—engage in COMBAT. A DEBATE is a battle with words, and when something was ABATEd, it was figuratively beaten down— now, eliminated ("abate the nuisance") or diminished ("the storm abated").

BATTERY has a more intricate evolution: its original sense was a severe beating (as in "assault and battery"), then a group of guns (which could beat down fortifications)— whence, improbably, a group of chemical "cells" producing electricity.]

BEL-, strong. L *debilis* meant deprived of strength—weakened—whence DEBILITATE. Strong things or people are often large, Russian *bol'shoi*, whence the BOLSHEVIKS— originally, the left wing of Russian socialists, led by Lenin, who sometimes were the majority—larger part—of the socialist movement.

■ "Bolshevik" is now a term of approval among some Soviet Communists and sharp disapproval almost anywhere else; the British still sometimes use "bolshy" to describe a "troublemaker."

BEND-, a protruding point, > Gc PEN and POUND (for animals), made of pointed stakes. To IMPOUND something is to put it in a pen, literally or figuratively.

BEU-, BHEU-, to swell—loosely speaking. Gc descendants include the swollen POCKs of chicken pox and smallpox, and the equally swollen POCKET and POUCH, whence POACHed eggs—originally cooked "in a pocket," whatever that meant. Also Gc are the swollen BOIL, the more pleasantly swollen BOSOM, the PUFF emitted from swollen cheeks, and the puffed-up BOAST.

L *bulla* meant a round ("swollen") object—notably, a bubble or ball (which, however, comes from a different root—see **bhel-2**). Its descendants include the BOWLING we do with balls and the "little [lead] ball" that was the original BULLET. A later L sense, the round seal placed on a document, gave us BULLETIN—originally posted with an official seal attached—and the "bulletins" or BILLS our creditors send us. The bills we sometimes pay with are a sort of bulletin, certifying that the government will "pay to the bearer the sum of" whatever it is.

L *bullire* meant to bubble ("swell") or BOIL; an EBULLIENT person is bubbling over with high spirits. A related word = to bubble up or stir > BUDGE; someone who won't budge won't stir (move). A less certain L descendant is *bucca*, (? swollen) cheek—compare PUFF above—whence *buccula*, the boss (raised center) of a shield, which, after an evolution too intricate to recount here, > BUCKLE in both senses—to bend under stress, and what we fasten a belt with.

BHA-1, to shine. Through Gc we get the shining BEACON or signal, which BECKONs those who see it, and—more remotely—the identifying sign or BANNER, under which a BAND of warriors fought. A possible but unlikely relative is BERRY, ?? the "shining" (bright-colored) fruit.

Gk *phos*, *phot-*, (shining) light, produced the "light-bearing" substance PHOSPHORUS, which emits light under certain conditions, and, of course, PHOTO- and all its kin—"photography" (literally, "writing with light"), See **ghrebh-2** "photosynthesis" and so on. A more remote Gk relative is *phantazein*, to make visible ("bring to light"), whence FANTASY, PHANTOM, and PANT ("gasp as if oppressed by a phantom or nightmare"). Yet another Gk relative is *phainein*, to show (make visible), whence the idiomatic EMPHASIS—originally = the appearance (outer show) of something, then a meaning implied but not stated. Somehow it got turned around to describe something stated EMPHATICally, not implied.

BHA-2, L *fari, fat-*, Gk *phonein*, to speak, has begotten a large and diverse family. Via L we get FATE—what was "spoken" by the gods—and the AFFABLE person who's easy to speak to. The related L *fabula*, a story (originally spoken, not written), > FABLE, whence FABULOUS—originally, as remarkable as the beasts found in fables. An INFANT ("not speaking") is a child too young to talk, which >, via Italian cavalrymen's slang, "the babies"— foot soldiers or INFANTRY.

L *fama*, rumor, reputation ("what people are saying"), > FAME, whence both FAMOUS and INFAMOUS; to DEFAME someone is to put down their reputation—perhaps by spreading rumors. A PREFACE is "spoken before" the text of a book; to CONFESS is to speak about one's crimes or sins; to PROFESS is to "speak forward" (publicly), which is certainly what a PROFESSOR does.

From Gk *phonē* (two syllables), voice, sound, come -PHONE, PHON(O)-, and their progeny (e.g., PHONETIC, TELEPHONE, PHONOGRAPH). A PROPHET is someone who speaks forth, a SYMPHONY is music written for many instruments sounding together, while an ANTHEM (originally, "antiphon") was a sort of liturgical response, but now a song of praise—especially of a nation. Gk *blasphemos*, evil-speaking, > both BLASPHEMY and BLAME (if someone blames you, they're speaking evil of you—though perhaps with good reason).

The Gc branch of the family harks back to a term meaning "speak officially"—proclaim or summon—whence BAN-ISH and BAN. By an intricate figurative process (see *BLM*), "ban" > BANAL; another complex evolution produced ABANDON. From the same Gc term, via Italian, comes BAN-DIT—one of a group "summoned" together for nefarious purposes; via MedL we get CONTRABAND—against (prohib-ited by) an official decree.

BHA-BHA-, BHA-UN-, Gc BEAN—originally, the broad or L FAVA bean, but now any kind (most modern beans originated in the New World).

BHAD-, good (!), whence Gc BETTER and BEST.

■ BAD itself is a far-from-obscure word of obscure origin; it has no clear connection with any other word in either Gc or English, where it first appeared during the thir-teenth century. By an ironic twist, it now means "good" in Black, and sometimes white teenage, slang.

BHAGHU-, arm, > Gc BOUGH—an "arm" of a tree.

BHAGO-, Gc BEECH, whence BOOK—originally, ? tablets of beechwood on which the early Germans carved runic in-scriptions (see below). Gc BUCKWHEAT is "wheat" whose grains resemble tiny beechnuts.

■ The beechwood tablets are mentioned by one or two late Roman writers—who may or may not have actually seen them. I suspect the story got garbled: the inscriptions were more likely carved on the beech tree's smooth, gray bark, where people still carve initials and other inscriptions.

BHAR-, BHOR-, projection, point, > Gc BRISTLE, BURR, the BASS with its prickly back fin, and ? the bristling BOAR with its pointed tusks.

BHARDA, L *barba*, Gc BEARD (? derived < preceding root). The L word gave us the BARBER who trims or shaves it, and, figuratively, the prickly BARB of a fishook or arrowhead.

■ The I-E term could also = ax (whence the medieval halberd—a pole-ax); both beard and ax were I-E symbols of patriarchal authority—compare **agwesi.**

BHAR(E)S-, Gc BARLEY; the Gc BARN was originally used to store it.

BHAU-, Gc BEAT or strike. Also Gc are BUTT (strike with one's head), the BUTTRESS that "butts" or thrusts against (ABUTS) the wall it supports, and, more remotely, the BUTTON that thrusts out from a piece of clothing. Via L we get REBUT—"strike back" at someone's argument. Perhaps from the same root, but more likely a separate one, is the BUTT (originally, thicker) end of something—which the BUTTOCKS certainly are.

BHE-, to warm; its Gc derivatives include the (warm) BATH—which, says the Roman historian Tacitus, the Germans of his day much enjoyed. (Given Germanic technology at the time, the bath was probably a sauna—see *OMNT.*) The Germans also "warmed"—BAKED—bread.

BHEDH-, L *fodere*, *foss-*, to dig, > the FOSSILS that scientists dig up. From Gc we get the soft, dug-up BED of a garden, whence (!) the soft bed you sleep in.

BHEG-, to break; its supposed Gc descendants—some of them probably illegitimate—include the BANG you hear when things break, the BUNGLEr who's always breaking things, and the BANK of earth or sand that "breaks" the contour of the ground or sea bottom. And you can use a bank of earth as a BENCH. Italian *banca* = the benches or tables that bankers sat at; a "broken bench" was a "broke"—BANKRUPT—bank (see *BLM*). And the original BANQUET was a snack you ate sitting on a bench; both the food and the seating are now much fancier.

See **reup-**

BHEGW-, to run away, > Gk *phebesthai*, flee in terror— what you feel like doing if you have a PHOBIA.

■ The two moons of Mars are named Phobos (Fear) and Deimos (Terror)—appropriate companions for the God of War.

BHEI-1, Gc BEE.

BHEI-2, to strike—what some birds do with their BILLs.

BHEID-, L *findere*, *fiss-*, to split, whence the FISSURE in a split rock and the FISSION of splitting atoms. Gc descendants concern other kinds of "splitting"—notably taking a BITE or BIT of food; the computer age has transferred the original bit into the smallest possible morsel of information and bite into BYTE—eight bits. Also, some BEETLES bite. Other Gc terms concern "splitting" (working) wood, as does the carpenter's bit—though it also "bites" a hole; a

BOAT was originally "split" (dug) out of a log—or ?? made of split planks, as later and larger Germanic boats were.

BHEIDH-, to persuade or trust, whence ? Gc ABIDE (? "await trustingly"). L descendants are more certain and more diverse; they include *fidere*, to trust or CONFIDE—perhaps involving CONFIDENTIAL information you're supposed to give out only if you're CONFIDENT the recipient is trustworthy. A related noun > FAITH, whence the FIANCÉ(E) whose FIDELITY you trust, the AFFIDAVIT whose truth you can (hopefully) trust, and the PERFIDY of the person you can't trust at all—plus the INFIDEL who has no faith in God (or anyway, *your* god).

As most people know, "Adeste Fidelis" (the Christmas carol) = "Come, (all) ye faithful!"

Another L relative, *foedus*, *foeder-*, meant a league or alliance (with someone you could, hopefully, trust)—whence the U.S. FEDERAL government, originally an "alliance" of the states, and the CONFEDERATE who's in league with a criminal.

BHEL-1, to shine, flash, or burn, whence the Gc BLAZE that can dazzle or BLIND you, and the BLACK of burned things. L *flamma*, FLAME, > FLAMMABLE, FLAMBOYANT ("flaming") colors or people, the flame-colored FLAMINGO, the INFLAMED wound that feels like it's on fire, the CONFLAGRATION with flames all around, and the FLAGRANT misdeed that blazes forth for everyone to see.

Other derivatives refer to (shining) white, whence Gc BLEACH (make white) and BLEAK—originally = white, whence the bleak look of a snow-covered landscape. Still other derivatives refer to various bright colors—notably Gc BLUE, also BLOND and BLUSH (turn red). More remote

Gc descendants are idiomatic BLEMISH (originally = to make pale, whence to damage) and BLEND (? originally = mix colors).

BHEL-2, to blow or swell, whence various round objects (compare **beu-**). Its Gc descendants include the round BOWL we eat from, the equally round BOLE of a tree, the more-or-less round BOULDER, and the "round" (rolled-up) BALE of cargo shipped in BULK. The tree bole ? > the BULWARK made of planks or beams.

Other round Gc derivatives include BALL, BALLOON, and BALLOT—originally, balls of different colors dropped into a box; the original sense survives in "to blackball" (exclude someone by vote). Another kind of balls are the BOLLOCKS (British for "testicles"), whence the BOLLIXed-up—balled-up—situation (see *BLM*).

The "swelling" sense of the root often involves the swollen Gk PHALLUS—the most notable feature of the Gc BULL. Less certainly related are Gc BOLD (? masculine, "ballsy"), and BAWDY—which bold remarks often are. But L *follis*, bellows, harks back to the "blow" sense—and even in Roman times was used as a metaphor for a windbag or FOOL.

BHEL-3, Gc BLOOM or thrive; also Gc is BLADE—originally, of thriving grass; later, of knives and weapons that, like a blade of grass, can cut you. L *flos*, *flor-*, a blooming FLOWER, gave us the FLORIST who deals in them, and FLORID (overflowery) writing or decoration. (A florid complexion, however, is not flowery but ruddy—though perhaps decorated with rum blossoms.) From the same source is FLOUR—originally, the "flower" of the grain, as contrasted with the bran husk.

See **kaul-**

See **per-2**

Also from the L word are CAULIFLOWER, the "flower" of the cabbage, and DEFLOWER—to remove a woman's "flower." (The association between "flower" and virginity is an old one; sometimes the flower is specifically a rose—once a symbol of the Virgin Mary.) FLOURISHing vegetation produces not just flowers but leaves (L *folia*) or FOLIAGE, whence the "leaves" of metal FOIL and the PORTFOLIO that holds "leaves" of paper.

BHEL-4, to cry out, BELLOW, or BAWL; a BELCH is a less emphatic "cry," and a BELL "cries out" when rung (all are Gc).

BHELD-, to strike or ? Gc BELT (someone). A Gc BOLT was originally a missile that struck you (as a thunderbolt still does); specifically, a stout arrow, but now a stout wood or metal fastening.

BHELG-, BHELK-, plank or Gc BA(U)LK (beam). (For the figurative sense of "balk" see *BLM*.) In Italian, the Gc term > a scaffold made of planks, whence BALCONY. DE-BAUCH has also been assigned to this root, but the connection—if any—is obscure.

BHELGH-, to swell (a relative of **bhel-2**). Its Gc descendants include the swelling BELLY, BELLOWS, BILLOW, and the BOLSTER on a couch or bed—later, figuratively, to prop up (as if on pillows). From L *bulga*, leather sack (< Gaulish), we get an old word for a (money) pouch—which, if we're lucky, BULGES. The BUDGET is the "pouch" containing personal or governmental expenditures—though nowadays it's more often flat than bulging.

BHENDH-, to tie or Gc BIND, plus several other Gc terms: the "BENDing" of ropes or cloth BANDs around a BUNDLE, and—eventually—the BOND that represents money the issuer is bound (obliged) to pay—or so we hope. In Brythonic (a Celtic tongue ancestral to Welsh), a manger (*binna*) was made of "bound" (woven) wicker; later it > a BIN. Finally, a Sanskrit word = to tie > BANDANNA—originally, made by tie-dyeing.

BHER-1, L *ferre*, Gc BEAR (carry), whether it's a BURDEN or a child (in Scotland, BAIRN); when a woman has carried a fetus long enough, she gives BIRTH. A corpse is borne on a BIER; goods, on a BARROW. And if you carry something to someone you BRING it to them. All these are Gc.

The L verb has given us FERTILE (? originally describing a woman who had borne many children), and a host of compounds, in many of which the "carry" sense has shifted to "hold." To TRANSFER something is to "carry" it across; to REFER it is to "carry" it back to someone; to OFFER it is to "hold" it toward someone; to PREFER it is to "hold" it before something else. When we CONFER, we "hold [a discussion] with" someone, in which we may DEFER ("hold back") to their opinion, or agree to DIFFER ("hold apart") from each other. When we INFER something, we're "carrying in" a meaning that wasn't actually stated; when we SUFFER we're "held under" something unpleasant.

A possible relative is L *fur*, the thief who carries things off FURTIVELY, whence the weasel-like FERRET ("little thief") that steals chickens and suchlike.

BHER-2, L *forare*, Gc BORE (pierce). Its L equivalent is PERFORATE.

BHER-3, Gc BROWN, whence BRUNET(TE), and the names for two brown animals, the BEAVER and BEAR (there are no black bears in Europe).

BHERDH-, to cut, whence the Gc BOARD cut from a log. Other Gc descendants, for no very clear reason, acquired the sense of "hut" (? "made of boards"), whence BOR-DELLO, a disreputable "little hut"; another obscure sense, "edge" (? of a cut board), gave us BORDER and STARBOARD—the steering "edge" (side) of a ship (see *BLM*).

BHER-4, to cook or bake, > L *frigere*, to roast or FRY.

BHERG-, to growl or Gc BARK.

BHERGH-1, to hide, protect, whence Gc BURY. Much more distantly related—if at all—are Gc BORROW (? "protect one's own interest"), and BARGAIN (another way of protecting oneself—from paying too much).

barrow

BHERGH-2, high, hill, hill fort, whence BELFRY, originally a high tower (its later connection with bells is pure coincidence). The fort > a (fortified) town or BOROUGH, whence the innumerable "-bergs," "-burghs," and "-burgs" of British, German, and U.S. town names, whence BURG—the quintessential American small town (also, a contemptuous term for any town or city). Town dwellers were BURGHERS or BOURGEOIS—though some were also BUR-GLARS. All these are Gc.

A less certain relative is L *fors*, *fort-*, strong (? < "strong fort"), whence such obvious descendants as FORCE, FORT, FORTIFY, FORTITUDE, and the FORTE of musicians who play "strongly" (loudly). Hardly less obvious are EFFORT, EN-FORCE, and REINFORCE. COMFORT originally = to support (give strength to), as in "aid and comfort to the enemy," whence the later sense of "relieve distress."

■ Whether this is a true word family is controversial. Some believe that the various "town" senses derive from the "protect" sense of **bhergh-1**. And L *fortis* and its descendants may come from **dher-2**, to hold firmly.

BHERhG-, Gc BRIGHT or white, whence the white BIRCH.

BHES-1, to rub, whence, after unusually intricate phonetic changes, Gc SAND—still glued to paper and used for rubbing down rough surfaces. (The phonetic shift, improbable as it looks, is certain—or as certain as anything is in this business.)

BHES-2, to breathe, whence Greek *psyche*, spirit, soul (compare **anh-**), whence PSYCHO- and all its kin (the best known are "-logy" and "-analysis"), and the PSYCHIC who communes with spirits.

BHEU-, Gc BE or exist, also dwell, grow; L FUTURE = "what is to be." The "dwell" sense begot Gc BUILD (a dwelling), BOOTH (a temporary building), HUSBAND ("dweller in the house"), and NEIGHBOR (someone dwelling near). A BOWER was originally a dwelling, and a servant (in the dwelling) was in BONDAGE (the word's sexual sense is very recent). More remote Gc descendants are BOUND for ("growing toward") a place and—possibly—BEAM, from a word = tree (? "growing thing"). The same root sense > Gk *physis*, growth, nature, which > PHYSICS—originally, the study of the natural world—whence the idiomatic PHYSICAL.

BHEUDH-, to be/make aware, whence Gc BID (originally = proclaim—what you do when you bid at an auction) and FORBID—"proclaim against."

■ "Bid" in all its senses represents the "fusion" of two distinct roots; for the other, see **gwhedh-**.

BHEUG-1, L *fugere*, to flee, whence the fleeing FUGITIVE who seeks REFUGE. *Subterfugere* meant to escape secretly, whence SUBTERFUGE—a secret action often used to escape the consequences of one's misdeeds.

BHEUG-2, to enjoy, ultimately > L *fungere*, *funct-*, to perform or FUNCTION; a related L word = discharged (from an obligation) or finished—which a DEFUNCT person is.

BHEUG-3, to bend, whence the bent BOW that propels an arrow, the even more bent BAGEL, and the polite BOW in which we bend at the waist. BUXOM originally meant "obedient"—someone who "bends" to another's command; for its subsequent evolution, see *OEtD*. All these are Gc, but BOG is < Celtic, referring to soft ground that "bends" beneath your feet.

BHLAG-, to strike, > L *flagrum*, a whip, whence FLOG.

BHLE-1, to howl, was toned down to BLEAT and amplified to BLARE, both Gc. L *flere*, to weep, begot FEEBLE—literally, "something to weep over," though I suspect the macho Romans also considered weeping a feeble thing to do.

BHLE-2, BHLA-, Gc BLOW (air), whence the blown-up BLADDER, the blowhard BLATHERer, and the violently blowing BLAST. From L *flare*, *flat-*, to blow, come INFLATE ("blow into"), DEFLATE— and the SOUFFLÉ that's "blown up" by beating air into it. Finally, L *flatus*, breath, fused with *foetor*, stench (origin unknown), to yield FLAVOR.

BHLEI-, to swell, whence ? Gc BLISTER.

■ This root and the next are related to **bhel-2**.

BHLEU-, to overflow, swell, > L *fluere*, to flow, whence the FLUID we FLUSH things with, and a host of figurative meanings. FLUENT speech flows freely; something that FLUCTUATES "flows" back and forth; if you're AFFLUENT, plenty of money has flowed to you; something SUPERFLUOUS is "overflowing" (in excess), while INFLUENCE "flows into" something or someone. INFLUENZA was originally ascribed to the malign influence of the stars.

BHLIG-, L *fligere*, *flict-*, to strike. If you're AFFLICTed, you're "struck" by something that someone or something has INFLICTed on you; in a CONFLICT, people are "striking with" one another, literally or figuratively.

BHOSO-, Gc BARE.

BHRAG-, L *fragrare*, to smell, whence FRAGRANT. Someone with FLAIR has a sharp nose for smelling out precisely what to do and/or when to do it.

BHRATER-, L *frater*, Sanskrit *bhrata*, Gc BROTHER. The L word has given us FRATERNAL and FRATERNITY (a "brotherhood" of sorts); the Sanskrit one, via Romany (Gypsy), PAL.

BHREG-, L *frangere*, *fract-*, Gc BREAK or BREACH (break a wall or a contract). From the L we get FRACTURE, FRAGILE, and FRAIL ("breakable"), as well as the FRACTIONS that things are "broken" into. If you INFRINGE someone's rights, you "break into" them; a lens REFRACTS (breaks the path of) light; the REFRAIN of a song is what the singer "breaks back" to after each verse. (For "refrain" = abstain, see **ghrendh-**.)

BHREI-, BHRI-, to break (? related to the preceding root), whence, via Gaulish and VL, DEBRIS—the broken pieces of something.

BREKW-, to cram together, whence L *frequens*, crowded or FREQUENT, and Gk *phragma*, fence (it keeps animals "crowded together"), whence DIAPHRAGM (see *BLM*).

BHREM-, to project; also a point, spike, or edge, whence, in Gc, prickly shrubs such as the BRAMBLE and BROOM—as well as the brooms originally made from the latter. The "edge" sense gives us Gc BRIM.

BHRES-, Gc BURST.

BHREU-1, to break up, whence Gc BRITTLE.

BHREU-2, Gc BOIL, bubble, burn. Other Gc derivatives include BREW (the yeast makes it bubble), the dough that is "brewed" with yeast into leavened BREAD, and the yeast itself, once called "barm"—whence the BARMY (bubble-brained) person (see *BLM*). Also from Gc is the BROODing (warming) of eggs by a female bird—part of the BREEDing process. L *fervere*, to boil or ferment, gives us both the lover's FERVENT ("boiling") passion and the EFFERVESCENce ("bubbling out") of fermentation and soda pop.

BHREUS-1, to swell, whence the pleasantly "swollen" BREAST; more distantly related are the swelling buds and shoots that some animals BROWSE on (both Gc).

BHREUS-2, to break, > Gc BRUISE. (As we now know, bruising is caused by broken capillaries.)

BHRU-, Gc eyeBROW; also ?? the Gc BRIDGE that crosses a stream as the eyebrow "bridges" the eye.

BHRUG-, L *fructus*, agricultural produce—such as FRUIT.

BHUDH-, L *fundus*, Gc BOTTOM or base. The L word > the FOUNDATION (base) of a building and the foundations FOUNDed and FUNDed by rich people, the FUNDAMENTAL things that are basic, and the PROFOUND idea that gets to the bottom of something.

BHUGO-, male animal, such as a Gc BUCK, and (< Gaulish via OF) the BUTCHER who kills and dresses it.

[North European BRAK-, Gc BREECHES, whence BREECH—originally, what the breeches covered; later, through soldiers' slang, the "ass end" of a gun.]

■ The root appears only in Gc and Celtic, indicating that it was borrowed from some aboriginal people of northern Europe, where the climate certainly encouraged the wearing of breeches. The Romans referred to the Gauls and Germans as *braccatae*, "wearing breeches," hence uncivilized, since they didn't wear tunics or togas like respectable people.

[Germanic BRUDHIZ, BRIDE.]

[Greek BURSA, hide, wineskin, whence the PURSE from which we DISBURSE money, sometimes to REIMBURSE someone.]

[Middle Dutch BUOLE (probably from West Gc), BULLY. The English word originally meant "sweetheart," then "fine fellow" (often ironic), then "swashbuckler," "pimp," and "tyrannical coward."]

[**Germanic BUSK-,** BUSH. A "little bush" of flowers is a BOUQUET, and someone in AMBUSH (via L) is hiding in the bushes.]

[**Latin CARCER,** prison (? from Etruscan), > INCARCER-ATE; the prison bars, *cancelli*, through an intricate metaphorical process, > CANCEL—"draw crossbars through" (see *BLM*).]

■ The Romans probably borrowed the word from their (temporary) Etruscan overlords (see Introduction), as the English later borrowed both "prison" and "jail/gaol" from their Norman overlords.

[**Latin CAUPO,** small tradesman, whence Gc CHEAP—originally = market, price, etc.; the modern sense comes from "good cheap" (a good price).]

■ A very early Gc borrowing from Roman merchants along the frontier.

[**Latin CURA,** care (which, however, comes from a different source—see **gar-**). A CURATOR takes care of a museum and a doctor who takes care of you will—hopefully—CURE you. Something done with care will be ACCURATE, and if you care about something you're probably CURIOUS too; a SINECURE is a job with no "care" (duties) attached (see *BLM*). To PROCURE something is a way of "caring for" someone's needs, or your own; if you're without care you're SECURE or SURE. This last has, in turn, begotten ENSURE (make something sure), ASSURE (make someone sure), and INSURE (secure yourself against loss).]

DA-, to divide, whence Gc TIME, which divides experience into days, weeks, and months; the TIDE that moves at a particular time, and TIDINGS—news of the times (or the *Times*). We find another kind of division in Gk *deme*, a township (division) of ancient Attica, whence *demos*, people (of the township), whence DEMOCRACY, rule by the people, and EPIDEMIC ("all over the people"); a PANDEMIC See **pant** is "all over all people"—e.g., the fourteenth-century Black Death, which devastated most of Europe.

Less certainly connected is Gk *daimon*, a divinity (originally ? "he who divides or apportions"), whence DEMON. The Gk term meant simply a spirit or demigod; the "modern" sense comes from a Gk translation of the Jewish scriptures: to the Jews, as to the Christians after them, any divinity but their own was—demonic.

DAIL-, to divide (probably related to the previous root, but found only in Gc and Celtic), whence DEAL—originally to divide or distribute, as it still is in cards. The DOLE is the money British governments deal out to the poor (equivalent to U.S. "welfare"), while an ORDEAL was originally a judgment apportioning proper shares. Its modern sense probably comes from "trial by ordeal," in which a person being tried was subjected to a painful physical experience (e.g., holding a red-hot iron ball for a few seconds); if he or she survived the ordeal, he or she wasn't guilty.

DAKRU-, Gc TEAR (from weeping).

[Germanic Dan-, low ground, > an animal's DEN (? "located in a hollow"), and ? DANE (Denmark, unlike the rest of Scandinavia, is almost entirely low ground).]

DAP-, to apportion in exchange. L *damnum* (< **dapnum*) meant something for which compensation—an INDEMNITY—was due in exchange; then DAMAGE of any sort. To CONDEMN someone is to render an adverse, sometimes DAMNing judgment on them. •

DE-, a demonstrative ("this," "that," etc.) root, but in Gc it took on the sense of "in the direction of" ("thataway"), TO, whence the idiomatic TOO. Sometimes assigned to this root are the L prefixes DE- and DIS-, but their senses— down, away from, the reverse of—make the connection dubious; for a more likely source, see **dwo-**.

DEIGH-, insect, "bug," whence ? Gc TICK—not really an insect, but to the ancient Germans (as still to many of us), anything that crawled was a bug.

DEIK-, to show, whence Gc TEACH—show someone what or how. Another way of showing begot L *dicere*, *dict-*, say, tell, which > DICTATE and DITTO—the last via Italian, where it meant "aforesaid." A DICTATOR, of course, tells everyone else what to do. To PREDICT is to tell beforehand; to CONTRADICT someone is to "say against" them. L *judex*, *judic-* was the JUDGE who tells us the law, provided it's within his or her JUDICIAL JURISDICTION. The jury tells the court its "true-saying" VERDICT—unless it's PREJUDICEd ("judging beforehand").

See **yewes**

See **wero-**

Other derivatives of the L verb include DITTY (originally, the words that a song "says"), BENEDICTION ("well-speaking"), and PREACH ("speak forth"). Idiomatic senses, with the original "say" sense stretched beyond recognition, include ADDICT, CONDITION, DEDICATE, ABDICATE, VINDICATE, REVENGE, and POLICY. (For details of these relationships, see *OEtD*.)

Another group of L relatives harks back to the original, "show" sense—physically showing something by pointing with a DIGIT, often the INDEX finger (whence INDICATE). (Gc TOE is sometimes assigned to this root, by analogy with "digit," but the connection is tenuous.) Finally, Gk *dikein*, throw ("direct an object"), > the DISCUS that athletes still throw, whence, by various, often intricate routes, DISH, DISK, and DESK (!).

DEIW-, to shine, but also the (shining) sky and the sky god who was the head Indo-European DEITY (< L). An obvious L relative is DIVINE; a less obvious one is ADIEU (literally, "to God"—"God be with you"). The god's name survives in many versions: Jove, whence the figurative JOVIAL (see *BLM*), Zeus, and the Gc Tiw, whose day was TUESDAY.

We find a rather different sense in L *dies*, *diurnum*, day— originally, the "shining" (daylight) hours—whence the DIARY or JOURNAL that records the day's events, a JOURNEY (originally, a day's march or ride), the DIAL that marks the day's hours ("The bawdy hand of the dial is on the prick of noon"—Shakespeare), the DIET that tells you how much to eat each day, and the meeting that's ADJOURNed—put off to another day or time. And L *dies malus*, evil day, is—DISMAL.

See **mel-5**

DEK-1, to take, accept. One group of descendants stems from L *docere*, teach ("cause to accept"), whence DOCTOR (originally = teacher), the DOCTRINE he or she teaches his or her DOCILE (teachable) DISCIPLES through proper DISCIPLINE, and DOCUMENT—originally, a lesson. Another L group centers on the idea of "acceptable," whence DECENT, DAINTY, DIGNITY, DECOROUS, DECORATE ("make more acceptable"), and INDIGNANT (originally considering something unacceptable or unworthy; later, how one feels after unacceptable treatment).

A more remote branch of the family stems from Gk *dokein*, to think, appear, seem (? "take into one's mind"), whence the ORTHODOX ("right-thinking") person, who may be a prisoner of DOGMA, and the PARADOX that is "beyond common sense."

DEK-2, something hanging down, such as a Gc TAIL or TAG, or projecting, like a Gc TACK.

DEKM, L *dekem*, Gk *deka*, Gc TEN. From Gc we get -TEEN (sixteen = "six and ten"); from L, the DECIMAL system of counting by tens, DECEMBER (originally, the tenth month—the Roman year began in March), DECIMATE (originally, execute one person in ten—see *BLM*), DIME (a tenth of a dollar), DOZEN (from L *duodecim*, "two and ten"), and ? DICKER, originally, ten hides or skins; the modern sense may come from the nineteenth-century

American fur trade, in which trappers and merchants dickered over the price of a dicker. Through Gk we get the ten-year-long DECADE, and DEAN—originally = chief of ten men (a sort of squad leader), then of ten monks, then the administrative head of a cathedral or college.

An elaboration of this root, **dekm-tom**, ten tens, > Gc HUNDRED, whence the "swollen hundred" or THOUSAND. The L equivalent, *centum* (originally pronounced "kentum") > CENTURY, CENT ($\frac{1}{100}$ of a dollar), and PERCENT— 20 percent = twenty per hundred.

See **teu(h)-**

DEKS-, right (side), whence (via L) DEXTEROUS—"right-handed"—and AMBIDEXTROUS—"right-handed with both hands." (Being myself left-handed, I take exception to these "handist" terms.)

■ The original root could also mean "south"—on one's right facing east. The Indo-Europeans took their directions from the east, rather than the north as we do—not surprisingly, given their reverence for the shining sky.

See **deiw-**

DEL-1, L *longus*, Gc LONG, whence LENGTH, LINGER (stay a long time), and the Gc term for spring, **langtinaz*, "time of lengthening [days]," whence LENT. From the L word we get ELONGATE (make longer in space) and PROLONG ("lengthen forward" in time), OBLONG ("somewhat long"—i.e., longer one way than the other), and LUNGE— originally, a sword thrust delivered by "elongating" oneself toward one's opponent.

DEL-2, to count, recount, or Gc TELL, whence TALE and TALK.

DEM(h)-, L *domus*, house, household, whence DOMICILE and DOMESTIC. An obvious relative is L *dominus*, master of a household, lord, whence DOMINATE, PREDOMINATE, DOMAIN, DOMINION, and even DANGER (originally, "power of a master"—which could be dangerous enough: he could toss you into a DUNGEON). The feminine *domina*, lady, > MADAM and MADONNA (both literally "my lady")—though not all madams are ladies. Gk *despotes*, "having power over the house," > DESPOT; from Gc we get TIMBER—originally = house; then, what it was built of.

See **poti-**

DEMh-, L *domare*, *domit-*, Gk *daman*, Gc TAME; also, constrain or force. From the L we get the INDOMITABLE person who can't be forced—or tamed; < Gk *adamas*, unconquerable, comes ADAMANT—originally, steel; later, DIAMOND; now the quality of being unyielding (see *BLM*).

DENK-, to bite, whence Gc TONGS, which "bit" a piece of red-hot metal so that the smith could hammer it on the anvil. A less obvious descendant is TOUGH—originally, tenacious (? "holding fast," as tongs do, or ? "hard to bite").

DENS-, L *densus*, DENSE; if you CONDENSE something you make it denser.

DENT-, L *dens*, *dent-*, Gc TOOTH, whence TUSK (originally, a canine tooth, as of a wild boar). From the L we get DENTAL, DENTIST, and the three-"toothed" TRIDENT. Something that's INDENTED is "toothed" or "tooth-marked," and the DANDELION is the "lion's tooth" (Fr *dent de lion*), from its toothed leaves.

See **trei-**

DEPH-, to stamp (on), whence (much later) the wax tablets (or leather sheets) that writing was "stamped" on, and eventually L *littera*, LETTER, whence LITERARY, LITERATE, and ILLITERATE, as well as LITERAL ("to the letter") and OBLITERATE—originally = erase (letters).

80

DER-1, run, walk, step, or Gc TREAD, whence TRAMP, TROT, and TRIP. Also Gc are TRADE—originally, the track one trod on (whence the trade winds, which follow a steady track); then the goods carried along it—and TRAP, something an animal steps into. From Greek *dromos*, a running, comes the DROMEDARY—a camel bred for running rather than carrying cargo.

DER-2, peel, flay, split, or Gc TEAR. A TURD is something you "split away" or separate yourself from; peeling or splitting something requires a sharp ("TART") implement. Other senses of the root have to do with (flayed) skin or leather, whence ? MedL *drappus*, cloth (< Gaulish), which > DRAPE.

DERBH-, to compress; a compressed slab of sod or peat is Gc TURF.

DERh-, to work, whence Gk *dran*, do, act. A DRAMA is acted on a stage, and DRASTIC remedies act strongly— perhaps, like many ancient medicines, too strongly for the patient's good.

DERK-, to see, whence Gk *drakon*, DRAGON (a monster supposedly having the evil eye), and, much later, RANKLE—a distortion of OF *draoncle*, a festering sore ("little dragon"). Things that rankle still fester in our minds.

DERU-, DREU-, firm, solid, steadfast, and various derived senses such as TREE, wooden objects such as TRAYS and TROUGHS, and the TAR of coniferous trees—all Gc. Greek *dendron*, tree, > the RHODODENDRON, a "rosy [flowered] tree."   See **wrod-**

The "steadfast" sense > Gc TRUE and TRUST, the BETROTHal in which two people agree to trust one another, and the TRUCE that hinges on (some) mutual trust. Old English *trymian*, strengthen, is clearly a relative, and is ? the source of TRIM (originally = well equipped). L *durus*, hard, may come from the "firm" sense of this root, or from **deuh-**, or ? a blend of the two.

DEU-1, to lack, be wanting, whence Gc TIRE—what happens to you when you lack energy.

DEU-2, to do, perform, show favor, revere. L *bonus*, good (favorable) > the BONUS that's good to get, the BONANZA that's even better, and other goodies—BONBON (literally, "good-good"), BOON, and BOUNTY. The equivalent L adverb, *bene*, well, > the BENEFIT you get when someone does well by you, the BENEVOLENT person who wills or wishes you well, and the BENIGN person who's a "good sort." An obvious L relative is *bellus*, *-a*, handsome, pretty ("looking well"), whence the pretty BELLE and her handsome BEAU, along with BEAUTY and EMBELLISH ("make beautiful").

See **dhe-**
See **wel-2**
See **gen(h)-**

A possible but very unlikely relative is Gk *dynasthai*, to be able or powerful, whence DYNAMIC, the powerful DYNASTY, the even more powerful DYNAMITE, and the power-generating DYNAMO.

DEUh-, DWAh-, long in time (DURATION), whence DURABLE (long-lasting) and DURING ("while [something] ENDURES")—all < L.

DEUK-, L *ducere*, *duct-*, to lead. A DUKE was originally a military leader; a DUCT "leads" water, air, or wiring from one place to another; a stream of water emerging from a duct can be used as a DOUCHE (< Fr *douche*, shower

bath), and a DOCK is a protected place (e.g., between two piers) into which a ship is "led"—in the United States, more often the pier itself; we find the original sense in "dry dock" (all L).

Figurative L uses include to CONDUCT ("lead with"), DEDUCE ("lead [a conclusion] from"), DEDUCT ("lead [money] from"), INDUCE ("lead into"), INTRODUCE ("lead between"), PRODUCE ("lead forth"), REDUCE (originally = "lead back"; now = "lead down"), SEDUCE ("lead apart" [astray]), SUBDUE ("lead under"), and EDUCATE ("lead forth" [someone's talents]).

The Gc senses often involve "leading" by force, as with TOW and TUG. Leading an animal usually involves TIEing something to it—and a group of people "tied" together is a TEAM (originally = clan or family).

DHABH-, to fit together (compare **ar-**). From L *fabrica*, the workshop where artisans fitted things together, we get both FABRICATE and FORGE—as well as the FABRICS made in some modern workshops.

DHE-, to set, put or Gc DO, whence the DEED that is done. Gc DOOM was originally a judgment set down, as in the Domesday Book, where William the Conqueror's clerks set down their judgments of the lands their master had seized. Its ominous modern sense probably comes from "doomsday," the final and inexorable Day of Judgment. Finally, the suffix -DOM means (among other things) the state or condition something is "put" (judged to be) in— e.g., "freedom."

L members of the family number in the dozens; most of them come from *facere, fact-,* to do or make. From the "do" sense we get FACT—something "done"—as, in another sense, is a FEAT. Something that's FEASIBLE is doable, FACILITY describes ease of doing (also, a place for doing things), something FACILE is done (too) easily, and something DIFFICULT isn't.

See **deu-**
See **op-1**

A BENEFACTOR BENEFITS—does well by—you; a MALEFACTOR does ill; an OFFICE is a place you do work, and an AFFAIR is something you do—for business or pleasure. A

See **dhwer-**
See **ar-**

FORFEIT was originally something done "outside" the law, but is now the penalty for doing it; an ARTIFICE is an artful way of doing something—and if you're DEFEATed, you're undone.

We get another large batch of words from the L "make" sense. A FEATURE of something is one of the things it's made up of; so, in a different sense, is a FACTOR. Something that's FASHIONed is made (often in a FACTORY), sometimes in a particular mode or fashion (the political FACTION was originally a political fashion).

A COUNTERFEIT is "made against" (the law), something with a DEFECT is mismade, but something PERFECT is made

See **man-2**

"completely." MANUFACTURES were originally made by hand, though now by machine, while CHAFE comes from

See **kelh-1**

L *calefacere*, make warm—what happens to your hands when you chafe (rub) them together. And to SACRIFICE

See **sak-**

something originally meant "make it sacred," as when an animal was ritually slaughtered.

Someone who's PROFICIENT has made progress (in learning)—and may well make a PROFIT; if he or she is insufficiently proficient, the profit is "made away" with and becomes a DEFICIT. SURFEIT comes from VL *superfactum*, made in excess—that is, more than SUFFICIENT.

But by far the commonest of the "make" terms is the suffix -FY, meaning to make something take on certain qualities (stupify, justify, notify, etc.). A more remote relative is L *efficere*, to work out, whence both EFFECT (what results from something working out) and EFFICIENT—working out well. From the related L *facies*, FACE (the form in which something is made), we get FACADE (the "face" of a building), SURFACE (what's "on the face" of something), DEFACE (damage the "face" or surface), and EFFACE (remove the "face").

L *inficere* takes us back to the original, "put" sense of the root: it meant to dip (put) something into (? a vat of dye), hence stain, hence taint—whence INFECT. Gk *tithenai*, put, > the THESIS that a scholar puts forward and the THEME put forward in a literary work.

DHE(I)-, L *fellare*, to suck, > FELLATIO. L *femina*, woman ("she who suckles"), > FEMALE and FEMININE; its relative, *fetus*, pregnancy, childbearing, offspring, > both FETUS and EFFETE ("worn out from childbearing").

DHEIGH-, L *fingere*, *fict-*, to form, build, whence the FIGURE into which something is formed (something DISFIGURED is "deformed") and the FICTION "built" by writers. Another sense of the L verb, contrive, > FEIGN and also FAINT, which originally = feigned, then weak. (The shift in sense suggests that fainting may have been seen as feigning—which it occasionally is.)

The Gc members of the family center on forming loaves of bread from DOUGH. DAIRY goes back to an OE word meaning a female servant who made bread, though for centuries it has meant the source of the milk, butter, and cheese consumed with bread; LADY originally meant "loaf kneader"—the female head of a household (in fact, she did much more supervising than kneading—see *BLM*). The most unlikely member of the "knead" group comes from an Iranian word = wall (originally built of kneaded mud bricks), whence PARADISE, literally "walled around" (e.g., a park or garden); for its modern, figurative sense see *BLM*.

DHEL-, a hollow, whence DALE (a regional English word for "valley") and the DELL the farmer was in. A remote but attested relative comes from Joachimsthal ("Joachim's Valley"), a medieval German silver-mining center. Coins struck there were called "Joachimstalers," then "talers," then—DOLLARS.

DHEN-, to flow, > L *fons*, *font-*, a flowing spring or FOUNTAIN.

DHER-1, to make muddy, also Gc DARKness. Likewise Gc are the "muddy" DREGS of, e.g., wine, whence DRIVEL.

DHER-2, to support, hold FIRMly (< L *firmus*, firm, strong). If you AFFIRM something, you say it strongly; if you CONFIRM what someone says, you're "strong with" them; and if you're INFIRM—feeling shaky—you're not strong at all. MedL *firma* was a "firm" (fixed) payment—whence a rented tract of land or FARM.

DHERS-, to be bold, or Gc DARE.

DHES-, a root of uncertain religious meaning. Various L words referring to (religious) holidays give us FESTIVAL, FAIR, FIESTA, FEAST, and FESTIVE. L *fanum*, temple, gave us both the (religious) FANATIC and PROFANE language used "outside the temple" (see *BLM*). We find another religious sense in Gk *theos*, god, whence the ENTHUSIASM ("possession by a god") of the religiously devout, and the ATHEIST who does without any god.

DHEU-1, another root of blurred meaning; its ultimate sense may have been a rising cloud of Gc DUST or smoke, but derivatives also refer to breath, and even to impaired ("clouded") wits. From the "dust" or "cloud" senses come Gc DOWN (? feathers "fine as dust"), DUSK (the "clouded" time of day), and DOVE ("the dusky bird"), as European doves indeed are.

In the "clouded wits" (or perceptions) group are Gc DIZZY, DOZE, DEAF, DUMB, and DULL. From the "breath" sense we get Gc DEER—originally, any living, breathing animal ("Rats and mice and such small deer"—Shakespeare), but now a particular family of horned mammals. Finally, L *fumus*, smoke, > both unpleasant FUMES and pleasant PERFUMES; THYME, though certainly "perfumed," is < a Gk word = a burned (smoking) sacrifice.

DHEU-2, to flow, whence Gc DEW.

DHEU-3, to become exhausted (whence Gc DWINDLE) or Gc DIE, whence DEAD and DEATH.

DHEUB-, hollow, or Gc DEEP (whence DEPTH); also Gc DIVE ("go deep in the water") and ? DIP.

See **dub-**

DHGHEM-, L *humus*, earth, whence the HUMUS treasured by gardeners and the HUMBLE person ("close to the earth"); to HUMILIATE someone is to humble them. The root ? also = earthling (man, human being), whence Gc BRIDEGROOM, the "bride's man." We find the same sense in L *homo*, *homin-*, HUMAN being, whence HUMANE (having "human" feelings)—though humans also go in for HOMICIDE.

See **brudhiz**

See **kah-id-**

DHGH(Y)ES-, Gc YESTERDAY.

DHIGW-, L *figere*, *fix-*, to stick or FIX (in place; the modern sense, "repair," is idiomatic), whence also FIXTURE (something fixed in place) and the grammarian's PREFIX and SUFFIX, which are, respectively, "fixed" before and after a word or root. Gc members seem to derive from sticking a spade into the earth, whence the DITCH you DIG and also a DIKE—originally, a ditch, but now the ridge of earth thrown up by digging one.

DHRAGH-, DHREG-, Gc to DRAW, whence DRAG and DRAFT in all its senses—draft animals, a draft (drawing or sketch) of something, a current of air drawn through a room, and beer drawn from a cask. In Gc **dhreg-** also had the special sense of "draw into the mouth," DRINK, whence DRUNK, referring both to past drinking and to its results. To DRENCH someone "causes them to drink"; to DROWN them does the same, in spades.

DHREIBH-, Gc to DRIVE—and driven snow DRIFTS.

DHREU-, to fall, Gc DROOP, flow, or Gc DRIP, whence the DROPS that drip, the DRIZZLE of a dripping day—which may well be DREARY (though the word originally referred to flowing blood). Akin to the "droop" sense is Gc DROWSE (originally = be sluggish).

DHREUGH-, to deceive—which a Gc DREAM can certainly do.

DHUGhTER-, Gc DAUGHTER.

[Celtic-Germanic DHUNO-, fortified, enclosed place—eventually, a Gc TOWN. A Gc term ? = hill (a logical site for a fortified place) > DUNE, the DOWNS of southern England—and the down that's where you go from the top of a dune or down.]

DHWEN-, to make a noise or Gc DIN.

DHWER-, Gc DOOR (originally, the gate to the fenced compound where the family and its animals lived). L *foras*, *foris* meant out of doors, whence FOREST, or outside, whence FOREIGN. And if a bank FORECLOSES on your home, it closes the door with you outside.

See **kleu-3**

DLK-U-, sweet, whence sugary Gk GLUCOSE and LICORICE, literally = sweet root.

See **wrad-**

DNGHU-, Gc TONGUE; the L equivalent, *lingua* (originally, *dingua*), gives us such obvious derivatives as LANGUAGE, LINGO, LINGUIST, and BILINGUAL ("two tongues").

DO-, L *dare*, *dat-*; *donare*, *donat-*; Gk *didonai*; Russian *dat'*, to give. *Donare* begot such obvious descendants as DONATE and DONOR and some not so obvious, since it could also mean PARDON; if you CONDONE something you're giving the perpetrator an unofficial pardon.

L *dare* survives in English only in figurative senses; DATA are (or is) what's "given"; so, in a different sense, is a DATE. An EDITION is (a piece of writing) "given out" (whence EDIT, prepare for publication), and if you "give" one number to another, you ADD them.

A TRADITION is "given across" from one generation to another, while a TRAITOR also "gives across" something— to the enemy (whence TREASON and BETRAY). If you RENDER something you give it up, as with RENT to a landlord or what you "render unto Caesar"; if you SURRENDER, you "give [yourself] under." A related L noun gives us DOWRY, the gift with which the bride's family ENDOWS the new couple.

The Gk verb gives us the DOSE a doctor gives you and the ANTIDOTE you get if the dose is too big. An ANECDOTE was originally "not given out" (published); some of the best anecdotes are still unpublished—as old newsmen say, "The best stories are the ones you can't print." The Russian *dat'*, finally, begot *izdat*, "give out"—publish (compare "edition" above), whence SAMIZDAT—publishing by oneself.

See **sem-1**

[**Latin DORSUM,** back, > the DORSAL fins of fish, the ENDORSEMENT you write on the back of a check, and DOSSIER—originally, a bundle of papers with a label on the back (modern dossiers are more often stored in government computers).]

DREM-, to sleep, whence (via L) the DORMITORY people sleep in and DORMANT, "sleeping" (as many plants are in winter).

[**Germanic DREUG-,** DRY, whence DROUGHT and the DRAIN that "dries" (remove water from) something.]

[**Germanic DUB-, DUP-,** to drop or dip. If you drop something suddenly, you DUMP it, while a "dip" in the skin is a DIMPLE. A more intricate evolution gives us DOPE, from a Dutch word meaning a sauce you dip things into, then a gooey mass of opium (see *BLM*).]

[**Germanic DUD-,** to shake or DODDER, as some elderly people do when they're in their DOTAGE—the time of life when they (supposedly) DOTE foolishly.]

[**Latin DUELLUM, later BELLUM,** war. The earlier form gives us the DUEL in which two people "make war"; the later, such obvious derivatives as the BELLIGERENT who carries on a war, and the REBEL who makes war, literally or figuratively, against a government—or "prevailing community standards." Rebels sometimes engage in noisy rioting; so, sometimes, do REVELErs.]

See **gerere**

[**Germanic DUNGA,** DUNG, ? specifically, dung used as fertilizer—see *OMNT*.]

DWEI-, to fear, whence L DIRE—something to be much feared—and Gk DINOSAUR, the "fearsome lizard." (In fact, dinosaurs weren't lizards and weren't necessarily fearsome: some were the size of chickens.)

■ This root, akin to the following one, originally = of two minds—which you may well be if you're fearful. Cf Macaulay's acount of the fearful, two-minded Etruscan army when "those behind cried 'Forward!' and those before cried 'Back!' "

DWO-, L *duo*, Gc TWO. Gc TWELVE means "two left" after you've counted over your ten fingers, TWENTY = TWICE ten—and TWINS come in twos. Gc BETWEEN usually involves two things, one on either side; TWILIGHT is the light between sunset and night. TWINE was originally made of two strands TWISTed together; a particular way of "twisting" (weaving) gives us TWILL and TWEED fabrics. And when a branch forks in two, you get a TWIG.

See **leip-**

See **leuk-**

The L word, through various channels, > DOUBLE, the DUET for two instruments or voices, and the DUPLICATE or twofold document, whence the DUPLICITY of the "twofold," two-faced person (see *BLM*). If you're in DOUBT or

See **plek-**

DUBIOUS, you're of two minds, and DOZEN comes from L *duodecem*, "two and ten."

A variant of this root may have = (broken or cut) in two, whence ? the ideas of separation, "away from," "down from," and even negation in the L prefixes DE- and DIS-.

ED-, L *edere*, *es-*, Gc to EAT, whence FRET, "eat at" (or be eaten at by) something; an ETCHing is made by "eating" a design (with acid) into a metal plate used to make a print. The L verb gives us EDIBLE—and the OBESE person who overeats.

EG, L *ego*, Gc I. From the L we get the EGOIST who's got a lot of "I" in his or her psychology.

EG-, L *egere*, to lack, whence the INDIGENT person who lacks nearly everything.

EG-2, to speak, say, whence L ADAGE (saying) and PRODIGY—originally, some extraordinary happening that "spoke before" (foretold) an important event, but now usually an extraordinary young person. PRODIGIOUS has taken on yet another shade of meaning: extraordinarily enormous.

EGHS, out, whence L *ex*, out of, away from, whence EX, EX-, sometimes softened to ES- or shortened to E-. Also L are the "outside" words EXTERIOR, EXTERNAL, EXTRA(-), STRANGE (outside one's usual experience), STRANGER ("outsider"), and EXTREME ("outermost").

EGNI-, L *ignis*, fire, whence IGNITE, and the molten, often fiery IGNEOUS rock that wells up from the depths of the earth.

EGWH-, to drink, whence L *ebrius*, drunk or INEBRIATEd. Someone who was "without drink" was *sobrius*, SOBER.

EI-1, L *ire*, *it-*, to go; English descendants are mostly prefixed forms of the L verb, used figuratively. AMBITION is a "going about" in search of advancement (see *BLM*); the AMBIENCE of something is the things going on around it; a CIRCUIT goes around a "circle" (as, from the negative back to the positive terminal of a battery). COITUS is a "going together," an EXIT is where you go out, an OBITUARY concerns someone who's "gone away" (permanently) or PERISHed ("gone completely"). See **sker-2**

SEDITION involves "going apart" (from the government), a TRANSIT system lets you "go across" from one place to another, a TRANSITIVE verb "goes across" from its subject to its direct object, and something TRANSIENT is always "going across"—that is, it's around only temporarily. L *comites* was originally a companion (one who "goes with" someone), but > the COUNT who was a "companion" of the king or emperor. Finally, *subire* was to go "under" (stealthily), and stealthy acts come without warning—SUDDENly.

A related L word, *iter*, journey ("a going") > ITINERARY (now, the schedule of a journey), the "journeying" ITINERANT worker, and even the traveling knight ERRANT. L *initium*, beginning (a "going in"), > INITIAL, INITIATE, and COMMENCE. It also = the doorway you go into, whence the Roman god Ianus, who presided over doorways (his two faces let him see both in and out) as a sort of celestial JANITOR; JANUARY marks the going out of one year and the coming in of another.

EI-2, reddish, Gc YEW (from its red berries).

EIK-, to be master of or Gc OWN. If you OWE someone, they "own" part of you—and you OUGHT (owe it to them) to pay up. FREIGHT is idiomatic; for its full pedigree, see *OEtD*.

See **arkhein**

See **gleubh**

EIS-1, source of various words meaning passion. L *ira*, anger, gives us IRE, IRATE, and IRASCIBLE. Gk *hieros*, filled with the divine passion, holy, > HIERARCHY—literally, "rule by priests"; the medieval Church was ruled by a hierarchy of priests, bishops, and cardinals, headed by the Pope. HIEROGLYPHICS were originally the "sacred carvings" of ancient Egyptian inscriptions, then any similar system of picture writing. Finally, a Gc term (probably < Celtic) = sacred metal > IRON.

■ The prehistoric "sacredness" of iron suggests that the Celts (or Germans) first encountered it in the form of iron meteorites, which have been worshiped in a number of cultures. Parallels to the term exist in other languages.

EIS-2, frost or Gc ICE.

See **pet(h)**

EKWO-, L *equus*, Gk *hippos*, horse (originally wild, not domesticated). The L word gives us EQUINE and EQUESTRIAN; the Gk one, HIPPOPOTAMUS—literally, "river horse." (As Hilaire Belloc remarked, "But why they call that thing a horse,/ That's what is Greek to me!")

■ Though a hippo looks nothing like a horse, it's also quite unlike any other animal the Greeks knew; you might say they did the best they could with the words they had. The suggestion by some scholars that **ekwo-** derives from **kwon-**, dog, is very dubious indeed; the Indo-Europeans, familiar with both animals, were well aware that they weren't at all alike in either appearance or habits.

EL-1, forearm or Gc ELBOW—literally, the "bow" (bend) where the forearm begins.

See
bheug-3

EL-2, red or brown, in tree and animal names, including the ELM, ALDER, and ELK. But not, I think, the AUK, as some scholars claim: the birds are conspicuously black and white. Moreover, they are not known south of the Baltic, meaning that the ancient Germans probably borrowed the word there (see Introduction).

[**Greek ELAIWA,** L *oliua*, *oliva*, OLIVE, whence the OIL pressed from its fruits. PETROLEUM is "rock oil."]

See **petra**

■ The L word may or may not have been borrowed < Gk, but both words certainly originated in some lost tongue of the Mediterranean lands, to which the olive is native.

ELK-ES-, a wound, > L ULCER.

EM-, to take, distribute, > L *emere*, to take, buy, whence the old phrase *Caveat emptor!* (Let the buyer beware!). Otherwise, it's reached English only in compounds; thus, from *exemere*, to take out, we get the SAMPLE and EXAMPLE "taken out" of a larger quantity or group; a PREEMPTive strike takes away in advance the enemy's capacity to retaliate—or so the generals tell us. From *peremere*, *perempt-*, take away entirely, we get the PEREMPTORY order that "takes away" any disobedience.

L *redimere*, buy back, > REDEEM, a related noun > the RANSOM paid to buy back a captive. L *promptus*, ready ("taken forth," as a sword from the scabbard), > PROMPT; *demere*, take away, > the VINTAGE when wine was "taken away" from the grapes ("trampling out the vintage"); now, more often wine you take away from the store at fancy prices.

See **w(o)in-**

Finally, *sumere*, take, obtain, buy, produced ASSUME, "take to [oneself]" ("Assume a virtue, if you have it not"—Shakespeare), CONSUME ("take with"), RESUME ("take again"), and PRESUME ("assume beforehand"); in Anglo-American law an accused person is presumed innocent until proven guilty).

EN, L *in(-)*, Gc IN, whence INNER—"farther in"—and ?? AND. From the L term (both a preposition and a prefix) we get the English prefixes EN- and IN-/IM-. (For the "negative" IN-/IM-, as in "insomnia" and "impossible," see **ne**.) The L preposition was elaborated into *intro*, inward, within, whence INTRODUCE ("lead within"), and *intra*, inside, within, whence ENTER, INTRA- (intramural sports are "within the walls" of a school or college), and INTRINSIC, referring to the "inside" qualities of something. Related L words gave us INTIMATE ("innermost"), INTESTINES—our "innards"—and, very remotely, the idiomatic INDUSTRY.

See **deuk-**

EN-ES-, L *onus*, burden. An ONUS is a figurative burden, something ONEROUS is burdensome, and to EXONERATE is to "take off the burden [of alleged guilt]."

ER-1, to move, set in motion. Possible Gc descendants are ARE and EARNEST, but the connection (if it exists) is not clear. More certain is L *oriri*, to arise, whence ORIGIN (where something arose) and ORIENT ("toward the rising sun"). The I-Es oriented themselves by facing the rising sun (see **deks-**); "the Orient" is the lands that (to Europeans) lie in that direction. *Aborire*, *abort-*, "arise away from," miscarry, > ABORT. / aboriginal

ER-2, Gc EARTH.

ERGH-, to mount; its two alleged descendants may or may not be legitimate. Gk *orkhein*, put in motion (? as a horse, after mounting it), > ORCHESTRA, originally, the part of a theater below the tiered seats, where the dancers moved about; now more often the musicians who occupy the front of that space. But Gk *orkhis*, testicle, whence OR-CHID (from the shape of its bulbs), is probably < a separate root.

ERh-1, to ROW or paddle (a canoe)—whence Gc RUDDER, originally the steering oar or paddle.

■ The Indo-Europeans almost certainly knew no water craft larger than a dugout, as shown by their borrowing of the words for ship (see **skipam**) and oar (see **airo**).

ERh-2, to separate. L *rarus* = widely separated, hence RARE; Gk *eremos* meant empty, desolate (even more "widely separated"), whence the HERMIT who lived in such places (notably, the Egyptian desert). Interestingly, the word has moved back toward its original sense: we now think of hermits as living not so much in desolate places as (self-)separated from the rest of humanity.

ERhD-, high, whence L *ardus*, high, steep; a high, steep slope is ARDUOUS to climb.

ERS-1, to be in motion, as in a Gc RACE. We find another kind of motion in L *errare*, wander, whence ERR, ERROR, ERRATIC, and ABERRATION—all of which involve wandering away from the truth or the normal course of things.

■ The relationship—if any—between this root and **ei-1** is unclear. What is certain is that their L descendants became badly confused in OF, so that a "knight errant" was both a journeying knight and a wandering knight—who may also have erred in the course of his travels.

ERS-2, to be wet, whence L *ros* ~~rosée~~ , dew. ROSEMARY was origi-

See **mori-** nally *ros marinus*, sea dew; it's a common seashore plant along the Mediterranean.

ES-, L *esse*, to be, whence the ESSENCE or "being" of something, ABSENT ("being away"), and PRESENT ("being in front [of one]"). A more remote relative is L *prodesse*, be of value, whence PROUD (of one's supposed value); even more remote is L *interest*, "it is between," hence, it makes a difference, matters—whence INTEREST (if you're interested in something, it matters to you). To REPRESENT originally meant "bring into one's PRESENCE" (where one is), but its modern senses are idiomatic.

Gc derivatives include IS and AM (parts of the verb "to be"), and the compound YES ("may it be so"); another compound gives us SIN, "what is real," which sin sometimes is (sometimes it's merely in the mind of the sinner). A related term > the obsolete "sooth," truth ("what is"). And if you tell people that they're saying sooth—"yes" them—you'll SOOTHE them (the evolution in meaning, though almost too good to be true, is well established).

ESEN-, harvest, > do harvest work, > work for wages, > Gc EARN.

ETI-, supposedly the root of Gc EIDER (duck). In fact, the duck, like the auk, does not migrate south of the Baltic, meaning that the Indo-Europeans could not have known—or named—it.

See **al-2**

EU-, L *vanus*, empty, lacking, whence VANISH ("leave empty"), VAIN (empty) boasting, and the equally "empty" VANITY. L *vacare* = to be empty or VACANT, whence the VACATION when we VACATE our normal haunts. Even more empty is a VACUUM or total VOID; to EVACUATE is to empty out, literally or figuratively. Finally, L *uastus/vastus* meant empty or WASTE (as land), whence DEVASTATE, lay waste, and VAST.

Gc derivatives come from the "lacking" sense; if you WANT something, whether it's a million dollars or a mate, you obviously lack it. A variant = become lacking or diminish—WANE, as the moon does for part of every month.

EUhDH-, Gc UDDER, > L *uber*, breast, fertile, whence the "bursting-out" EXUBERANT fertility of vegetation—and the bursting-out spirits of exuberant people.

EUS-, to burn, > L COMBUSTION and, after the fire dies down, Gc EMBERS.

[**Latin FERRUM,** iron (almost certainly < Etruscan), whence the chemist's FERROUS and FERRIC (iron-containing) and the FARRIER who shoes horses with iron. But the suggestion that BRASS comes from the same source is highly unlikely, to say the least, on both phonetic and semantic grounds.]

■ The Etruscans pretty certainly migrated to Italy, from Asia Minor, shortly before 1500 B.C.—that is, soon after the invention of ironworking in precisely that part of the world. And archaeology tells us that they were highly skilled ironworkers. It seems very likely, then, that the Romans borrowed both the technology and the word from them.

But "brass" is Gc—and the Germans had little or no contact with the Etruscans. More: they had their own word for iron, hence would hardly have borrowed (and grossly distorted) the Etruscan word, let alone transferred it to a conspicuously different metal.

See **eis-1**

[**Germanic FRANKON-,** javelin, whence the Germanic Franks who fought with it—successfully enough to give their name to FRANCE and the FRENCH. As conquerers, the Franks were the only altogether free people in France—hence, you might say, the only ones who could speak freely or FRANKly.]

gegen

[**Germanic GAGINA,** in a direct line with, hence AGAINST ("face-to-face"—compare **ant-**). AGAIN originally = in the opposite ("against") direction; later, "in return," whence its present meaning, "once more." To GAINSAY something is to "say against" it, while UNGAINLY goes back to the basic sense: it originally meant "not straight"—i.e., not in line with.]

GAL-1, bald, naked; Gc CALLOW originally = without feathers (a naked young bird), whence its current sense, "immature."

GAL-2, to shout or Gc CALL, whence noisy CLATTER.

GAR-, to call or cry, whence Gc CARE—originally = grieve, lament ("cry"). If you're CHARY of doing something (e.g., giving praise), you do it with care—if at all. From L *garrire*, to chatter, comes the chattering, GARRULOUS person; from Gaelic *slugorne*, war cry, comes SLOGAN—which is, indeed, a politician's or businessman's "war cry."

[**Germanic GARWIAN,** to make, prepare, equip; your GEAR is your equipment, as is your GARB.]

GAU-, L *gaudere*, to REJOICE, whence both JOY and ENJOY. (GAUDY is sometimes assigned to this family, but is probably from an obscure Gc root.)

[**Greek GE,** the earth, whence GEO- (-graphy, -logy, etc.).]

GEI-, to sprout or split open (like a sprouting bud), whence Gc CHINK, as in a split board.

GEL-, to form into a ball—the alleged base of many loosely related words (see below). One group concerns masses or lumps of something—Gc CLUMP, CLUB, CLOUD (originally, a hill; now a "hill" in the sky), CLOD, CLOT, KLUTZ (literally a lump; figuratively a lumpish fellow), and CLUE (originally, a ball of yarn—see *BLM*). A possible L relative is GLOBE.

More dubiously related is a group of words meaning to stick or Gc CLING to, whence CLENCH, CLINCH, CLUTCH, CLAW, and CLIMB (if you're climbing rocks, you'd better cling tight!). Probably akin to these are words meaning to fasten, such as Gc CLIP, CLAMP, and the CLAM whose shells clamp shut; others refer to sticky substances that cling to you—Gc CLAY and L GLUE. Gc CLAMMY originally = sticky; its modern sense—cold and moist—comes from "clam."

■ I think the experts may have gone overboard in, well, clumping all these words together. More likely, we're dealing with at least two distinct roots, one referring to lumps, the other to sticking to or clutching something.

GEL-2, bright, shining, whence Gc CLEAN ("the schoolboy, with shining morning face . . ."—Shakespeare).

GEL-3, to freeze, also Gc COLD, whence COOL and CHILL. From L we get CONGEAL ("freeze together"), as well as GELATIN and JELLY, which also congeal, though not by freezing. A more remote L relative is GLACIER.

GEMBH-, tooth (also fingernail), whence the toothed Gc COMB and the "uncombed," UNKEMPT person.

GEMh-, Gk *gamein*, to marry, whence the -GAMY in "monogamy," etc.

GEN-, like **gel-1**, another catchall root (see below). Its supposed meaning was "compress into a ball," whence KNEAD, but also ? various Gc words describing compressed, KNOBby things and ?? others meaning sharp blows. The "knobs" include CLUB, NUB, KNUCKLE, KNOLL (a "knob" of ground), and ? KNOT, whence KNIT (originally = tie with a knot). The "sharp blows" group includes KNOCK, KNACK (originally = sharp blow), and KNACKWURST—a sausage that cracks (German *knackt*) sharply when cut or bitten. More remotely connected—if at all—is KNIFE.

■ The very diverse descendants of this alleged root suggest that here, too, we're actually dealing with two or more different ones—probably not even Indo-European. Their descendants are found only in Gc—which, incidentally, was rich in non–I-E words beginning with KN- (modern examples are "knave" and "knight," which five centuries ago were pronounced as spelled). So—why not call it a Germanic root and be done with it? Ask the experts!

GEN(h)-, to beget, give birth, with derivatives referring to children (L PROGENY), families (Gc KIN), and tribal groups (which originated as extended families). Gc descendants come from the "family" sense; they include KIND, both the noun (What kind is it? = What is it AKIN to?) and the adjective (if someone is kind to you, they're treating you like kin). Cf. Hamlet's bitter play on words, when he calls his infamous uncle "a little more than kin, and less than kind."

The L family members are much more diverse. Most directly related to the root sense (beget/birth) are the GENITAL organs we beget with, PREGNANT ("before birth"), the

CONGENITAL traits we're born with (usually GENETIC), which are also the INNATE ones born in us—our NATURE. More distant are NATION (originally = race, breed), whose people are INDIGENOUS ("born in [a particular place]"), and RENAISSANCE, a figurative rebirth.

L *genius* originally = a god of procreation, then the innate qualities that were one's GENIUS. An ENGINE was originally any device invented by an INGENIOUS (naturally talented) person. In BENIGN (good-natured) and MALIGN (evil-natured), the GEN- has been compressed to -GN.

A side branch of this part of the family centers not on being born but on what one is born into. If you were well-born you were GENTEEL, a GENTLEMAN or -WOMAN (whence GENTLE), while GENEROUS originally = nobly born (the nobles could afford to be). NATIVE, by contrast, originally = lowborn (specifically, born a serf or slave) and therefore NAIVE. PUNY, finally, comes from French *puis ne*, later born, younger, hence inferior in size or strength.

GENERATE originally meant to produce offspring, but now to produce power and other things; DEGENERATE is < a Latin word meaning "away from one's kind"—in a bad sense, of course ("not our kind of person"). Also in this group, though more loosely related, are the L GERMs that sometimes GERMINATE in our bodies, and Gk GENESIS (from a word = nativity, hence beginning—see below).

A second L group centers around the notion of tribe—the biologist's GENUS—or kind—the original meaning of GENDER. GENEALOGY is the study of "tribes" (families); GENOCIDE, the killing off of an entire "tribe." What's GENERALly true of a group of things is true of the whole "tribe"; a military general—originally, "general officer"—commands, you might say, a whole tribe of soldiers.

■ Genesis is, of course, the book of the Bible that deals with the beginning of everything. However, a seventeenth-century Scottish translation is said to have called it "The Buke of Swiving" (screwing)—presumably through confusion with the act of generation. Considering how often one or another of the Patriarchs in Genesis "knew his wife and begat," the mistranslation (if it actually occurred) was not inappropriate.

GENU-1, Gc KNEE, whence KNEEL; also angle, corner, Gk *gonia*, whence DIAGONAL—"across from corner to corner."

GENU-2, jawbone or Gc CHIN.

GER-1, to gather, whence Gc CRAM—the result of energetic gathering. Gathering animals into a flock (L *grex*, *greg-*) has given us the GREGARIOUS person who likes to "flock" with others, AGGREGATE ("flock or gather toward"), CON-GREGATE ("flock with"—a preacher's congregation is his or her flock), SEGREGATE ("gather apart"), and EGREGIOUS ("out of the flock"—see *BLM*).

Gk *agora*, a marketplace or place of assembly (where people gathered together), > *agoreuein*, to speak (in the agora), whence ALLEGORY, "speaking otherwise" (i.e., in figurative language) and the idiomatic CATEGORY, < a verb = accuse ("speak down"), but long ago softened to its present sense.

GER-2, ? to bend, is another "hypothetical" (or pseudo-) I-E root (compare **gen-**); its descendants, found only in Gc words beginning with GR- and KR-, all refer ultimately to bent, curved, or CROOKED objects, or actions involving them. They include the seaman's hooked GRAPNEL with which he GRAPPLES for submerged objects. (In British slang, a crooked person is "bent.")

Other family members are the "bent-over" CRIPPLE and the bent CRUTCH with which he or she CREEPS about; CREEK (originally, and still in Britain, a crooked inlet from the sea); the CRAMP that bends us over in pain; the bent, mechanical CRANK—and the human crank with a "bent" mind. Verbs in the family include CRIMP (as a nail, by bending it over), CRINGE (bend away), CROUCH (bend down), CRUMPLE, and CRINKLEd CURLS.

Other crooked things or actions include ENCROACH (originally, to seize or "hook" something), the twisted CRULLER, LACROSSE (played with a bent stick), and the idiomatic GRAPE, < Gc *krappon*, a hook; later, a bunch of grapes (F *grappe*) harvested with a sharpened hook; finally, a single fruit on the bunch.

Allegedly related (and "allegedly" is the operative word) is a group of terms = a rounded mass, hence, a collection, hence a container used to collect or hold things. The "masses" include CRUMB and CROP (originally, a bundle of grain); the containers, CROCK, CRIB, CRADLE, and CART.

GERBH-, Gk *graphein*, to scratch. Gc family members include the scratchy CRAB, the almost equally scratchy CRAYFISH or crawfish, CARVE (originally = to cut), and ? CRAWL ("move like a crab").

Gk *graphein* could also mean draw or write ("scratch" lines or letters), whence the GRAPH drawn to GRAPHICally show a relationship—DIAGRAM it (< *gramma*, picture, letter, writing, whence also GRAMMAR). From the same source are -GRAPH (TELEGRAPH = distant writing; autograph = one's own writing), the PARAGRAPHs in a piece of writing, the GRAPHITE sometimes used for writing (it's the "lead" in a pencil), the PROGRAM that originally = public writing (a notice), and the GRAFFITO written on a wall.

[**Latin GERERE**, **GEST-,** carry on or out, act, do, whence the BELLIGERENT who carries on a war. A GESTURE was originally your bearing—the way you act—and a JEST was originally any deed (action) or exploit, though now only a funny one. Other descendants are figurative: CON-GEST (< *congestus*, heaped together), DIGEST (< *digestus*, arranged, dissolved), REGISTER (< *regestus*, recorded), and SUGGEST (< *suggestus*, carried—now, to "carry" an idea into the mind).]

See **duellum**

GERh-1, to grow old, whence Gk GERIATRICS.

GERh-2, to cry hoarsely, also the hoarse-crying L GRACKLE and Gc CRANE and CROW—both the bird and what a rooster does. The "hoarse cry" sense > Gc CROON, CRACK, and ?? the hoarsely growling CUR; the "crane" sense > the builder's crane (see *BLM*) and the Gc CRANBERRY, supposedly relished by cranes; the Gk GERANIUM has fruits shaped like a crane's bill.

G(E)U-LO-, a glowing COAL.

GEUS-, to taste or Gc CHOOSE, whence CHOICE. From L come both the GUSTO with which you consume tasty things and the DISGUST evoked by distasteful ones.

GHABH-, GHEBH-, to receive or Gc GIVE, whence GIFT. Also Gc is FORGIVE, originally = give up (one's anger). L *habere*, *habit-*, possess, hold, have (something given to you), > ABLE (have the power to do something), -ABLE,

-IBLE, and ABILITY. From the same L verb come EXHIBIT ("hold out"), INHIBIT ("hold in"), and PROHIBIT ("hold back" [people from doing something]). A related verb, *habitare, habitat-*, to dwell, > the HABITAT an animal habitually INHABITS, the HABITS that "dwell" in us, and COHABIT (dwell together). Finally, L *debere, debit-*, to owe (? "be obliged to give back"), > the DEBT that's DUE your creditor, which it's your DUTY to pay.

■ The fact that the same root could = both give and receive may reflect the importance in I-E life of reciprocal giving and receiving—both goods and hospitality; see **ghos-ti-**.

GHABHOLO-, fork or branch of a tree, hence (via Gaulish and OF) the JAVELIN made from the branch.

GHAI-, Gc to YAWN or GAPE, whence GASP and GAP. A gap in something is a L HIATUS; an enormous gap is a Gk CHASM.

GHAIDO-, Gc GOAT.

GHAIS-, L *haerere, haesit-*, to cling, stick or ADHERE; also, to HESITATE—what you do in a sticky situation. When things "stick together," they COHERE.

GHAISO-, a stick or spear, whence Gc GORE—a bull "spearing" with his horns—and ? the gore that flows when he does. Also Gc is GARLIC, the "spear leek," from its pointed cloves.

GHALGH-, a tree branch—the original Gc GALLOWS—or a rod, whence the rod or Gc GAUGE you measure things by.

GHANS-, Gc GOOSE and GANDER, whence GANNET, reputed to be as foolish at sea as the goose is on land (some species of gannets are called ''boobies'').

GHASTO-, rod, whence the rod used to measure feet and Gc YARDS.

GHE-, to release, whence Gc GO (''be released'') and AGO (five years ago = five years gone by). FOR(E)GO originally = ''cause to go away,'' hence pass over, abstain from; one's GAIT is the way one goes (both Gc). A possible relative is L *heres*, HEIR (? someone whose parents have ''gone''), whence INHERIT, HERITAGE, and HEREDITY.

GHEBH-EL-, head, whence ? the ''head'' or Gc GABLE of a pitched roof.

GHEDH-, to join, fit, or Gc GATHER things TOGETHER; things that are ''fitting'' are Gc GOOD.

GHEI-1, to prick or Gc GOAD (an animal).

GHEI-2, L *hiems*, winter, whence HIBERNATE—what some animals do in winter.

GHEIS-, (to) fear, fearsome, whence Gc GHOST, GHASTLY, and AGHAST.

GHEL-1, to call or Gc YELL, whence YELP. Later Gc derivatives = to sing, whence the NIGHTINGALE who sings at night.

GHEL-2, to shine, whence words denoting bright colors and colored things. The ''shining'' sense > a host of Gc words, including GLEAM, GLINT, GLITTER, GLIMMER, GLOAM-ING ("the twilight's last gleaming"), GLISTEN, GLARE, GLOSS, GLASS, GLOW, and even GLIMPSE (if you glimpse something shiny you get just a gleam of it). If your face is shining, you're GLAD, whence GLEE; if it's "shining" unpleasantly, you GLOWER or GLOAT.

The "color" words include Gc YELLOW and GOLD (whence GILD), Gk CHLORINE—a yellowish gas—and, via Arabic, AR-SENIC, ultimately < Persian *zar*, gold (some ores of arsenic are bright yellow). Gc GALL (bile) is greenish yellow; from the Gk equivalent, *khole*, we get CHOLER and MELAN-CHOLY—moods once ascribed to an excess of bile and "black bile" respectively (see *BLM*).

Very dubious relatives are a group of Gc words dealing with sliding or slipping; they include GLIDE; the GLITCH (slip) in, say, a computer program, and the GLIB, slippery person.

GHEL-3, to cut, whence Gc GELD (a gelded animal is still sometimes called "cut").

GHELDH-, to pay, whence (via Yiddish) the GELT some-one pays you—or you're forced to YIELD (both Gc).

■ The root occurs only in Germanic and Slavonic. Histori-cally, it crops up in "Danegeld"—the protection money that the early English were forced to pay Danish pirates.

GHELD-UNA, jaw, whence the Gc GILLS of a fish.

GHEN-, Gc to GNAW; possible Gc relatives are NAG (to "gnaw" at someone), NOSH (to "gnaw" at a snack), and ?? the GNAT that "gnaws" at you.

■ This is another "hypothetical" I-E root; more likely, it's pure Gc.

GHE(N)D-, to seize or take, whence Gc GET, FORGET ("take away" [a memory]), BEGET (originally = acquire), and GUESS—originally = take aim (we don't always hit what we're aiming—or guessing—at).

L family members mostly derive from *pre(he)ndere*, to seize, grasp, or get hold of, whence the PRISON that "seizes" and holds you, the IMPREGNABLE fortress that can't be seized, and the PRIZE (enemy ship) seized in wartime. (The prize you strive for, however, is related to "price"—see **per-6**.)

To APPREHEND and COMPREHEND are both ways of grasping ideas (on the figurative meaning of APPREHENSIVE, see *BLM*), while an APPRENTICE is being trained to "grasp" (learn) a skilled trade. An ENTERPRISE is "work taken in hand" (grasped), hence a business undertaking launched by an ENTREPRENEUR; a SURPRISE "seizes" you suddenly. A related L word, *praeda*, booty, > PREY, PREDATOR, and ?? SPREE.

GHER-1, to grasp, enclose, hence an enclosure such as a Gc YARD, ORCHARD, or GARDEN, whence KINDERGARTEN—a "garden" for children (German *Kinder*); also Gc is the GIRDLE that encloses one's waist or hips. L *hortus*, garden, > HORTICULTURE; another kind of enclosure was a COURT, whence the enclosures where kings and judges hold forth—COURTEOUSly (in theory). A COURTESAN courts the favor of her lover(s) or customers.

Less certainly related is Gk *khoros*, a dancing ground (? enclosed area), whence the CHORUS of dancers or singers, whence CHOIR and CHORALE.

GHER-2, to call out, hence Gc GREET.

GHER-3, to shine, glow, whence ? Gc GRAY.

GHER-4, to scratch, whence Gk *kharassein*, to carve, cut, whence GASH. From the same Gk source is CHARACTER—originally, a distinctive (carved) mark; now usually the distinctive marks that heredity and experience have "carved" into our personalities. The metaphor dates from ancient times.

GHER-5, to like, want, or Gc YEARN for something; if you want it very much, you may get Gc GREEDY. If you L EXHORT someone, you're trying to make them want something.

GHERh-, Gk *khorde*, gut, string, or Gc CORD, whence YARN—the "cord" you knit or weave with. If part of your gut protrudes through your abdominal wall, you have a L HERNIA.

■ The gut/string relationship reflects the fact that animal intestines, only marginally edible, were "recycled" into tough cordage; until quite recently, many musical strings, subject to great tension, were made of gut. The "chord" of musical notes sounding together is unrelated; it derives from "accord"—see **kerd-1**.

GHERS-, to bristle, whence the bristly Gc GORSE bush and L URCHIN—originally, the prickly hedgehog; now the equally prickly sea urchin, as well as "prickly" (irritating) little boys. Also L are HORROR and things you ABHOR, which make your hair bristle ("stand on end")—see *BLM*.

GHESLO-, ? thousand, whence L MILLI- (millimeter = $\frac{1}{1000}$ of a meter) and MILE (a Roman mile was a thousand paces—*mille passuum*); also MILLENNIUM. The Gk equivalent was *khilioi*, whence KILO- (one kilometer = 1,000 meters).

■ A dubious root: the Indo-Europeans had few or no opportunities to count by thousands. Note that the Gc word for "thousand" is an independent coinage (see **dekm**), and the same may well be true of the L and Gk terms.

GHESOR-, Gk *kheir*, hand, whence the SURGEON who operates on you (with his hands) rather than changing your diet or giving you drugs as other physicians do.

GHEU-1, L *fundere*, *fus-*, to pour, whence the FUNNEL through which you pour things, and the FOUNDRY in which FUSEd (molten) metal is poured into molds. Figurative uses include CONFUSE ("pour together"), DIFFUSE ("pour apart"), PROFUSE ("pouring forth"), TRANSFUSE ("pour across"), and REFUND ("pour back"). To REFUSE is another kind of "pouring back"—though some derive the word from a quite different root. A more remote L relative is *futilis*, easily emptied, leaky; pouring water into a leaky vessel is FUTILE.

Gc members of the tribe include GUSH, GUST (a "gush" of wind), the GEYSER from which hot water gushes, and— improbably but pretty certainly—GUT (? because the guts of a butchered animal "pour out").

GHEU-, to yawn or gape (? related to **ghai-**), whence the GUMS you expose when you do. A Gk word for a yawning chasm gave us CHAOS, from which a seventeenth-century Dutch scientist coined GAS.

GHEU(h)-, to call, invoke, whence the Gc GOD one invokes, and GIDDY—a word much weakened from its original sense, "possessed by a god, insane."

GHOS-TI-, Gc GUEST, L HOST—more precisely, "someone with whom one has reciprocal duties of L HOSPITALITY"—see below. Also < L are words for institutions offering various sorts of hospitality: HOSPITALs to the ill, HOSTELs to young travelers, and HOTELs to anyone who can pay. But a guest could also be a stranger—who might be HOSTILE (note that "host" can also = army). A hostage is an involuntary "guest," but the word comes from a quite different root—see **sed-1**.

■ This root implies that to the Indo-Europeans, as to many of their linguistic descendants, the host/guest relationship was semisacred. We know from history that in ancient Greece an important institution was "guest friendship": a host's obligation to shelter the guest within his walls, and the guest's obligation to offer reciprocal hospitality in the future. The resulting network of mutual obligations helped bind society together beyond the bounds of the individual extended family.

GHOW-E-, to revere or worship; we still sometimes Gc GAWK at those we revere—and hope they will L FAVOR us. (Not all experts accept these derivations, and I'm not so sure myself.)

GHRE-, Gc to GROW or become GREEN, whence GRASS.

GHREBH-1, to reach, seize, Gc GRASP or GRAB.

GHREBH-2, to scratch or dig, hence bury. The "scratch" sense > Gc GROOVE and ENGRAVE ("scratch" a design onto a piece of metal); the "dig/bury" sense > Gc GRAVE.

GHREDH-, L *gradi*, *gress-*, to walk, step, or go; its English descendants are all figurative. A CONGRESS "walks together," though often contentiously; if it PROGRESSES, it "walks forward," if it REGRESSES or RETROGRESSES, backward. Its members may speak AGGRESSIVELY ("walking toward" [an opponent]), often DIGRESS ("walk away from" [the point]), and sometimes TRANSGRESS ("walk across") the boundaries of ethical conduct. The related L noun = step has given us GRADE and DEGREE—the "steps" by which we rank things. Someone or something DEGRADEd has lost rank, while RETROGRADE motion "steps backward."

GHREI-, to rub, whence Gk CHRIST—literally, "the anointed one" (i.e., rubbed with perfumed oil)—whence CHRISTIAN and CHRISTMAS. In some Christian denominations, a baby is CHRISTENed by being literally "anointed"—smeared with consecrated oil. Less certain relatives are Gc GRISLY (? "rubbing or grating on the mind") and GRIME (? "rubbed-in dirt").

GHREIB-, Gc to GRIP, whence GROPE—and the GRIPPE that "grips" us so tightly and unpleasantly.

GHREM-, angry, whence Gc GRIM and the GRIMACEs angry people make—unless they merely GRUMBLE. Through Russian we get POGROM, literally "like thunder" (? "anger of the gods"), hence destruction. The anti-Jewish pogroms of Czarist Russia did indeed fall on their miserable victims like thunder.

GHRENDH-, Gc to GRIND. In L the root > *frenum* [*frein*], the bit on which a horse's teeth grind—and which forces it to REFRAIN from running away. ?Grendel

115

GHREU-, to grind (? related to previous root), whence the
Gc GRIT produced by grinding, and (via Gaulish and OF)
GRAVEL—originally, coarse sand. We find the same idea in
Gc GREAT, originally, coarse or thick. A less certain Gc
relative is GRUESOME (? the quality of "grinding" on one's
sensibilities). Even less certain is Gk *khroma*, skin (??
"rough surface"), hence complexion, color, whence
CHROMATIC (having to do with color) and CHROMIUM,
from its colorful compounds, many of them used as pigments.

GHWER-, wild beast, whence L *ferus*, wild, untamed,
whence FIERCE and FEROCIOUS; a domestic animal that has
gone wild is FERAL.

GLEUBH-, to cut or Gc CLEAVE, whence the CLOVE of garlic
that can be easily cleaved from the bulb. CLEVER ?? comes
from an Old Norse word = easy to split, whence ? skillful,
but the connection is tenuous.

GNO-, L *(g)noscere*, *cognoscere*, Gc to KNOW, whence
CAN—originally, having the knowhow, KNOWLEDGE, or
CUNNING to do something. Also Gc is UNCOUTH—origi-
nally, unknown or unfamiliar. From the L verbs we get
many words dealing with various kinds of knowing: NO-
TICE ("something [made] known"), NOTIFY (cause some-
one to know), NOTION (something you know), NOTORI-
OUS (originally, well-known; now, all too well known),
RECOGNIZE ("know again"), IGNORANT (not knowing), IG-
NORE ("not [choose to] know"), the "known" or famous
NOBLE—and the CONNOISSEUR who really knows some field
such as art.

QUAINT (originally = skilled, knowledgeable) comes
from the same L source, but its evolution is intricate in

both sound and sense (see *OEtD*). From Gk we get the doctor's DIAGNOSIS (originally = discernment), in which he sets forth what he knows or discerns about the patient's illness, and the PROGNOSIS, in which he "discerns forward" its probable outcome. More distantly related is L NARRATE (? "tell what one knows"), but NOTE (originally, a sign or symbol), though it resembles "notice," etc., almost certainly comes from some other, unknown source.

[**Germanic GRAT-, KRAT-,** to SCRATCH, whence the GRATEr with which one "scratches" food into small bits.]

GREUT-, to compress or push, whence the compressed, pushing Gc CROWD and the pressed Gc CURD of sour milk. (According to the Roman historian Tacitus, curds—equivalent to our cottage cheese—were a major item in the primitive Germanic diet.)

GREN-NO-, L GRAIN and Gc CORN (originally, and still in Great Britain, grain of any kind; U.S. corn was originally "Indian corn"). Also from L are GRANITE (from its grainy texture) and GRENADE, an intricate metaphor involving the pomegranate ("grainy apple")—see *BLM*.

GRU-, Gc to GRUNT, whence GRUDGE (if you do something grudgingly, you do it with a grumbling grunt).

GWA-, GWEM-, to go or Gc COME; someone who is "well come" is WELCOME. From L *venire*, to come, we get the EVENT or ADVENTURE that comes to you, the AVENUE along which people come or approach, and the INVENTion that "comes into" your mind. A CONVENT is a "coming together" of religious folk; at a CONVENTION, it's the laity who get together.

Also < L are INTERVENE (originally, "come between" two disputants), REVENUE (the income that "comes back" from property to its owner—or from taxpayers to the government), and the SOUVENIR that makes a memory come back to you. From Gk *banein*, to go, walk, or step, we get the BASE (? "step") on which buildings and other things stand, and the ACROBAT who steps on tiptoe.

See **ak-**

GWEBH-, Gk *baptein*, to dip, whence BAPTIZE; some Christian denominations still baptize by dipping or immersion, as John the BAPTIST did Christ in the river Jordan.

GWEI(h)-, L *vivere*, to live, whence VIVACIOUS and VIVID, both = lively, and the VICTUALS and VITAMINS that are VITAL to life. To REVIVE is to "live again"; to SURVIVE, to "live on." From Gc we get QUICK, originally = alive ("the quick and the dead"), then lively, then rapid. In Gk the root begot three rather different descendants. From *bios*, life, we get BIO- (-logy, -chemistry, etc.), AMPHIBIOUS ("living both ways"), and MICROBE ("tiny life"). From *zoon*, living thing, we get ZOO- (-logy, etc.) and, of course, the "zoological garden" we now call a ZOO. Finally, from *hygies*, healthy ("living well"), comes HYGIENE.

See **(am)bho**
See **sme-**

GWEL-1, pierce, whence Gc KILL, also QUELL, which originally = the same thing. Piercing, with a knife or a bullet, is still the commonest way of killing.

GWEL-2, L *volare, volat-*, to fly, whence the VOLATILE substance that "flies" into the air (as a gas), and the VOLLEY that "flies" in a different way.

GWEL-3, L *gula*, throat or GULLET; from a related L term comes the GLUTTON who GLUTS himself or herself. KEEL has been assigned to this root (?? "throat" of a vessel), but is more likely exotic, borrowed by the Germans from the aboriginal Baltic people who taught them to construct keeled vessels (see Introduction, and compare **skipam** and **airo**).

GWELBH-, Gk *delphus*, womb, whence ?? DOLPHIN (presumably from its shape) and DELPHINIUM, from the dolphinlike shape of part of its flower.

■ The supposed relationship between the animal and the organ seems to me farfetched, even if we accept their rather remote similarity in shape: the dolphin was almost certainly named by sailors—few of whom could ever have seen a womb. I'd guess the Greeks borrowed the original word from the seagoing Minoans (see Introduction) and, by the process called "folk etymology," distorted it into something that sounded like a Greek word.

GWELh-1, to reach or throw, Gk *ballein*, whence various figurative terms (most of them via L). A PROBLEM "throws forth" (a question), a PARABLE compares two things ("throws" them side by side), but SYMBOL (literally, "throw together") is idiomatic. From the same source is L *parabolare*, to talk (? "throw forth" words), whence the PARLIAMENT and PARLOR where different kinds of talking take place.

A related Gk word, *diabolos*, to slander (? "throw dirt on"), was used to mistranslate Hebrew "Satan" as "slanderer" (actually it = enemy), whence (via L) DEVIL and DIABOLIC. Yet another Gk relative = to dance (? "throw one's body about") > the professional BALLET, the non-professional BALL, and BALLAD, from a Portuguese word = dance tune.

GWELh-2, L *glans*, *gland-*, acorn, whence GLAND—presumably from the shape of some glands.

See **leg-1**

GWEN-, Greek *gyne*, woman, whence GYNECOLOGY, the study of women—specifically, their diseases. From Gc we get QUEEN, originally any woman, now a very special one.

GWERh-1, L *gravis*, Gk *barys*, heavy. The L word, used figuratively, > GRAVE (we still speak of grave matters as "heavy"), GRIEVE ("be heavy-hearted"), GRAVITY (what makes things heavy), and AGGRAVATE (originally = make heavier). From the same original root is L *brutus*, heavy, dull, stupid, whence BRUTE and BRUTAL. From the Gk word, finally, we get the "heavy"-voiced BARITONE and the BAROMETER that measures the "heaviness" (pressure) of the atmosphere.

GWERh-2, to praise, whence L *gratus*, pleasing ("praiseworthy"), GRATIFYing or AGREEable, also GRATEFUL—whence GRATITUDE. Other L descendants include pleasing qualities or things such as GRACE, GRACIOUSness, and GRATUITY, as well as CONGRATULATE (express one's pleasure). Via Celtic, finally, we get the BARD who praised kings or chieftains.

GWERh-3, to swallow, whence L *vorare*, to swallow VORACIOUSly or DEVOUR; a variant form > L *gurges*, throat, whence GORGE—as a verb, devour; as a noun, the narrow "throat" through which a river runs. From Gk *bronkhos*, throat or windpipe, comes BRONCHITIS.

GWET-1, to speak, whence Gc BEQUEATH, originally = the same thing, then "speak one's will" (in early English times, wills were literally "spoken" [dictated] by the testator to someone who could write).

GWET-2, L *botulus*, intestine, BOWEL.

GWHEDH-, to ask, whence Gc BID (see also **bheudh-**); also, to pray, whence Gc BEAD—originally a prayer, then a rosary used to count off prayers, then one of its beads.

GWHEN-, to strike or kill, whence Gc BANE—originally = killer, then poison (for its figurative use, see *BLM*). From a lost L verb, **fendere*, *fens-*, to strike, we get OFFEND ("strike toward"), DEFEND ("strike away"), and DEFENSE, whence the FENCE that "defends" our possessions.

GWHER-, to warm or heat, whence Gc BURN, the burning (fire)BRAND that figuratively > the sword one BRAN-DISHes, and BRANDY, originally "brandewine"—"burned" (distilled) wine. From L *fornax*, oven, we get FURNACE and ? FORNICATE—what low-grade Roman whores did beneath the ovenlike vaulting of public buildings. A much more obvious descendant is Gk *thermos*, hot, whence THERMO- (-meter, -dynamic, etc.).

GWHI-, tendon or thread, L *filum*, whence FILAMENT, FILE (originally, a string on which papers were filed—see *BLM*), and FILLET—originally, a "thread" (band) around the forehead, then a "band" (slice) of meat or fish. FILI-GREE is jewelry combining "threads" of gold or silver with "grains"—beads or jewels. A PROFILE is "drawn with a thread"—i.e., in outline.

See
gren-no-

■ This root must be very ancient indeed, dating from the days before people had learned to spin plant fibers and therefore sewed skins together with threads split from tendons.

GWHRE-, to smell or Gc BREATHe.

GWHREN-, to think, whence Gk *phren*, mind, whence the FRENETIC, disordered mind of FRENZY. More remote is Gk *phrasis*, manner of speaking, which > PHRASE.

GWLTUR-, L *vultur*, VULTURE (an uncertain root).

GWOU-, bull, ox, or Gc COW, which yields both L BEEF and Gk BUTTER. Also < Gk is BUCOLIC, "pertaining to herds-men," hence pastoral or rustic. bovine

GWRES-, fat or thick, L *grossus*, whence GROSS; a GROCER was originally a merchant who bought and sold "in gross"—wholesale.

GYEU-, GEU-, Gc to CHEW.

See **es-**

I-, a pronoun root that has evolved or been incorporated into various terms, most of them not pronouns; the connections are hard to explain in detail. From Gc we get YES ("may it be so"), YONDER, YET, and IF. L *id*, it, > Freud's famous ID; the related *idem*, (it is) the same, > IDENTICAL, IDENTITY (originally = sameness), and IDENTIFY.

■ Freud's original writings (in German, of course) referred to the "I," the "it," and the "super-I" (*Über-ich*). His English translators, presumably feeling that these commonplace terms didn't sound "scientific" enough, Latinized them into "ego," "id," and "super-ego." There was nothing new about such upgrading: three centuries earlier, an English critic wrote bitingly about writers who larded their language with Latinate terms to make it sound "as if they spoke by some revelation."

KA-, to like or desire, whence L CHERISH, the idiomatic CHARITY (see below), and CARESS—what we often do to people or animals we like or desire. In Gc, the root > a word = lover ("someone desired"), then adulterer (an illicit lover), whence WHORE—also illicit, but paid. Sanskrit *kamah*, love, desire, > the KAMASUTRA, that supposedly definitive textbook on physical love—though some of its "lessons" are practicable only by contortionists.

■ In the Latin Bible, *caritas* = love: "Though I speak with the tongues of angels and have not charity [love], it is as a sounding brass and a tinkling cymbal." Translated into English, the word gradually took on its present predominant meaning: demonstrating one's supposed love for one's fellows by giving them money.

KAD-1, L *cadere*, *cas-*, to fall, whence the falling water of a CASCADE, the musician's "falling" CADENCE of notes or chords, and the CHUTE down which things fall or slide; a PARACHUTE "wards off" a fall. From the same L verb are terms for things that "fall on" or befall you: CASE (e.g., a legal case), CHANCE, ACCIDENT, INCIDENT, and OCCASION. Something that DECAYS "falls away" from its original

See **per-1**

state; so does the DECADENT person or institution (see *BLM*).

KAD-2, sorrow or Gc HATEred, whence (via OF) HEINOUS ("hateful").

KADH-, to shelter or cover, whence the Gc HAT and HOOD that cover the head.

KAh-ID-, L *caedere*, *caes-*, to strike, whence the additional L sense of "strike down" (kill), whence -CIDE (sui-, homi-, etc.). But the main sense of the L verb was "cut," whence CHISEL, SCISSORS, and the surgeon's INCISION ("cutting in"). A CONCISE statement has been "cut" for maximum brevity, but PRECISE is idiomatic (its L original = cut short). Also idiomatic is DECIDE, literally = cut away, but its L original = cut the knot.

See
(s)ter-n-

KAGH-, to catch, seize, also wickerwork or a (wicker) fence (? that could "catch" straying animals). A HEDGE can serve as a fence, and can also "catch" you—especially if it's full of HAWTHORN. Gaulish *caio* was a retaining wall (a sort of fence), whence QUAY—a "wall" in a harbor to which boats can tie up. A possible relative is L *colum*, (? wickerwork) sieve, whence COLANDER, and its relative *colare*, to filter, whence PERCOLATE ("filter through"); more remotely related is Fr *coulée*, a flow, whence COULEE—a deep ravine in Western North America cut by flowing water.

KAGHLO-, pebble or Gc HAIL.

KAI-, Gc HEAT, whence HOT.

KAILO-, Gc WHOLE, uninjured, or HALE, whence HEALTH and WHOLESOME. The root could also = of good omen, whence Gc HOLY, HALLOW ("hallowed be Thy name"), and HALLOWEEN, the eve of All Hallows (Saints) Day.

KAITO-, forest, uncultivated land, whence Gc HEATH (HEATHER, though it grows on heaths, is unrelated). A "heath dweller" was presumed to be HEATHEN (see *BLM*).

[**Germanic KAK-,** a round object, such as a CAKE, COOKIE (< Dutch "little cake"), or QUICHE.]

KAK(K)A-, to defecate, whence (via L and Dutch) POP-PYCOCK—literally, "soft [pappy] shit."

■ The word originated among Dutch urchins on the streets of New York or its predecessor, New Amsterdam, but was borrowed in all innocence by the Victorian English. The same root > Gk *kakos*, bad ("shitty"), which we find in such words as "cacophony," very unpleasant sound.

KAL-1, cup, whence L CHALICE.

KAL-2, hard, whence the hard L CALLUS, as on the foot, and the CALLOUS, hard-hearted person.

KAMER-, to bend, whence Gk *kamara*, a vault (with a "bent" [arched] ceiling), whence CHAMBER and COM-RADE—originally, a roommate or ? barracks mate. CAMERA is < L *camera obscura*, "dark room," with a pinhole in one of its shutters or curtains; light shining through the pinhole would form an image of the scene outside, on the opposite wall. Nowadays, of course, the "room" is a small box, the "pinhole" is a lens, and the image is formed on film, but the name has stuck.

■ Some say the "vault" sense goes back to I-E, but—had the primitive I-E farmers ever seen vaults? I don't believe it! Conceivably the "vault" was the "bent" ceiling of a thatched hut.

KAMP-, to bend (?? related to the last root), whence Gk *kampe*, a bending or joint. Via L and Italian *gamba*, leg, it > GAMBOL ("kick up one's legs") and GAMBIT ("trip up")—now a chess term for a series of opening moves that will (hopefully) trip up one's opponent, but also used figuratively.

KAN-, L *canere*, to sing, whence CANTOR, CHANT, and CHARM—originally, the chanted INCANTATION used in EN-CHANTMENTs. L ACCENT was originally the "song added" (to speech). A remote relative is Gc HEN—originally = the *chanticleer* < singer (the vocal rooster—German *Hahn*); in English it somehow got transferred to the rooster's clucking mate.

KAND-, L *candere*, to shine, whence CANDLE, and the CANDIDATE clad in a shining white toga (see *BLM*)—whose speeches might or might not be CANDID. From a lost L verb, **candere*, to kindle ("cause to shine"), comes the INCENDIARY who kindles things and the INCENSE that is "kindled" in some churches.

■ "Kindle" itself looks as if it ought to be part of this family, but the experts agree that it isn't. Such linguistic coincidences aren't common, but they happen.

KANNABIS, Gk *kannabis*, Gc HEMP. Gk CANVAS was originally woven of hemp, but CANNABIS now refers to the "by-products" of hemp (marijuana and hashish)—much commoner today than hemp cordage or canvas.

■ This is not a native I-E word, say the experts, but was borrowed early on from some unknown source. Such borrowings often come through trade, suggesting that the Indo-Europeans were either buying hemp fiber (unlikely) or—dealing dope.

KANTO-, a bending, whence ? the idiomatic CANTEEN—in Britain, a shop selling food and drink to soldiers, but in the United States, a portable container for drink.

KAP-, to grasp or hold, whence Gc HAVE ("to have and to hold"), the HAFT ("grasping part") of a tool, the HAWK that grasps its prey, and HAVEN, originally = harbor (? "place that holds ships"). Also Gc are HEAVE (what you do when you grasp a rope), whence HEAVY (if it's heavy, you have to heave at it). From L *capsa*, box (that holds something), we get CAPSULE, CASE, CASH (originally = money box), and CHASSIS, originally = CASEMENT (window frame), then the frame of a carriage or auto.

L *capere*, to take, seize, or CATCH, has contributed a host of words, including CHASE; most of its other descendants are figurative. From the "take" sense we get ACCEPT ("take to" [oneself]), ANTICIPATE ("take in advance"), CONCEIVE ("be taken with"—either an idea or a baby), and EXCEPT ("take out"); also PARTICIPATE (take part in), PERCEIVE ("take into" [the mind]), RECEIVE ("take back" [to oneself]), RECEIPT (for what one has received), and the RECIPE that lists the ingredients you "take" to cook something. MUNICIPAL originally referred to taking or accepting an office in the community (see below).   See **mei-1**

From the "catch/seize" sense we get CAPTURE, the person who CAPTIVATES us—figuratively makes us CAPTIVE—and perhaps DECEIVES ("catch in a trap") us as well. A CABLE was a heavy hawser that "seized" a ship being towed— and a CAPTION (originally = capture) seizes the reader's attention. To INTERCEPT is to "seize [something] between" the sender and the intended receiver, as in American football.

■ In later Roman times, municipal offices were sometimes compulsory; you might say that the office took the officeholder rather than vice versa.

KAP(H)O-, Gc HOOF.

KAPRO-, L *caper*, he-goat, whence CAPER (as goats do). [*chèvre*] Two other family members, though improbable, are legitimate. In Roman builder's slang, *capreolus*, "little goat," = two pieces of wood fixed together like rafters (? a goat's horns)—that is, in the shape of a CHEVRON. Much later, Fr *cabriolet*, a light, springy carriage that "leaped about" like a goat, was borrowed into English and shortened to CAB.

KAPUT, L *caput*, *capit-*, Gc HEAD; the L word has given us a host of figurative terms, many discussed in *BLM*. A CAPE is a headland, the garment by the same name was originally worn over the head, and to ESCAPE originally = to slip out of one's cape. A CAPITAL is the head city (in capital punishment the victim was DECAPITATEd), and a CAPTAIN is the head man or CHIEF of a ship or group of soldiers (a CADET was originally a "little chief"—junior officer). A KERCHIEF is worn over the head (a HANDKERCHIEF is, of course, a "kerchief" held in the hand), and a CHAPTER is one of the headings under which a book is organized.

[also chef]

A PRECIPITOUS slope is one you can fall (or jump) down headlong; you figuratively do the same thing if you PRECIPITATE yourself into a situation. More remotely related are CATTLE (? so many "head"), which were the original form of portable wealth (capital), and MISCHIEF, originally = misfortune—something that "came to a head" badly.

KAR-1, Gc HARD, whence HARDY (i.e., tough). From Gk *kratos*, strength ("toughness"), power, comes -CRACY (demo-, aristo-, etc.); from L *cancer*, crab (with a hard shell), come both the constellation and the CANCER that, like a crab, claws at our flesh. (The scientist's "carcino-" comes from a related Gk word meaning both crab and cancer.)

KAS-, gray, whence the gray Gc HARE.

KAU-, to strike or Gc HEW, whence "hewed down" HAY and the HOE used to "hew" (break up) ground.

KAUL-, L *caula*, stem; later, cabbage stalk, whence KALE, CAULIFLOWER ("cabbage flower"), and COLESLAW (cabbage salad).

See **bhel-3**
See **sal-1**

KED-, L *cedere*, *cess-*, to go, yield, give up. The "go" sense > DECEASE ("go away"), INTERCEDE ("go between"), PRECEDE (go ahead of), PROCEED (go forward), RECEDE (go back), SECEDE ("go away"), EXCEED ("go out of" [what is needed or desired]), and the ANCESTORS who "go before" you. Also < this sense is SUCCEED; its L original = go or come close after, which > the idiomatic "achieve a good conclusion"; both senses survive in English. Also idiomatic is ABSCESS, literally "gone away."

The "give up/yield" sense > CEASE, ACCEDE (yield to), whence the idiomatic ACCESS, and CONCEDE (also "yield to''), whence CONCESSION. Finally, a special sense of the verb, ''withdraw'' (what people often do when they give up), > NECESSARY—''not to be withdrawn from.''

KEG-, Gc HOOK, whence HACK (as with a hooked tool or weapon). Also Gc is HECKLE, a metal comb with hooked teeth used to untangle flax fibers; for its figurative use see *BLM*.

KEI-1, to lie, whence bed or couch; also (though not in English) beloved, dear (the quality of one you bed with). From the ''bed'' sense we get Gk *koiman*, put to sleep, whence the CEMETERY where the dead are put ''to sleep, perchance to dream.'' In L and some other languages the root acquired the special sense of ''member of a household'' (? who beds down there), whence *civis*, *civit-*, CITIZEN, CITY (originally, the citizenry of Rome, not the physical town), CIVIC, CIVIL (pertaining to or befitting a citizen, ''CIVILIZEd''), and CIVILIAN.

KEI-2, source of various adjectives of color or Gc HUE.

KEI-3, L *ciere*, *cit-*, set in motion, whence EXCITE and IN-CITE (either sets someone into motion, literally or otherwise) and RESUSCITATE (''set in motion again''). From Gk *kinein*, to move, come KINETIC (kinetic energy is energy of motion) and CINEMA, originally, ''cinematograph''—moving picture.

KEL-1, to strike or cut, whence the Gc HILT you hold when you strike someone with a weapon. From Gaulish comes L *gladius*, sword, whence the GLADIATORS who fought with them—and the GLADIOLUS whose leaves are ''little swords.''

From Gk *kolaphos*, a blow, come COPE, originally "come to blows with" but now simply "deal with," and COUP, originally (in Fr) a blow, but now the sudden "blow" that overthrows a government (for other figurative senses see *BLM*). And a L CALAMITY is, of course, a severe blow. A secondary sense of the root was something cut off, as a twig, whence Gk CLONE. Also Gk, but idiomatic, are CLERGY and CLERK—the latter originally a clergyman, then anyone literate (as few but the clergy were), then someone dealing with records and accounts.

KEL-2, to cover, hence L CONCEAL or protect. Gc derivatives refer to coverings or covered places: HALL, HULL (of a vegetable or vessel), the HOLLOW HOLE, the HOLSTER that covers a pistol, the HOUSING that covers part of a machine (but "house" is of unknown origin), and the HELMET that covers and protects the head. HELL was the "covered place"— the underworld.

L descendants are more diverse. The "cover" sense > *cilium*, the eyelid that covers the eye, > *supercilium*, eyebrow ("above the eyelid"), whence the SUPERCILIOUS person whose eyebrows are continually raised; *cella*, storeroom (compare HALL above), > CELL and CELLAR. The "conceal" sense > CLANDESTINE (concealed) actions— which sometimes lead to a cover-up; OCCULT knowledge is "concealed" from most people.

KEL-3, to drive, set in swift motion, L ACCELERATE. Other descendants are less certain; they include Gc HOLD (originally, ? drive cattle, hence possess them) and ?? HALT (the opposite of "accelerate"!). L *celeber*, much frequented (? "much motion around"), > renowned or CELEBRATEd, whence CELEBRITY.

KEL-4, to lean, tilt, or Gc HEEL, as a vessel does.

KEL-5, to be prominent; also, Gc HILL. From L *excellare*, to raise up (make prominent), we get EXCEL; from *culmen*, summit (of a hill), we get CULMINATE ("reach the summit"), and from *columna*, originally a projecting ("elevated") object, come COLUMN and COLONEL—originally, the leader of a column of troops.

KEL-6, to prick, whence the prickly Gc HOLLY.

KEL-7, L *calvi*, to deceive or trick, whence CALUMNY, a false accusation, and CHALLENGE—originally, an accusation of any sort.

KELB-, Gc to HELP.

See **dhe-**

KELh-1, to warm, whence various L descendants: SCALD, CHAFE ("make warm," as by rubbing the hands together), the CALDRON in which things are "warmed" and the CHOWDER we "warm" there, NONCHALANT ("not warm"— "cool"), and CALORIE—technically, a measure of heat, hence of the heat or energy content of food. From Gc comes the LEE side of a vessel, which being away from the wind is marginally "warmer" than the opposite or weather side.

KELh-2, to shout, whence L *clamare*, call, cry out, CLAMOR, whence CLAIM—originally, a "called-out" demand—and RECLAIM ("call back"). Other derivatives are EXCLAIM ("call out"), PROCLAIM ("call forth"), ACCLAIM ("call toward"), and COUNCIL (a "calling together")— which may or may not CONCILIATE clashing factions in it. CALENDAR is < L *kalendae*, the first day of the month, when the dates of the other significant days (nones and ides) were publicly proclaimed.

Less certainly related is L *clarus*, CLEAR (? having a nature that "calls out"), whence DECLARE ("make clear") and (!) ECLAIR—an idiomatic (not to say arbitrary) use of a Fr word = lightning. L *classis* was originally a "called out" summons, hence a CLASS of citizens drafted for military service (whence its later sense of fleet or army). Even less certain is Gc HAUL (?? "call together").

KELP-, to grasp, whence the HELVE of a tool and the HELM of a boat that you grasp, and the HALTER that "grasps" an animal (later, also the noose that "grasped" a criminal's neck).

KEM-1, hornless, short (? < "cut short"), whence Gc SCANT.

KEM-2, to compress, whence double over, as in the Gc HEM of a garment.

KEM-3, Gc to HUM.

KEN-1, to be active, whence Gk *diakonos*, servant, whence DEACON, a "servant" of the congregation.

KEN-2, another hypothetical base of various Gc words that may or may not be related: their meanings include pinch, as in NIP, NIBBLE, and ? NIGGARD (a penny-pincher), and close the eyes (? pinch the lids together), whence NAP and NOD.

KEN-3, L *recens*, fresh, young, new, whence RECENT.

KEN-4, yet another hypothetical root, concerned with compression, including Gc NECK (where the body is "compressed") and NUT (a hard, "compressed" fruit), and L *nucleus*, kernel, whence NUCLEUS, first the "kernel" of a comet, then of a cell or atom. More dubious is Gc NOOK, originally = corner (?? "compressed space").

K(E)NhKO-, yellow, golden, whence Gc HONEY.

KENI-, dust or ashes, whence L INCINERATE ("make into ashes").

KENK-1, to bind or gird (L *cingere, cinct-*), whence the CINCH that girds a horse, PRECINCT (an area "girded in" by boundaries), the SUCCINCT ("tightly girded") statement, and SHINGLES, an unpleasant skin disease that sometimes covers the middle of the body like a girdle.

KENK-2, to suffer from thirst or Gc HUNGER.

KENK-3, Gc HEEL (of the foot).

KENS-, to proclaim, whence L *censere*, to judge or assess, whence CENSOR and CENSUS.

KENT-, Gk *kentein*, to prick, whence a point "pricked" at the CENTER of, e.g., a circle. Something ECCENTRIC is off center; so, figuratively, is an eccentric person.

KER-1, L *cornu*, Gk *keras*, Gc HORN, whence also head (? "place where the horns are"), and various horn-shaped or projecting things. The Gc HORNET carries a tiny "horn" in its tail, and the REINDEER is a "horned animal." Through L we get the one-horned UNICORN, and CORNET—a different kind of horn (though its remote an-

See **dheu-1**

cestor was an animal horn); from Gk, the RHINOCEROS, with a horn on its nose. *keratin*

Horn-shaped objects include Gk CARROT and (< Sanskrit) GINGER; the "head" sense > Gk CRANIUM and CHEER (originally = face, disposition, as in "be of good cheer"), both via L. Gk CARAT, finally, originally = the weight of a single, horny carob bean; it came into English via Arabic and Fr.

KER-2, an imitative root referring to various noises—Gc SCREECH, SCREAM, RINGing, and RETCHing—and noisy birds, including the Gc ROOK and RAVEN; also Gc (and noisy) is the CRICKET. From L *crepare*, *crepit-*, to creak, hence to crack, come the cracked-open CREVICE and the DECREPIT ("creaking") person.

KER-3, L *crescere*, to grow, whence INCREASE and its opposite, DECREASE. From the same L word, but more remote, are CRESCENT (originally = the "growing" moon), the musician's CRESCENDO (growing volume), the CONCRETE that hardens ("grows together") when mixed with water, the RECRUITS used to reinforce ("cause to grow again") a body of troops; a related term for reinforcements gave us CREW. Less certainly related is L SINCERE—originally, not falsified or adulterated (? "of one growth").

Another L verb, *creare*, *creat-*, to CREATE ("cause to grow"), > PROCREATE—a sort of creation that most of us engage in occasionally. Finally, the Roman goddess CERES, who presided over growing crops, > CEREALS—originally, grain crops; now also various foods made from them.

KER-4, heat, fire, whence Gc HEARTH, L CARBON (originally = charcoal), and CREMATE; also (probably) Gk CERAMIC (ceramics are, of course, fired in a kiln).

KER-5, KERh-, to injure, whence the L CARIES that injures our teeth.

KER-6, Gk *kerasos*, CHERRY (originally wild, not cultivated).

KERD-1, L *cors*, *cord-*, Gc HEART, whence a host of figurative meanings, most of them discussed in *BLM*. Some probably date from I-E times, since they occur in both L and Gc; thus a L CORDIAL greeting is also Gc HEARTY, and L DISCOURAGE = Gc DISHEARTEN.

An unquestionably I-E metaphor is **ker-dhe-*, "put in one's heart," hence trust, believe, whence the L CREED one believes, CREDIT (another kind of belief), CREDIBLE (believable), CREDULOUS (believing too easily) and MISCREANT (originally, a heretic or "misbeliever"). A more intricate evolution > GRANT—originally = agree ("give credence") to; RECORD originally = get by heart. Other L metaphors derive from the idea of the heart as seat of the feelings: COURAGE, ACCORD ("hearts together"), and DISCORD ("hearts apart").

KERDH-, Gc HERD.

KERh-, to cook, whence mix, whence confuse (too many cooks?). The "cook" sense is ? the source of Gc RARE (half-cooked); the "mix" sense, of Gk CRATER, originally a mixing vessel; the "confuse" sense > Gc UPROAR.

KERP-, to gather, pluck, or Gc HARVEST. From L *carpere*, *carpt-*, to pluck, we get the EXCERPT "plucked out" of a larger work, and the idiomatic SCARCE and CARPET.

KERS-, L *currere*, *curs*-, to run, whence COURIER ("runner"), the COURSE on which horses or people run, the running CURRENT of water or electricity, the CORRIDOR that (often) runs the length of a building, CAREER—originally, run rapidly, but now also the way one's (professional) life runs—and the CURSOR that "runs" on a computer's visual display terminal.

Figurative senses, all L, include CONCUR ("run with" [someone's opinion]), and the DISCOURSE that often "runs to and fro"—is DISCURSIVE, in fact. An EXCURSION "runs out" somewhere, INTERCOURSE is a "running between," a PRECURSOR is a forerunner, RECOURSE and RECUR both refer to different kinds of "running back," something that OCCURS "runs to meet" us, and someone who SUCCORS us "runs under" or supports us.

Another branch of the family stems from Gaulish *carros*, a CART (running on wheels), which > L CARRIAGE, CAR, and CHARIOT, plus the CARPENTER who made the wagon and the CARGO it was used to CARRY—i.e., was CHARGEd with, in its original sense (burdened). CARICATURE is idiomatic; its Italian original = load, burden, hence exaggeration.

A controversial member of the family is Gc HORSE, which Eric Partridge once suggested could mean "the runner." It makes some sense phonetically—the K-to-H shift is standard in Gc (see Introduction)—and also semantically: the domesticated horse could draw a light cart or chariot at a run, while its predecessor, the ox, could at best achieve a shambling trot (see *OMNT*).

KERT-, to turn, entwine, whence both Gc and L terms meaning a "twined" (wickerwork) frame or Gc HURDLE (originally, and still in Britain, used to pen animals; its athletic sense is very recent). Through L we get CRATE (originally, made of wickerwork), as well as GRATE, GRAT- ING, GRID, and GRIDDLE, all of which vaguely resemble wickerwork.

KES-1, to cut, whence L CASTRATE. Other L descendants are figurative, and fairly intricate: a CASTLE was ? a "cut-off" (separated) place, a CHASTE person is "cut off" from sexual activity, while CASTE comes from a Portuguese word = pure (? "cut off" from adulterants).

KES-2, to put in order, whence Gk *kosmos*, the "order" of the universe, whence COSMIC.

KEU-1, hKEU-, to perceive, see, or Gc HEAR, whence Gc SHOW (originally = look at). From Gk *akouein*, to hear, we get ACOUSTIC.

KEU-2, to bend, whence various round and/or hollow ob- jects such as the rounded Gc HEAP, HIP, and HIVE, and the rounded, hollow L CUP. Gk *kumbe*, bowl, > the bowl- shaped CYMBALS and ? the CHIME they emit; also Gk is CUBE—originally = the hollow enclosed by the hipbones. The "bend" sense > Gc HIGH ("bent upward"), whence HEIGHT; ? HOP (by bending the legs), and the HAWKER or HUCKSTER bent beneath his peddler's pack.

L *cubare*, lie down on ("bend down"), > the CUBICLE we lie down in, the CONCUBINE we lie down with, and INCU- BATE—what a female bird does when she "lies down" on her eggs. A closely related verb > the INCUMBENT who "lies down in" a particular job (sometimes all too liter- ally!) and SUCCUMB ("lie down under").

KEU-3, to burn, whence Gk CAUSTIC—literally or figuratively burning—and HOLOCAUST—"wholly burnt" (see *BLM*). A related Gk word = heat (of the day) > CALM (? heat of the day > siesta > quiet time). See **sol-**

KEUh-1, to pay attention, whence L *cauere*, to beware, whence CAUTION and PRECAUTION—"caution in advance."

KEUh-2, to swell; also, for some reason, a hole, whence L *cavea*, a hollow, whence CAVE, CAVERN, CAGE, JAIL/GAOL, CONCAVE, EXCAVATE ("hollow out"), and DECOY—originally, a pool surrounded with a "cage" of nets to capture wildfowl. Gk *kodeia*, the hollow poppy head, > CODEINE. The "swell" sense > L *cumulus*, a ("swollen") heap, whence heaped-up CUMULUS clouds and ACCUMULATE ("heap up"). A variant of the root meant strong, powerful, "big" ("swelled up"), whence Gk *kyrios*, lord, whence CHURCH (Scottish KIRK), originally *kyriakos doma*, the Lord's house.

KEWERO-, north wind—which in northern Europe often brings a storm or Gc SHOWER. ·

[Germanic KIDH-, KID (young goat, but recently young person).]

KISTA, Gk *kiste*, basket, whence (via L) containers such as CHESTS, CISTERNS, and KEISTERS (originally = suitcases; see *BLM*).

KLEG-, to cry or sound, whence Gc LAUGH and L CLANG.

KLEI-, L *clinare*, Gc to LEAN, whence the LADDER that leans against a wall. The Gk word for ladder > CLIMAX, originally a "ladder" of musical notes, later the top of some "ladder" (see *BLM*). The lost L verb has given us INCLINE ("lean toward"), DECLINE ("lean away from"), RECLINE ("lean backward"), and PROCLIVITY—what someone "leans toward" doing.

L *cliens*, *client-*, a dependent who "leaned on" some powerful person, > CLIENT; Gk *klima*, the "leaning" (sloping) surface of the earth, > a region or zone on that surface with a particular CLIMATE. And Gk *kline*, the bed we recline on, > CLINIC. Finally, a secondary sense of the root, to bend (? "lean over"), ? > Gc LID—what "bends over" a container. But this word may derive from **kel-2**, to cover.

KLENG-, to bend or turn, whence Gc LINK (originally, a loop of chain). Also Gc are the LANKY (thin, "bendable") person, the FLANK, where the body bends, and FLINCH—bend or turn aside.

KLEU-1, to hear, whence Gc LISTEN and LOUD (if it's loud, it's heard).

KLEU-2, to wash, whence the Gk CATACLYSM in which everything is "washed away."

KLEU-3, ? hook, peg, whence L *claudere*, *claus-*, CLOSE (? "lock with a hook or peg"), whence things ENCLOSEd or INCLUDEd ("closed in") or EXCLUDEd ("closed out"). A SECLUDEd place is "closed away," and something CONCLUDEd is brought to a close. From the original "peg" sense comes L *clavis*, nail—for centuries, usually a wooden peg—whence the spicy, nail-shaped CLOVE. Possible members of this family are Gc LOT, ALLOT, and LOTTERY, but the connection (if any) is remote. *cloy*

KLOU-, seen by some as the I-E source of various Gc words, but these are more likely of Folkish origin (see Introduction). They include LEAP, LOPE, ELOPE ("leap away" into the arms of a lover), GALLOP, and (with a L prefix) INTER-LOPER—someone who "leaps" into something he or she shouldn't.

KNEIGWH-, to lean together, whence L *conivere*, close the eyes ("lean the eyelids together"), then CONNIVE—"close one's eyes" to someone's misdeed, though now more often to take part in it.

KNID-, Gc NIT.

KO-1, root of demonstrative pronouns (this, that, etc.), whence Gc HE ("this person"), HIM, HIS, and HER. Other Gc descendants are HERE ("in this place"), and ?? BEHIND, HINDER ("keep [something] behind"), and HINTERLAND, the "behind land"—back country. Another dubious relative is L *cetera*, the other part (? "those others"), whence ET CETERA.

KO-2, to sharpen or whet, as on a Gc HONE; a possible relative is the sharp-pointed Gk CONE.

KOB-, to suit, fit, succeed, whence Gc HAPPY and its opposite, HAPLESS. A secondary Gc sense, occur by chance, > HAPPEN and MISHAP—a "bad chance."

KOKSA, unidentified body part, whence L *coxa*, hip, whence the CUSHION you put under your, uh, hip.

KOM, beside, near, with, whence Old L *com*, with, whence the later L prefixes CO-, COM-, and CON-. A variant > L CONTRA, opposite (beside = face-to-face), whence COUN-

TRY ("the land opposite"—spread before—one); also, opposed to ("eyeball-to-eyeball"), whence CONTRA-, CONTRARY, COUNTER (act in opposition), COUNTER-, and ENCOUNTER (originally = meet in conflict)—not to mention the U.S.-backed CONTRAS in Nicaragua.

KONhMO-, (shin)bone, whence ?? Gc HAM, but this is more likely < some root akin to **kamp-**, to bend, since it originally = the bend of the knee.

KONK-, Gc to HANG, whence the HINGE a door hangs on, and HANKER—originally = "hang around" someone.

KONK(H)O-, shellfish, whence Gk COCKLE and CONCH.

KORMO-, pain, whence Gc HARM.

KORO-, war, war band, army, whence HARRY—what armies do to their enemies. A Gc compound meaning fort ("army hill") eventually came to mean merely army quarters, then any lodging, whence the HARBOR where ships are lodged, and HARBINGER—originally, an advance man who arranged lodgings for a traveling army or royal party (see *BLM*). Another compound > HERALD, originally = army leader, then the spokesman of such a leader, then anyone who announced something ("Hark the herald angels sing").

KOSELO-, Gc HAZEL (tree and nut).

KOST-, bone (probably related to **ost-**), whence L *costa*, rib, side. A CUTLET was originally sliced from the ribs of an animal, while the COAST is the "side" of a country or region. And to ACCOST (someone) originally = come alongside.

KRAU-, KRU-, to hide, whence Gk CRYPTIC, CRYPTO- (cryptography = "hidden writing"), and the "hidden" (underground) CRYPT of a church.

KREI-, to sift, hence L DISCRIMINATE ("sift apart"), distinguish. The "sift" sense > Gc RIDDLE, originally a sieve, now "make a sieve of," as with bullets (see *BLM*), and L GARBLE —originally = to sift, then (via Arabic) to "sift" (information) maliciously. L *cernere*, *cert-*, *cret-*, to sift, hence separate, decide, > CERTAIN (decided), CONCERN (originally = DISCERN, "sift apart"), DECREE (a decision), DISCREET (originally = showing good judgment), and SECRET ("sifted away" [from public view]). SECRETE is idiomatic.

L *crimen*, *crimin-*, judgment, hence offense, > CRIME and CRIMINAL; Gk *krinein*, to separate, decide, judge, > the CRITIC who judges things, CRISIS (originally, the decisive moment or turning point, as of a disease), and the idiomatic HYPOCRITE—originally = actor, hence dissembler.

KREK-1, to beat or weave (the connection is unclear), whence the Gc REEL used to wind yarn or thread, whence the REELING drunk with winding steps.

KREK-2, frog spawn or fish eggs—Gc ROE.

KRET-, to shake, whence the idiomatic Gc RATHER, originally = more quickly, hence sooner ("I'd rather do it" = "I'd do it sooner" [than I'd do something else]).

KREUh-, Gc RAW meat, whence L *crudus*, raw (whence CRUDE) or bloody (whence CRUEL).

KREUP-, scab, become encrusted, whence the Gc sense of rough; to RUFFLE something is to "roughen" it in various ways, and a GRUFF voice is a rough one.

KREUS-, to begin to freeze, form a L CRUST, whence the crusty CROUTON and the CRUSTACEAN with its external "crust" (shell). The "freeze" sense > Gk *crystallos*, ice, whence CRYSTAL (ice is still the kind of crystal most of us know best).

KREUT-, KREUDH-, Gc REED.

KROPO-, Gc ROOF.

KSERO-, Gk *xeros*, dry, whence XEROGRAPHY, "dry writing" (contrasted with "wet writing" using ink); the term was the source of one of the world's best-known trademarks, XEROX. Another sense of the Gk word, a dry powder for treating wounds, may have > Arabic *al ixsir*, the ELIXIR. Another possible relative is L *serenus*, dry, clear, calm, whence SERENE (clear, dry weather is usually serene as well).

[**Germanic KU-,** the supposed root of various loosely related terms, centering on the idea of a hollow space or place, hence an enclosing object, but also ? a round object or lump. The "enclosure" group includes CUBBY, COTTAGE, CUTTLEFISH (from its ink bag), and—CUNT, certainly an enclosing object. More dubious are CUDGEL and COWER; even more dubious is CHICKEN, generally considered a diminutive of MedL *coccus*—an obviously imitative word ("Cock-a-doodle-do!") that > COCK.]

KUS-, Gc KISS.

KWED-, to sharpen, or Gc WHET.

KWEI-, to hiss or Gc WHISTLE, whence WHISPER and WHINE.

KWEI-1, to atone, compensate, pay a L PENALTY (< Gk *poine*), whence PUNISH, PAIN, and IMPUNITY ("unpunishment"). A SUBPOENA orders the recipient to appear and testify in court, "under penalty" of a contempt charge if he or she doesn't show up.

KWEI-2, to pile up, build, make, whence Gk *poiein*, to make or create, whence POET and POEM.

KWEIh-, to rest, be L QUIET, whence ? L TRANQUIL, ACQUIESCE (originally = remain quiet), and REQUIEM (from the L *requiem aeternam donat eis*, give him eternal rest). Gc WHILE (originally = time, as in "quite a while") is generally considered a member of this family, but the connection is obscure.

KWEIT-, to shine, Gc WHITE, whence WHEAT, from the white flour it yields contrasted with darker rye meal.

■ Rye, hardier than wheat, has been widely cultivated around the Baltic since prehistoric times. Modern light-colored "rye" bread is made from a mixture of wheat and rye flours.

KWEL-1, to turn, move around, hence dwell in ("hang around"). The "turn" sense > Gc WHEEL and Gk CYCLE, BICYCLE, CYCLONE (a storm in which the winds circle around a low-pressure area), and the POLE the earth turns on, whence PULLEY. A L COLLAR goes around the neck— what the head turns on. The "dwell" sense > L COLONY, CULTIVATE, CULTURE, and CULT—a religious group with which one "dwells."

■ "Cyclone" is sometimes used to = tornado (see **(s)tenh-**), but technically means a much larger but less violent storm.

KWEL-2, far in space or time, whence Gk *tele*, far away, whence TELE- (-scope, -vision, etc.), and Gk *palai*, long ago, whence PALEO-; paleontology deals with long-ago life, paleography, with ancient documents, etc.

KWELP-, to arch, whence Gk *kolpos*, bosom, whence GULF, a "bosomlike" indentation of the coast.

KWENT(H)-, Gk *paskein*, L *pati*, *pass-* (? < Gk), to suffer. Gk *pathos*, suffering, passions, emotions, > PA-THOS, PATHETIC, PATHOLOGY (the science of "suffering"—disease), and SYMPATHY ("suffering together").

KWEP-, to smoke, cook, ? hence move violently (? "boil"), be agitated—the supposed root of various loosely related words. Clearly akin to the "smoke" sense is L *vapor*, steam or VAPOR, whence EVAPORATE; the "cook" sense > L VAPID ("cooked too long"). More dubious relatives (? from the "agitated" sense) are L COVET and CUPID, who makes lovers "covet" each other.

KWERP-, to turn oneself, whence Gc WHIRL; also WHARF—"place where people move around."

KWES-, to pant or Gc WHEEZE. From L *queri*, to complain, come QUERULOUS and QUARREL.

KWET-, L *quatere*, *quass-* (in compounds, *-cuss-*), to shake or strike, whence the CONCUSSION that can both shake and strike us, PERCUSSION instruments that are struck (rather than bowed or blown), and DISCUSS (originally = disperse—"strike apart"—then investigate, then investigate by argument); RESCUE results from an intricate idiomatic evolution (see *OEtD*). From the same L root are

SQUASH ("strike flat"), and—via German *quetshen*, to crush—the Yiddish KVETCH who crushes us beneath constant complaints.

■ The vegetable squash, though "squashy" when cooked, is < an unrelated Native American word (the plant was first cultivated in Mexico).

KWETWER-, L *quatuor*, Gc FOUR. Obvious Gc descendants are FORTY, FOURTEEN, and FOURTH; obvious L ones are QUARTER, QUART (one fourth of a gallon), and, less obviously, QUARANTINE, which traditionally lasted forty days (see *BLM*). Other L descendants have to do with the four-sided SQUARE; they include SQUAD (originally, a square formation of soldiers), QUADRILLE (an old French square dance), and the QUARRY that produces squared-off blocks of stone.

KWO-, KWI-, the root of many relative and interrogative pronouns, including Gc WHO, WHOM, WHOSE, WHAT, WHICH, HOW, WHEN, WHITHER, and WHERE. WHETHER comes from a compound meaning "which of two"—to which the answer may be EITHER or NEITHER. From L come QUORUM, "whose"—i.e., those whose presence is necessary—and QUOTA ("how many"), of which QUOTE is an idiomatic variant. Two related L terms > QUANTITY (what amount) and QUALITY (what kind). L *uter*, either of two (compare WHETHER above), > NEUTER and NEUTRAL (both = neither one thing nor the other), while L *ibi*, there, > ALIBI ("I wasn't there!"). See **al-1**

KWON-, L *canis*, Gk *kuon*, dog. From the L we get CANINE and KENNEL; from the Gk, the CYNIC who led a dog's life (see *BLM*). The Gc equivalent, **hundaz*, still = dog in most Gc tongues (e.g., German *Hund*), but in English has become a particular class of dog, the HOUND.

■ "Dog" itself is a word of obscure origin that appeared in English, out of nowhere, something over a thousand years ago. It may originally have referred to a particular breed of dog, but what that breed was, and why its owners chose that name for it, are unknown.

KWREP-, L *corpus*, body, whence CORPSE, CORPULENT ("abounding in body"), and the CORPUSCLES ("little bodies") of the blood. A CORPORATION is a body of business-people; a CORPS, a body of troops; a CORPORAL is in charge of such a body (though a much smaller one than an army corps), and corporal punishment is applied to the body. A CORSAGE was originally a bodice, now a bunch of flowers pinned there, and a CORSET is a "little body"—worn to slim down big bodies.

KWRMI-, Sanskrit *krmi*, worm, whence CRIMSON—originally, a red dye obtained from "worms" (pregnant females of an insect akin to the cochineal beetle).

carmine

LA-, the "echoic" root of various sounds, notably the ones that Gc LULL a baby to sleep; also L LAMENT and ? Gc LOON, the diving bird whose wavering cry rings out across so many northern lakes. But I suspect this last has been influenced by "lunatic," since the cry rather resembles maniacal laughter. LOLL is sometimes assigned to this root but more likely derives from **leb-1**.

LAB-, Gc LAPping or smacking the lips, whence Fr *lamper*, gulp down, whence the boozer's toast *Lampons!* (Let's drink!), whence ? LAMPOON, though the connection is unclear.

LAKS-, large salmonlike fish, whence Gc LOX.

■ Some scholars flatly define this root as "salmon," but the "true" (Atlantic) salmon is found only in streams draining into the Atlantic or Baltic—i.e., not in the Danube basin, where many people believe the Indo-Europeans originated. More likely, then, I-E* *laksos* referred to one or more of the large salmonids that abound in that region. Worth noting is that in the American Northwest, known for its salmon fisheries, the word refers to three or four different species of fish.

LAKU-, body of water, whence L LAKE and Gaelic LOCH. The latter word shows up on the map of Ireland, but is spelled L-O-U-G-H.

LAP-, to set fire to, burn, whence Gk LAMP and LANTERN.

LAS-, to be eager, hence wanton, whence Gc LUST and L LASCIVIOUS.

LE-1, to get, whence the L LARCENY that gets the thief his (or her) loot.

LE-2, to slacken, Gc LET go; more remotely related is Gc LATE (? originally = "slack," sluggish), whence LATTER and LAST ("latest").

LEB-1, the source of various tenuously related words centering on the notion of "hanging loosely." They include Gc LIMP, LUMP, SLUMP, SLOB, and LABEL (originally, a hanging ribbon or strip), also ? LOLL. More dubious relatives are Gc SLAM and SLAP.

A more likely relative is L *labi*, *laps-*, slip or fall, whence LAPSE (a "slip," as of the memory), ELAPSE ("slip away," as time does), COLLAPSE ("fall together"), and RELAPSE ("fall back"). Perhaps < the same ultimate source is L *labor*, LABOR, toil, exertion (? < a burden under which one slips or falls), whence COLLABORATE ("labor together").

LEB-2, Gc LIP.

LEG-1, Gk *legein*, L *legere*, *lect-*, to gather or COLLECT. The L word also = to choose or SELECT ("gather [pick] out"), or read (? "gather words"), whence LEGIBLE, LECTURE, and LEGEND. SACRILEGE comes < a word = one who "collected" (stole) sacred things.

The Gk verb > CATALOGUE ("thorough gathering"); it also = speak (? "collect [one's] words"), whence DIALECT ("speech apart," as in a particular region), the DIALOGUE among two or more speakers, the PROLOGUE spoken before (a play), and the EPILOGUE spoken afterward. The related noun *logos*, word, speech, reasoning, > LOGIC and -LOGY ("reasoning about" some specialized subject), plus the APOLOGY that "speaks away" one's offense.

A less certain relative is L *lex*, *leg-*, law (? collection of rules), whence LEGAL, LEGITIMATE, LEGISLATOR ("law giver"), and LOYAL. A PRIVILEGE is a "private law"—for the privileged classes, naturally ("one law for the rich, another for the poor"). Another dubious relative is L *legare*, *legat-*, to depute, commission, charge, whence ALLEGE (originally = charge before a court), the DELEGATE who is "deputed away" (e.g., to a convention), and COLLEAGUE—someone one is deputed with, hence a partner.

LEG-2, to dribble or trickle, whence Gc LEAK and LACK—the normal result of a leak.

LEGH-, Gc to LIE or LAY (they're still causing confusion centuries later). Also Gc are LOW ("laid down"), the LAIR an animal lies in, LEDGE (originally, a shelf things were laid on), and LEDGER (originally, a book lying permanently in one place). LAGER beer has been aged by lying in a cellar or warehouse, the LAW is "what is laid down"—and a FELLOW was originally someone who laid down a "fee" (money) in a business partnership.

See **peku-**

LEGWH-, L *levis*, Gc LIGHT (weight), whence the LEAVEN-ing that makes dough "lighter" and the lightweight LUNGS (one imagines the lungs of a butchered animal floating off down a stream). From the L word and its relative, *levare*, to lighten, hence lift, come ALLEVIATE ("make lighter"), RELIEVE (lighten, as a burden), ELEVATE (lift up), and the LEVER used in lifting. CARNIVAL has a more complex evolution: it comes from MedL *carneleva-men*, the cessation ("lifting") of meat eating. In Medieval Europe, the carnival season came immediately before Lent, when meat eating became a sin.

See **sker-1**

■ In an earlier book I mistakenly—though plausibly—derived "carnival" from L *carne vale*, farewell to meat; the moral is that in this business you can't take *anything* for granted.

LEI-, SLEI-, Gc SLIMY, also SLIP(PERY), SLICK, and LOAM (originally = clay). More dubious Gc relatives are SLIGHT and SCHLEP (literally, to drag—? slide something along). More certain is L *oblivisci*, to forget (? "let slip from the mind"), whence OBLIVION. LINIMENT comes from a remotely related L verb meaning smear or anoint (with something slippery).

LEID-, L *ludere*, to play; the L verb also = to jest, whence LUDICROUS ("You've got to be joking!"). ALLUDE originally = play with (verbally), hence refer to indirectly; to DELUDE is to "play false"—perhaps by fostering the victim's ILLUSIONS. A PRELUDE was "played beforehand"; an INTERLUDE was "played between"; ELUDE ("slip away" [from]) is idiomatic.

LEIG-1, L *ligare*, to bind, whence the LEAGUE that OBLIGES (binds) one ALLY to support another—which both parties can, hopefully, RELY on. From the same source are LIEN, a binding right on some sort of property, and the ALLOY that "binds" two or more metals together. RALLY originally = reassemble ("rebind"), as in "rally troops," but today it usually = merely assemble or assembly.

LEIGH-, Gc to LICK—whence the lip-licking LECHER.

LEIKW-, L *linquere*, *lict-*, Gk *lepein*, to leave. From L come RELINQUISH ("leave [give] back") and DERELICT (left behind, as an abandoned ship; now a person similarly "left behind" by life). Gk *eklepein*, literally = leave out, hence fail to appear, > the astronomical ECLIPSE, in which the sun or moon temporarily "fails" to appear. From Gc we get LEND ("leave to," give), whence LOAN.

LEIP-, to stick, adhere, also "sticky" fat, but in Gc the "stick" sense > continue (as in "stick to" a task), whence the continuing LIFE we LIVE—until we have to LEAVE it (let it "stick" behind). Some claim that LIVER comes from the same root, because it was thought to produce the blood that is vital for life.

LEIS-1, track, furrow, whence Gc LAST (continue; "follow a track") and LEARN (follow a "track" of study). L *lira*, furrow, > DELIRIUM ("out of the furrow"—see *BLM*).

LEIS-2, small, whence Gc LESS and LEAST.

LEIT-1, to detest or Gc LOATHE.

LEIT-2, to go forth (also die), whence Gc LEAD and LOAD (originally = journey, way).

LEIZD-, border, band (? of cloth), whence Gc LIST ("strip of paper").

LEK-, to tear or L LACERATE.

LEM-, to break in pieces, also broken, crippled, Gc LAME. Other Gc relatives are LAM (originally, "cripple by beating") and ? LUMBER—move with a "lame" gait.

LENDH-1, L *lumbus*, LOIN (lower back), whence the LUMBAGO that pains us there, and SIRLOIN ("over the loin"), the upper part of a loin of beef.

■ Legend has it that "sirloin" was originally "Sir Loin"—a loin of beef so delicious that an English king knighted it. A charming tale—but there's not a word of truth in it!

LENDH-2, open Gc LAND, whence LANDSCAPE (originally = tract of land) and LAWN (originally = pasture).

LENTO-, L *lentus*, flexible or Gc LITHE, whence LINDEN (from its flexible inner bark). The L word > RELENT ("bend back").

LEP-, to be flat, hence the flat sole or palm, whence Gc GLOVE.

LETRO-, Gc LEATHER.

LEU-1, L *solvere*, *solut-*, Gk *lyein*, Gc to LOOSE(N). Gc descendants include LOSE (what often happens with loose things), LOSS, and FORLORN (originally = abandoned— "lost"; later, forsaken or desolate). L family members include the SOLUTION that SOLVES or RESOLVES ("loosens") a knotty problem, or in which something has been DIS-SOLVED ("loosened away")—assuming the problem, or substance, is SOLUBLE; something ABSOLUTE is free ("loos-ened") from qualification. From Gk we get the ANALYSIS that "loosens" the components of a problem or chemical compound and the PARALYSIS that "loosens" (disables) one's limb(s).

LEU-2, dirt, make dirty, whence L *lutum*, mud, whence POLLUTE ("put mud into").

LEUBH-, to care, desire (whence L LIBIDO), or Gc LOVE, whence BELIEVE (hold dear, hence trust). Love also implies pleasure ("I'd as LIEF do it") and even permission—giving someone LEAVE to do something, whence the soldier's FUR-LOUGH (all Gc).

LEUD-, Gc LITTLE.

LEUDH-, to mount up, grow, whence ? L *liber*, free, whence LIBERAL, LIBERTY, LIBERATE (but not "deliberate"— see **lithra**), and LIBERTINE (see *BLM*). To DELIVER something originally = to set it free, whence the modern sense of hand over.

LEU(h)-, L *lauare* (in some compounds -*luere*), to wash, whence the LOTION used to "wash" our skins, the LAUNDRY things are washed in, the DELUGE that washes away everything, and DILUTE—add water to ("wash"). L *latrina* was first a washing place (bathroom), then a privy or LATRINE. Gc descendants include LATHER and LYE (used in soap making).

LEUG-, to bend, turn, or wind, as does a Gc LOCK of hair; the lock on a door ? comes from the idea of "bending together" (shutting). L *luxus* originally described a plant bending because it had grown excessively, hence the later sense of excess or extravagance, whence LUXURY. And L *luctare*, to wrestle ("bend") or struggle, > the RELUCTANT person who "struggles back" against doing something.

LEUGH-, Gc to tell a LIE.

LEUK-, L *lux*, *luc*-, brightness or Gc LIGHT. From the L we get the LUSTER of bright things, LUCID (originally = shining), ILLUSTRATE (originally = throw light on or ELUCIDATE), and the TRANSLUCENT substance that light shines *lucent* through. Other L relatives are *lumen*, light, whence LUMINOUS and ILLUMINATE, and *luna*, the bright, shining moon, whence LUNAR and the LUNATIC, whose frenzied outbursts were supposedly caused or influenced by the moon.

LEUP-, to peel or break off, as a Gc LEAF in the fall. LODGE and LOBBY come < a Gc term = roof made from (peeled) bark, hence a shelter. Gc *luftaz*, sky (? "roof of the world") may be from this root but is more likely purely Gc; it is the source of ALOFT and the LOFT (attic) of a building, not to mention the Nazi Luftwaffe ("air weapon").

[**Germanic LIK-,** had many meanings: body, form (LIKE-NESS), ALIKE, LIKE (all senses), whence LIKELY and the idiomatic EACH. But easily the commonest member of this family is the adverbial (occasionally adjectival) suffix -LY (originally, -*lic*); thus "stupidly" literally = stupidlike—an expression still used in some dialects of English. We find the earlier form in the borrowed (< Dutch) word FROLIC, literally "joylike"—which a frolic indeed is.]

LINO-, L *linum*, flax, whence LINEN, LINSEED, LINOLEUM (originally containing linseed oil), LINGERIE (originally = linen garments), and LINT (originally = surgical dressing made by scraping linen); LINAMENT, too, originally = dressing. Also < L are LINE (originally, a linen cord) and the (linen) LINING of a garment.

[**Mediterranean LITHRA,** L *libra*, a scale (balance), also a pound (LB.), whence LEVEL (originally, the tool still used by carpenters and masons to "balance" the line of a wall or frame). To DELIBERATE is to balance the alternatives; EQUILIBRIUM is the "equal balance" we sometimes lose. Gk *litra*, a unit of weight, eventually > the modern coinage LITER/LITRE.]

[Latin LOCUS, place, whence LOCATE, LOCAL (in or around a particular place), and in LIEU (place) of.]

LUS-, Gc LOUSE.

MA-1, good, hence at a good (seasonable, early) time, whence L *maturus*, seasonable, ripe, MATURE; a PREMATURE baby is, of course, born before it's "ripe." A MATINEE is a "morning" (early) performance of any sort—normally, in the afternoon.

MA-2, MA-MA-, imitation of an infant's "instinctive" cry for the breast, whence the MAMMALs whose females possess "breasts" (milk glands). MAMA, a much later (sixteenth-century) English "reinvention" of the same term, > MOM(MA) and MUM.

■ The root has been called a vocalization of the infant's sucking motions, which are, of course, universal. So (almost) is the word: it occurs in many languages outside the I-E family—e.g., Chinese.

MA-3, damp, whence Gc MOOR, originally marshland, now wasteland.

[Latin MACULA, spot, blemish, whence IMMACULATE, "unspotted," as in the old carol "A Virgin Unspotted." (The modern poet T. S. Eliot showed off his learning by writing of "the maculate giraffe.")]

MAD-, moist, wet; also, various qualities of food and even food itself, whence Gc MEAT—originally, food of any sort; what we call meat was "flesh-meat." Your MATE is one with whom you share food—in the United States, usually a husband or wife; in England and Australia, also a chum.

MAG-, MAK-, to knead, fit, or Gc MAKE, whence MASON, a particular kind of maker. The "fit" sense > Gc MATCH (a matchmaker "fits" two people together); the "knead" sense > "mix," whence Gc MINGLE, MONGREL (of mixed breed), and AMONG ("mixed in with"). And Gk *maza*, a (kneaded) lump or barley cake, > MASS and MASSIVE.

MAGH-1, be able, have the power, whence Gc MIGHT (power), MAY (originally = be able), and DISMAY ("remove [someone's] power"). Gk *mekhanes*, device (which enables one to do something), > MACHINE, MECHA-NISM, and the MECHANIC who tends them. Also < Gk is MAGIC—originally, the supposed powers of the magi, a caste of priests in ancient Persia.

MAGHU-, young person, whence MAIDEN and MAID (the domestic maid is ? from "maidservant").

MAI-1, to cut, whence Gc (via OF) MAIM, MANGLE, and MAYHEM. A Gc variant = the biter > ANT and the tiny MITE.

MAI-2, ? to soil, defile, whence the MOLE that "soils" the skin.

MAK-, long, thin, whence the L EMACIATEd person who lives on a MEAGER diet.

MAN-1, MON-, Gc MAN (person); later also male person. WOMAN comes from OE *wyfman*, female person.   See **wyf**

MAN-2, L *manus*, hand. Its descendants include MANAGE ("take in hand"—originally, a horse), MANUAL (done with the hands; also, a handbook), MAINTAIN ("hold in hand"—support), and MANEUVER ("work [something] with the hand"); MANNER and MANIPULATE (ultimately < a L word = handful) are idiomatic.

Compounds include MANICURE, care of the hands, and   See **cura**
MANIFEST = "struck with the hand," hence obvious ("It   See **gwhen**
hits you in the face!"); a MANUSCRIPT was originally writ-   See **skribh-**
ten by hand, MANUFACTURES were originally made by   See **dhe-**
hand, and to EMANCIPATE is to "let out of the hand" (see *BLM*).

The L compound *mandare*, *mandat-*, entrust ("give into   See **do-**
the hand"), COMMAND, > COUNTERMAND, COMMANDO, DE-MAND, and (via a different route) COMMEND and RECOM-MEND.

[**Latin MAPPA,** cloth, towel, > NAPKIN, APRON, MAP (< MedL *mappa mundi*, "sheet of the world"), and ? MOP.]

■ Quintilian, a first-century Roman writer, claimed that the L word was borrowed from the Carthaginians, who spoke a Semitic tongue related to Hebrew. Since no one has turned up any Semitic root akin to it, the word (if indeed it came from North Africa) may have been borrowed from some indigenous tongue of that region, akin to modern Berber.

MARI-, young woman, hence bride, whence Gc MARRY.

MARKO-, horse, whence Gc MARE. MARSHAL has a much more intricate history: it started as a compound of "mare" with a Gc word meaning slave or servant; the "horse servant" was later upgraded to a cavalry leader and finally to a top military officer.

[**Latin MAS,** MALE, whence MASCULINE, EMASCULATE (remove the masculine organs, literally or figuratively), and—of course—MACHO.]

MAT-, a tool of some sort, whence (via VL) MATTOCK.

See **pelh-3**

MATER-, (< **ma-2**), L *mater*, Gk *meter*, Gc MOTHER. From the L we get MATERNAL, MATRIMONY, and through a different route, MATRIX (in L, a breeding female, hence womb, hence the "womb" that forms or holds something). L *materia*, originally the hard part of a tree (seen as the "mother" of the tender shoots), > MATERIAL and MATTER. From Gk we get METROPOLIS, the "mother city" (e.g., Athens in ancient Attica); now, of course, any major city. The METRO in Paris, Washington, and various other cities was originally short for "metropolitan railway."

MATH-, worm, whence Gc MOTH (the larvae of moths are indeed "worms"—caterpillars).

[**Italic MAWORT-,** a pre–I-E deity adopted by the Romans as MARS, their war god, whence MARTIAL. The god's name was also transferred to the sun's reddish ("bloody") fourth planet, and to the month of MARCH.]

MAZDO-, rod, pole, whence Gc MAST.

■ Some scholars give "mast" as one of the original (I-E) senses of the root, but this assumes that the I-Es had water craft with masts and sails—which I doubt.

ME-1, first-person singular pronoun in all but the nominative (subject) case (see **eg**), whence Gc ME, MY, MYSELF, and MINE.

ME-2, L *metiri*, *mens-*, to MEASURE, whence DIMENSION and IMMENSE ("immeasurable"). Gk *metron*, measure, > the METER/METRE that "measures" verse, the meter (or -METER) that measures other things, and the meters/metres distances are measured in. Also the DIAMETER that "measures through" the center of a circle, and GEOMETRY ("measuring the earth"). More remotely allied is Gc MEAL, originally = measure, then an appointed ("measured") time for eating.

See **ge**

Another branch of the family centers on the Gc MOON (whence MONDAY), used around the world to measure off the Gc MONTH. L *mensis*, month, gave us MENSTRUATE and SEMESTER—literally "six-month" (half a year) but now half a school or college year. The Gk equivalent gave us MENARCHE (the beginning of menstruation) and MENO-PAUSE.

See **arkhein**
See **paus-**

ME-3, big, whence Gc MORE and MOST.

ME-4, Gc to MOW (grass or grain), whence the "mowed" MEADOW and the AFTERMATH, originally = grass springing up after a field was mowed—see *BLM*.

MED-, "take appropriate measures," hence deal with, look after, whence L *medere*, look after, heal, which > MEDICINE, MEDICAL, and REMEDY. L *meditari*, to think about (? "plan appropriate measures"), > MEDITATE; *moderare*, *moderat-* keep within measure, > MODEST and MODERATE. And L *modus* variously meant size (whence MODEL and MOLD/MOULD), limit (whence MODIFY), and manner (whence MODE and MODERN—"in today's mode").

A COMMODITY was something of "due measure," hence convenient or useful; to ACCOMMODATE is to make suitable ("of the proper measure"). Possible but unlikely Gc relatives are EMPTY (? "not meeting the proper measure") and ?? MUST.

MEDHU-, honey, or its fermented product, Gc MEAD. From Gk *methuein*, to be intoxicated, comes the AMETHYST that supposedly charmed its wearer against getting drunk.

MEDHYO-, L *medius*, Gc MIDDLE, whence AMID. From the L we get MEAN (average), MEDIAN, MEDIUM, MEDIOCRE, MEDIATE (a mediator is "in the middle"), and INTERMEDIATE ("in the middle between"). Compounds include MEDIEVAL (in the Middle Ages), MEDITERRANEAN ("in the middle of the land"), and MERIDIAN, literally = middle of the day, as in *ante meridian* (A.M.) and *post meridian* (P.M.).

See **aiw-**

See **ters-**

See **deiw-**

MEG-, L *magnus*, Gk *megas*, Sanskrit *maha-*, great. From the L we get MAGNIFY ("make great"), MAGNIFICENT, and MAGNANIMOUS ("great-minded"); L *major*, greater, > MAJOR, MAJORITY, and MAYOR; *maximus*, greatest, > MAXIMUM. L *maiestas*, greatness, > MAJESTY (Your Majesty = Your Greatness), while *magister*, MASTER ("he who is great"), > MISTER, MISTRESS, MISS, MISSUS, and MAESTRO; a secondary sense, "high [great] official," > MAGISTRATE. From the Gk we get MEGA- (as in "megabyte"); from the Sanskrit, MAHARAJAH, "great king." Gc MUCH, of course, = great quantity.

See **anh-**

See **reg-1**

MEI-1. A root of broad (or vague) meaning: change, go, move, with relatives having to to with the movement (exchange) of goods and services, and the L COMMUNITY

162

within which the exchange occurred. The "change" sense > Gc MAD and MIS- ("changed for the worse"), whence AMISS and MISTAKE; L *mutare*, change, > MOLT (change plumage), MUTATE, and COMMUTE (originally = "change with," exchange; the modern sense—what a commuter does—is idiomatic). Also < L are MIGRATE (change where one lives), whence EMIGRATE (migrate out of) and IMMIGRATE (migrate into). From Gk, finally, we get the AMOEBA that is "without [a constant] shape."

See **tak-**

From the "go" sense we get Gc MISS ("go wrong") and L *meare*, go, pass, whence PERMEATE, "go through." The "exchange" sense > L MUTUAL, while the "community" sense > many derivatives in both Gc and L. Gc MEAN, originally = in L COMMON use, then inferior or ignoble ("But down these mean streets a man must go who is not himself mean"—Raymond Chandler). MUNICIPAL comes from L *munus*, a civic (community) office, whence ? a public spectacle paid for by officeholders, hence a gift, whence REMUNERATE and MUNIFICENT. *Immunus* meant exempt—IMMUNE—from (the burdens of) public office, which under the late empire could be pretty severe.

In some L words the "exchange" sense > "share," as in COMMUNE and COMMUNISM, in both of which goods are (theoretically) shared equally, and COMMUNICATE (originally = share, now share information).

MEI-2, small, > L *minor*, less, lesser, whence MINOR, MINUS ($10 - 5 =$ ten less five), MINUTE (very small, and a "minute" period of time), DIMINISH (make smaller), MINCE (chop small), and the purely idiomatic MENU. By an odd coincidence, the L adjective also came to mean badly, wrongly, whence the prefix MIS- in words of L origin (e.g., "mischance"); practically, it now has the same meaning as Gc MIS- (see previous entry). Finally, L *minister* was an inferior or servant, whence the MINISTER who is a "servant" of the government, or God, and MINESTRONE, originally = large serving, which a plate of minestrone generally is.

MEI-3, to fix; also, build fences or fortifications, whence L *murus*, wall, whence MURAL paintings. From L *munire*, to fortify, strengthen, come both MUNITIONS and AMMUNITION.

MEI-4, mild, whence L MITIGATE, "make milder."

MEIGH-, to urinate, hence Gc MIST ("It's pissing down").

MEIK-, L *miscere*, *mixt-*, MIX, whence MEDDLE ("mix into"), and the MEDLEY or MÉLANGE that is a MISCELLANEOUS MIXTURE. MASH was originally malt mixed with water (as it still is to brewers), and a PROMISCUOUS person has a "mixed" character—to say the least. miscible

MEI-NO-, opinion, Meinung intention, whence MEAN (what you mean is what you intend to say). In Gc the term also = complaint, whence MOAN.

MEL-1, soft, whence Gc MILD, MELT (soften), SCHMALTZ (literally = melted fat, but see *BLM*), and ? MALT (grain soaked—"softened"—in water). From L we get the soft-bodied (though often hard-shelled) MOLLUSK, and ?? from Gaulish **molto-*, sheep (? "the soft-fleeced animal"), MUTTON.

■ Since there is good reason to think that the Gauls were not the first sheepherders in Western Europe, **molto-* was more likely borrowed from some earlier, non–I-E people—as were Gc "sheep," "ram," and "lamb."

MEL-2, Gk *melos*, limb, whence a "limb" (phrase) of music—a MELODY, whence MELODRAMA—originally, a play with music.

MEL-3, darkish in color, whence Gk *melas*, black, whence MELANCHOLY, literally "black bile" (see *BLM*).

MEL-4, strong, great, whence L *multus*, much, many, whence MULTI- and MULTITUDE.

MEL-5, L *malus*, bad, whence MAL- and a host of bad or MALIGN things or qualities, including MALICE, MALADY, MALEFACTOR, MALEVOLENT, and DISMAL ("bad day").   See **deiw-**

MEL(h)-, to crush or grind, whence ground Gc MEAL and the L MILL that grinds it. Also < L are our MOLAR (grinding) teeth, and, via a different route, the MALLET and MAUL that "crush" (pound) things.

■ The (water) mill was the first artificially powered machine used on land. As such, its name > almost a generic term for any powered device or factory, as in "steel mill," "cotton mill," and even—humorously—"gin mill."

MELG-, Gc to MILK (also, rub off). From an apparently unrelated I-E root (? **(ga)lak-**) are the Gk and L words for milk; from the Gk comes the GALAXY—the Milky Way; from the L, LETTUCE (some varieties have or had a milky juice).

MELIT-, honey, whence L MOLASSES and Gk MARMELADE—originally, a quince preserve.

■ Since honey was for thousands of years the only sweetener known in Europe, its name was transferred to various other sweet things.

MELO-, SMELO-, Gc SMALL animal.

[**Greek MELON,** apple or any seed-bearing fruit, whence MELON and, after intricate changes, MARMELADE (see **melit-** above). Probably borrowed < some Mediterranean language.]

MEMS-, meat, whence L *membrum*, limb (a joint of meat), whence MEMBER—a "limb" of an organization.

MEN-1, to think, whence Gc MIND and REMIND (though the "re-" is < L). Wholly L are MENTAL and DEMENTED ("mind away"). A related L noun = REMEMBER ("think back") > REMINISCE. From the Gk root *mnes-*, remember, come AMNESIA (not remembering) and the AMNESTY in which someone's offense (real or alleged) is legally "forgotten."

The root could also mean various aspects of thinking, good or bad, as in Gk MANIA. L *monere* meant to remind, warn, advise, or ADMONISH; a MONUMENT was originally a gravestone that reminded passers-by of the departed; a MONSTER was originally an extraordinary event that served as a divine PREMONITION ("warning in advance"). And a SUMMONS is a "warning" to appear, as in traffic court.

Four other family members evolved by more intricate processes. The Gk muses were goddesses of "thinking" (learning and the arts), whence MUSEUM and MUSIC. And—this is *really* complicated—the Roman goddess June was sometimes known as *Juno* [Moneta, "Juno the
{ cf. Keats

166

Admonisher"; her temple in Rome, called the Moneta, was where the MINT was located—whence MONEY.

MEN-2, to project, whence various projecting body parts such as the Gc MOUTH. L *minae* were projecting points (? as in a line of spearmen), hence threats or MENACES. An EMINENT or PROMINENT person "projects" (sticks out) from the crowd; an IMMINENT event is "projected." A MOUNTAIN or MOUNT sticks out from the surrounding terrain; the verb "to mount" (as a mountain) > AMOUNT = rise to a certain level ("Your bill amounts to . . .").

MEN-3, L *manere*, to REMAIN, whence the MANORS and MANSIONS in which some people "remain"; something PERMANENT "remains completely."

MEN-4, small, isolated, whence Gk MONO-, MONK (originally, a solitary hermit), and MONASTERY; also ? various small fish called Gc MINNOWS.

MEND-, physical defect, fault, which needs to be L MENDed or AMENDed; also < L is the character defect of the lying, MENDACIOUS person.

MENDH-1, to learn, whence Gk MATHEMATICS.
polymath
■ Some Greek philosophers considered mathematics the highest form of learning, because it always produced the same conclusions.

MENDH-2, to chew, whence the L MANGER where some domestic animals chew their fodder, and the Gk MUS-TACHE that sits above the human chewing apparatus.

MENEGH-, copious or Gc MANY.

MENG-, to polish or furbish, whence L *mango*, gem polisher, swindler (who "polished up" shoddy wares), whence -MONGER.

■ In VL, *mango* was applied to (among others) Roman traders along the German frontier—who no doubt tried hard to swindle their unlettered customers. Borrowed into Gc, it sometimes took on a neutral coloration, as in British "fishmonger" and "ironmonger" (hardware dealer), but never completely lost its low-life connotations, as in "scandalmonger," "whoremonger," and "warmonger." Indeed, even "fishmonger" has been used (by Shakespeare, among others) to mean whoremonger.

MER-1, to flicker, whence Gc MURKY (dim) light of various sorts, as in early Gc MORNING—whence TOMORROW, "at the [next] morrow." A more intricate (and less than certain) evolution > L *merus*, unmixed (wine), whence MERE—originally = unmixed; later, only.

MER-2, to rub away, harm (? by "rubbing away" skin), but the "rub" sense is all but extinct in English except in the L MORTAR used to "rub" (grind) spices and pigments. The "harm" sense survives in Gc NIGHTMARE ("night" + an extinct word = [harmful] goblin). A possible relative is L *mordere*, to bite, whence the MORSEL you bite off and the REMORSE that "bites again."

Possibly the same I-E root, but more likely a different one, = to die (?? "be harmed"), whence Gc MURDER. L *mors*, *mort-*, death, > MORBID, MORTAL, MORIBUND, and MORTIFY (originally = kill, but its modern senses are all figurative); a MORTGAGE was originally a "dead pledge"—a debt that could be collected even if the debtor was dead, as a mortgage indeed can be.

MER-3, to tie, whence Gc MOOR (a boat).

MERG-, boundary, borderland; in Gc also a LANDMARK (originally = boundary marker), and the ceremony of MARKing a boundary by MARCHing around it. From L we get only the MARGIN that borders a page.

[**Italic MERK-** (? from Etruscan), referring to trade, whence L *merx*, *merc-*, MERCHANDISE, whence the MER-CHANT engaged in COMMERCE ("trade together"), the "commercial" MERCENARY soldier, and idiomatic MERCY—ultimately < a L noun = reward or fee. Probably < the same root is the Roman god MERCURY, messenger of the gods and patron of merchants—and thieves. The transfer of his name to the planet may reflect its (relatively) speedy motion across the skies, or its thieflike elusiveness: it can be seen, if at all, only at twilight or dawn. The metal mercury is idiomatic.]

[**Greek MERPH-,** form. Its direct English descendants are all scholarly, but it may also be the source (? via Etruscan) of L *forma*, FORM, shape, whence FORMAL, FOR-MULA (the "form"—recipe or rule—for doing something), CONFORM ("shape with"), and DEFORM ("shape away from").]

MERS-, to trouble, hence injure or Gc MAR.

MEU-, damp, wet, whence swampy ground (Gc MIRE) and its vegetation (Gc MOSS); QUAGMIRE probably = quaking bog. More remotely related is L *mustus*, newborn ("wet"), new, whence "must," newly pressed (unfermented) grape juice—and the ground seed of MUSTARD mixed with it.

MEUh-, to push away, whence L *movere*, *mot-*, to MOVE, whence MOTION, COMMOTION, the MOTOR that moves things, and the MOTIVES and EMOTIONS that move us. To PROMOTE something moves it forward; to REMOVE it moves it away—perhaps to a REMOTE place. L *mobilis*, changeable ("given to movement"), hence fickle, begot the phrase *mobile vulgus*, "the fickle crowd," which seventeenth-century English snobs clipped to MOB. Closely related is L *momentum*, moving power, whence MOMENTUM—and a MOMENT of moving time.

MEUG-1, to act surreptitiously, whence MOOCH (Gc or Gaulish, via OF).

MEUG-2, slimy, slippery, whence L MUCUS, MUCILAGE, and MOIST. Gk *myxa*, mucus, also = the wick of a lamp—which, like mucus, emerged from the nozzle ("nostril"), whence MATCH—originally, a wicklike contrivance used to set fire to, say, the powder in a gun.

Gc family members are very diverse: MUGGY (originally = drizzly) weather can be "slippery," to SMUGGLE contraband is to "slip" it through, and a MEEK person is "soft," as slippery things often are. More tenuously related is another Gc group centering on the notion of "adorn" (? "slick down"), whence the SMUG ("sleek") person, SMOCK, and after an intricate evolution, SCHMUCK. Originally this = jewel, adornment, then a man's most precious "jewel," then (via Yiddish) "prick" (unpleasant fool).

MEZG-1, L *mergere*, *mers-*, to dip, dive or plunge, whence MERGE (originally = plunge), IMMERSE (dip into), SUB-MERGE ("dip/dive under") and EMERGE ("dive out").

MEZG-2, to knot, hence make a Gc MESH.

■ Some define this root as "to knit." But knitting wasn't invented until a few centuries ago (the word originally = fasten with a knot), so that the I-Es surely had no word for it.

[**Greek MIMOS,** a MIME, whence MIMIC.]

[**Latin MISER,** wretched, unfortunate, whence MISERA-BLE, MISERY, and the wretched MISER.]

MO-, to exert oneself, whence L *molestus*, labored (requiring exertion), hence difficult, troublesome, whence MO-LEST. L *moliri*, to construct (laboriously) > DEMOLISH—"deconstruct."

MOD-, to assemble or Gc MEET.

MOLKO-, (skin) bag, whence Gc MAIL—still carried in bags, sometimes made of tanned skin.

MON-, neck, whence the Gc MANE on the neck of a horse.

MORI-, body of water, ?? sea, whence Gc MERE (in Britain, a lake or pond), MARSH (waterlogged land), and MORASS. Latin *mare*, sea, > MARINE, MARITIME, and Italian MARINARA ("sailor-style") sauce.

■ This root could have meant "sea" only if the I-Es were a maritime people—which few authorities believe.

MORMOR-, L MURMUR.

MO(U)RO-, Gk *moros*, foolish, whence MORON.

MOZGO-, Gc MARROW.

MREGH-M(N)O-, Gc BRAIN.

MREGH-U-, short, whence L BRIEF, ABBREVIATE, and
brachiate ABRIDGE. Gk *brakhion* = shorter, also = the shorter
(upper) part of the arm, whence (via various routes) EM-
BRACE (throw one's arms around), PRETZEL (originally, in
the shape of an armlet—ring), and BRASSIERE ("arm
guard"—see below). Gc derivatives relate shortness to
pleasantness ("A short life and a MERRY one"), whence
MIRTH.

■ "Brassiere" shows how sex taboos can influence language. Its original sense was "arm guard," which of course
a brassiere is not; its French equivalent, *soutien gorge*,
means "throat supporter"—which again it is not. Only
the Germans seem to have been forthright enough to call
it what it is: *Bustenhalter*, busts-holder.

MU-I-, a root imitating various inarticulate sounds that
people MUTTER or MUMBLE—unless they keep MUM completely; MUMPS can also make you mumble. All these are
Gc, but MUTE is < L. A much more intricate evolution
began with Gk *muein*, close the lips, the source of a word
meaning the secret rites of the so-called MYSTERY religions,
which initiates were expected to be close-mouthed about;
MYSTIC is < the same source.

MU-2, a fly, gnat, or Gc MIDGE; from L via Spanish comes
MOSQUITO ("little fly") and, via Italian soldiers' slang,

MUSKET (originally = crossbow)—a "little fly" that could really sting.

MUS-, Gc MOUSE; L MUSCLE is a "little mouse" that scuttles beneath the skin—see *BLM*.

[Medieval Latin MUSUM, MUZZLE.]

MUT-, cut short, whence L MUTILATE.

NANA, baby talk for a nurse or other female "caretaker" other than the mother (compare **ma-2**), whence L NUN (medieval nuns often nursed the sick, as some still do). NANNY is probably a "reinvention" of this term.

NAS-, Gc NOSE, whence NOSTRIL, and L NASAL. Gc NUZZLE = press the nose against, and Gc NOZZLE is the "nose" of, say, a hose.

NAU-1, to be exhausted, hence death, but its modern descendants have been much softened: NEED comes from an OE word = distress; NUDGE, from a Russian one (via Yiddish) = tedious ("exhausting")—which a "nudge" (pronounced "nooj") indeed is. The term has probably been influenced by the unrelated verb "nudge" (push); a "nudge" is always pushing you.

NAU-2, boat, whence L *navis*, ship, whence NAVY, NAVAL, and NAVIGATE. From Gk *naus*, ship, comes the NAUSEA   See **ag-**

many people feel on shipboard, whence NOISE (see *BLM*); *nautes*, sailor, > NAUTICAL and -NAUT (astro-, cosmo-).

NDHER-, Gc UNDER. Via L we get INTER-, INFERIOR ("more under," lower), and INFERNO, originally the INFERNAL ("lower") regions, as in Dante's famous epic of that name.

NE, Gc NOT, along with most other English NEGATIVES— words that DENY or NEGATE an idea (the last three < L). From Gc come NO, NEITHER, NOR, NEVER, NONE, NOTHING, and NAUGHT (formerly = nothing; later, zero), whence NAUGHTY (originally, a person possessing naught—who, having naught to lose, might well become "naughty"). From L *nullus*, none, come NULL, NULLIFY ("make null"), and ANNUL; L *nihil*, nothing, > ANNIHILATE ("turn to nothing").

Other obvious L negatives are NON- and RENEGADE, someone who "re-denies" a cause or doctrine, whence RENEGE. NEGLECT originated as "not choose," hence ignore; a NEGLIGEE is an informal, "neglected" dress. And from L *negotium*, business ("not leisure"), comes NEGOTIATE— which businesspeople spend much time doing.

NEBH-, L *nebula*, cloud, whence the NEBULAS ("cloudy objects" of several kinds) that astronomers study—and NEBULOUS (cloudy, hence insubstantial) ideas or theories.

nuance

NED-, to bind or tie, whence Gc NET and ? NETTLE (which may have been used to make cordage, as the related hemp plant is). From L come the DENOUEMENT that "unknots" a drama, ANNEX ("bind to"), and CONNECT ("bind together").

NEGW-RO-, various colors, including L *niger*, black, whence NEGRO and DENIGRATE, "blacken" (someone) ("throw mud at").

■ The negative senses of *niger*, like those of "black," have nothing to do with skin color: dirt is often black; so are threatening storm clouds, and so is night—when both evil spirits and evil people are abroad.

[**Germanic NEHW-IZ,** NEAR, whence NEXT ("nearest") and NEIGHBOR (near dweller).] See **bheu-**

NEI-, to be excited, shine (connection unclear), whence L *nitidus*, shining, clean, whence NEAT and also NET (as in "income"—see *BLM*).

NEK-1, death, whence L *nocere*, to harm, whence NOXIOUS, OBNOXIOUS, PERNICIOUS ("very harmful"), and NUISANCE (originally = harm), plus INNOCENT and INNOCUOUS, both = not harmful. NECTAR was the drink of the Greek gods, which made them immortal; its literal meaning is "overcoming death." See **terh-2**

NEK-2, to reach, attain; if you reach successfully you attain Gc ENOUGH.

NEKW-T-, L *nox*, *noct-*, Gc NIGHT; the L word > NOCTURNAL and EQUINOX, when the length of night equals that of day. (EQUI- is from a non–I-E word = level, even.)

NEM-, to assign, allot; the Gk goddess NEMESIS gave people the justice (usually unpleasant) they deserved (were allotted)—see *BLM*. Other Gk derivatives centered on the idea of divide, arrange, manage, whence AUTONOMOUS (self-managing) and -NOMY (e.g., astro-, eco-). Gk *nome*, (divided) pastureland, > the NOMADs who wander in search of pasture for their herds. A possible relative is L *numerus*, division, NUMBER, whence ENUMERATE ("number off"). In Gc, the root > take or seize, whence NIMBLE ("quick at seizing") and NUMB (from a "seizure").

NEPOT-, grandson, L NEPHEW; from the same source are NIECE and the figurative NEPOTISM (see *BLM*).

NER-1, under, also on the left (see note), hence (if you're facing east) Gc NORTH. The NORMANS were pirates from the north (Scandinavia), some of whom settled in Normandy; soon after, they conquered England.

■ The under/left connection may reflect the widespread feeling in many cultures that there's something wrong or "sub" about the left hand.

NER-2, hNER-, Gk *aner*, *andr-*, man (human being), whence the PHILANDERer who "loves men" (more often, women). Possibly from the same root is Gk *anthropos*, man, whence ANTHROPOLOGY (the study of mankind) and PHILANTHROPY—another kind of "loving."

NES-1, to return safely home, whence Gk NOSTALGIA, originally = homesickness; now, a desire to return "home" to the past.

nostos [handwritten above "to return"]

NES-2, first-person plural pronoun except as subject of sentence (see **we-1**)—Gc US, OUR, OURS.

NETR-, snake, whence Gc ADDER (the N was detached when "a nadder" > "an adder").

NEU-1, to shout, whence L **nuntiare*, give a message, whence ANNOUNCE ("message given to"), DENOUNCE ("message given against"), PRONOUNCE ("message given forth"), and RENOUNCE ("message given back").

NEU-2, L **nuere*, to nod, whence the INNUENDO conveyed by a "nod" (or a wink—traditionally just as good) rather than in words.

NEWN, L *novem*, Gc NINE, whence NINETEEN and NINETY; from the L we get NOVEMBER, the "ninth" month (see **dekm**).

NEWO-, L *novus*, Gk *newos*, Gc NEW, whence RENEW ("make new again"). From the L we get NOVA (a "new" star), the NOVICE who's new to some institution or skill, the NOVEL (new) thing—a NOVELTY—whence the novel that's (supposedly) a new story. To INNOVATE is to create something new, while to RENOVATE something is to renew it. From Gk we get NEON (a new gas when it was first discovered) and NEO- (as in -conservative—though most neoconservative doctrines are pretty musty).

■ The root is related to **nu**, the source of "now"; something "now" is something new.

NI, down, whence Gc BENEATH, UNDERNEATH, and NETHER ("more down," hence lower); the NETHERLANDS are the lowlands of Europe.

NIZDO-, Gc NEST, whence NESTLE (settle into a "nest"); *niche*

NOBH-, OMBH-, L *umbilicus*, Gc NAVEL, later the navel-like "nave" (hub) of a wheel (see *OMNT*), whence the

omphalos

See **ghaiso-**

AUGER ("hub piercer"), originally used to drill the axle hole in the nave. The L word, of course, > the UMBILICAL cord.

NOGH-, hHOGH-, ONGH-, claw or Gc NAIL.

NOGW-, Gk *gymnos*, L NUDE, Gc NAKED. The Gk word > GYMNASIUM, "naked place" (Greek men stripped before exercising), whence GYMNAST.

NO-MEN-, L *nomen*, *nomin-*, Gk *onoma*, Gc NAME. From the L we get NOMINAL (various senses, including "in name only"), NOMINATE (put someone's name forward), NOUN (the name of something), the PRONOUN that "stands for" it, and MISNOMER (wrong name). The L word also = reputation, whence RENOWN and IGNOMINY ("no reputation"). From the Gk word we get ANONYMOUS (no name), PSEUDONYM (false name), SYNONYM ("same name"), and ANTONYM ("opposite name"). *onomatopoeia*

See also **newo-**

NU-, Gc NOW.

olfactory ?redolent
OD-1, Gk *ozein*, L *olere*, to smell, whence ODOR. Gk OZONE is a sharp-smelling form of oxygen found in the upper atmosphere—in decreasing quantities.

OD-2, to hate, whence L *odi*, I hate, which was softened to ANNOY and ENNUI.

OG-, fruit, berry, whence Gc ACORN, the "berry" of the oak.

OID-, Gk *odein*, to swell, whence EDEMA (swelling in tissues; also the excess fluid that often induces it). OAT (not Gc but pure English) is ?? from this root, but more likely borrowed from some aboriginal people in northwest Europe, where the grain probably originated.

OI-NO-, L *unus*, Gc ONE, whence ELEVEN ("one left"), ONCE, ONLY ("just one"), A, AN, ALONE (by oneself), LONELY, ANY and its negative, NONE, and, surprisingly, ATONE—literally, put oneself "at one" with God or one's fellows. From the L are such obvious relatives as UNION ("oneness"), UNITE, UNITY, UNANIMOUS ("of one mind"), the one-horned UNICORN, and UNIVERSE—"everything turned into one." The L word for some reason > *uncia*, a twelfth, whence INCH (¹⁄12 ft) and OUNCE (¹⁄12 lb. Troy weight). A secondary sense of the original root was L UNIQUE—"one of a kind." See **leip-**

See **anh-**
See **ker-1**
See **wer-3**

OITO-, Gc OATH.

OKTO(U), L *octo*, Gk *okto*, Gc EIGHT. From L we get OCTAVE—the eight tones of the diatonic scale, and the "eighth" month, OCTOBER; from Gk, the eight-"footed" OCTOPUS. See **ped-1**

OKW-, to see, whence Gc EYE and DAISY, the "day's eye" (see *BLM*); also WINDOW, the "wind's eye" (you see out of it—and the wind blows into it). From L we get EYELET ("little eye"), INVEIGLE ("blind the eyes of"—see *BLM*), and INOCULATE—originally, implant an "eye" (bud or graft); now, "implant" a microbe or vaccine.

From various Gk words for eye we get a host of medico-scientific terms, of which the best known are -OPIA (as in "myopia") and OPHTHALMO- (as in "ophthalmologist"). More generally known are terms from Gk *opsis*, *opt-*, sight, seeing, whence OPTIC, SYNOPSIS ("seeing [everything] together"), and AUTOPSY, literally "seen by an eye-witness"; the present sense is idiomatic.

ONGW-, L to ANOINT, whence OINTMENT and the "oily" UNCTUOUS person (see *BLM*).

OP-1, to work, hence produce abundantly; we find the "work" sense in several L descendants—notably OPERATE and COOPERATE (work together). An OPUS is a (usually) musical work; an OPERA, a particular kind of musical work. A L compound, "work with the hand(s)," > MANEUVER and MANURE (originally = to cultivate). The "abundance" sense > L *copia*, plenty, whence COPIOUS and COPY (copying a document makes it more abundant); more remotely related is L *omnis*, all, whence OMNIBUS (a vehicle "for all"), which was clipped to BUS.

See **man-2**

OP-2, L *opere*, to choose, whence ADOPT ("choose to yourself," as a child), the OPTION you choose to exercise—or not—and the OPINION you choose to hold.

OR-, to pronounce a ritual formula, whence L *orare*, to pray, hence plead, speak, whence the ORATOR and his or her ORATION. The "pray" sense > ADORE, originally = worship religiously; now "worship" in any way.

ORBH-, to separate, whence the Gk ORPHAN separated from its parents by death, and Old Slavonic *rabu*, slave ("separated from freedom"), whence ROBOT, a mechanical "slave."

ORS-, Gc ARSE/ASS, buttocks. Gk *ouros*, tail, > SQUIRREL   See **skot-**
("shadow-tail").

■ The shift from buttocks to tail, or vice versa, has occurred independently in several languages, including English,
in which "tail" = (woman's) buttocks.

OS-1, Gc ASH tree.

OS-2, L *os*, *or-*, mouth, whence ORAL; L *ostium*, door (the
"mouth" of a room or building), > the doorkeeper or
USHER.

OST-, bone; also (in several families) shell, whence L OYS-
TER and Gk *ostrakon*, shell, potsherd, whence OSTRACIZE
(see *BLM*).

OUS-, AUS-, L **aus*, *aur-*, Gc EAR. The L word begot *aus-*
cultare, listen ("incline the ear"), whence the (military)   See **klei-**
SCOUT who keeps his ear inclined for sounds of enemy
activity.

OWI-, sheep, whence Gc EWE.

PA-, to protect or Gc FEED, whence FOOD, FODDER, and FOR-
AGE; the "protect" sense > Gc FUR and the FOSTER parent
who both feeds and protects a child. From L come the
PASTURE where animals feed, the PASTOR who protects
them (and the pastor who protects his religious "flock"),

and the REPAST at which we "feed intensively." Also < L
are ANTIPASTO ("before the repast") and ? PESTER, from a
VL word meaning "tie up" (an animal), but more likely
from L *pestis*, plague (people who pester you plague you).

Also from the "feed" sense is L *panis*, bread (in ancient
Rome, as still in many places, the staple food), whence the
PANTRY where bread was kept and the COMPANION one
"shares bread with." COMPANY = either those we invite
to share bread ("Company tonight!") or a group of businesspeople who hope to share "bread" (see *BLM*).

PAG-, PAK-, L *pangere*, *pact-*, fasten, fix, whence COM-
PACT ("fixed together") and PEACE (when enemies are
"fastened together" by a PACT), whence PACIFY ("make
peaceful"), APPEASE (act peacefully toward), and PACIFIC.
Gc FANG originally = seize ("fasten onto"), then one of
the teeth with which an animal seizes its prey.

L *palus*, a stake (fixed in the ground), > the PALE or
PALING made of stakes or POLES. MedL *trepalium*, an instrument of torture (presumably made of three stakes),
> TRAVEL, which often was (and sometimes still is) tor-
ture—see *BLM*. Also < the "stake" sense is L *pagus*,
(staked out) boundary, hence village, hence countryside,
whence PEASANT; *paganus*, countryman, hence civilian,
> PAGAN (a "civilian" not in the army of Christ). L
pagina, trellis (made of stakes), > a column or PAGE of
writing.

■ This root is associated with some notable historical iro-
nies. The Pacific is, of course, no more "pacific" than any
other sea, and less than some; Magellan so named it because, it is said, he wanted to encourage further explora-
tion. And "pacify" recalls the British chieftain who said

of Roman "pacification" in his land: "They make a desert—and call it peace." Much the same could be said of recent "pacifications" in Vietnam and Afghanistan—among other places.

PAN-, cloth, whence Gc VANE, originally = banner; the present sense was ? influenced by "fan." L *pannus*, piece of cloth, > PANE and PANEL.

See **we-2**

PANT-, Gk *pas*, *pant-*, all, whence PAN- (pandemic, Pan-American); the Roman Pantheon was a temple to all the gods.

■ The root occurs only in Gk and Tocharian, an extinct I-E tongue of Central Asia; presumably it was "lost" elsewhere, since borrowing in either direction seems almost impossible.

PAP-, teat, hence food (a "baby-talk" root), whence L PAP, soft (baby) food, whence POPPYCOCK, literally = soft shit. Gc PAMPER, originally = cram with food. L *pupillus*, little child, > PUPIL (student); for the pupil of the eye, see *BLM*.

See **kak(k)a-**

PAPA, father, > PAPA, POP, and POPE (the head "father" of the Roman church); all are < Gk via L.

■ The word, like **ma-2**, is < baby talk, hence found in many non–I-E languages.

PAST-, solid, firm, whence Gc FAST (firmly FASTENed), STEADFAST ("standing firmly"), the FAST when you firmly abstain from eating, and the BREAKFAST that "breaks" your (overnight) fast.

See **sta-**

PAU-, _paucity_ small or Gc FEW. L POOR describes someone with few resources; a PAUPER is one who "produces little," hence lives in POVERTY, and a PUSILLANIMOUS person has a "very small soul." Another group of descendants concerns various small animals: Gc FOAL and FILLY and L PONY and PULLET. From Gk _pais_, _paid-_, child, comes the PEDIATRICIAN who deals with children's ailments, and _paideia_, education (originally of children), whence ENCYCLOPEDIA, originally the "circle" of arts and sciences that the Greeks considered essential for a comprehensive education.

See **perh-1**

See **anh-**

See **kwel-1**

PAUS-, to desert, leave (off), stop, whence L PAUSE, POSE ("stop moving," as a model does), REPOSE, and ? COMPOSE.

■ In VL _pausa_ became confused with _positus_, placed; "compose" ("place together") and "pose" may represent a blend of the two.

PED-1, L _pes_, _ped-_, Gk _pous_, _pod-_, Gc FOOT, whence FETCH, to bring (on foot). From L are PAWN, originally a foot soldier (see _BLM_), the PEDESTRIAN who goes on foot, and the PEDALS footed by those who prefer to bike. The Gk word > the PODIATRIST who cares for people's feet, the eight-footed OCTOPUS, and the photographer's three-footed TRIPOD. And from Persian _pai_, foot or leg, come the PAJAMAS that cover some people's legs.

Another branch of the family involves Gc FETTERing the feet; they include L IMPEDE and EXPEDITE ("put on/remove fetters"—see _BLM_). IMPEACH involves another kind of fettering—and DISPATCH, ? another kind of unfettering. Yet another group centers on stumbling (feet), whence L _peccare_, to stumble or sin, whence PECADILLO (a "little sin") and IMPECCABLE (without "sin"); L _pejor_, worse ("more stumbling"), > IMPAIR (make worse); _pessimus_, worst, > the PESSIMIST who always expects it.

More dubious relatives are CALIBER, from Arabic *qualib*, casting mold, ? shoemaker's last, which ? comes from Gk *kalapous*, "wooden foot," and Gk PILOT, which is certainly < *peda*, steering oars—but where do the feet come in? More likely, I think, the term is a Mediterranean word borrowed by Greek sailors (much as the Germans borrowed their term for "oar"), who then assimilated it into something like their own word for foot. Compare DOLPHIN under **gwelbh-**.

See **airo**

PED-2, container, whence Gc VAT. A less certain relative comes from an old Gc word meaning clothes (? containers for the body), whence ? the rags or fragments that we FRITTER away. This word, in turn, probably influenced the fritters we eat: their basic source is akin to "fry," but they also usually contain fragments of meat, vegetables, or fruit.

See **bher-4**

PEG-, breast, chest, whence L EXPECTORATE ("expel from the chest"). pectoral

P(E)I-, to hurt, whence ? L *pati, pass-*, to suffer, whence PASSION (originally = suffering, as in "The Passion of Christ") and the PATIENT who suffers PASSIVELY and hopes for his or her fellows' COMPASSION ("suffering with"). More distantly related is Gc FIEND, originally = enemy ("hurtful person")—as "sex fiends" still are.

PEIG-, PEIK-1, to cut, whence the Gc FILE that cuts away metal; also, mark (with a cut), whence L *pingere, pict-*, to embroider, tattoo, PAINT, PICTURE, or DEPICT. Other L derivatives include PIGMENT, PICTURESQUE ("like a picture"), and the Mexican PINTO, a "painted" (particolored) horse—the U.S. cowboy's "Old Paint."

PEIG-, PEIK-2, evil-minded, hostile, whence Gc FOE, FEUD, and FICKLE (originally = treacherous).

PEI(h)-, to swell, be Gc FAT. Possible relatives are L PINE, from its "fatty" (inflammable) resin (pine kindling is still called "fatwood" in the southern United States), and IRISH (< Celtic), because of the "fat" (fertile) land they inhabited.

PEIS-1, to crush, whence the L PESTLE that crushes things in a mortar, whence PISTON (< an Italian word = pestle); also ?? L *pilum*, javelin, which > the PILE that supports a wharf or building.

See **porko-**

PEISK-, Gc FISH, L PISCES (the celestial Fishes), whence PORPOISE ("pig fish").

See **ekwo-**

■ This is another case of people naming unfamiliar things with familiar words. The porpoise doesn't look much like a pig—but the hippopotamus looks even less like a horse.

PEK-1, to make pretty or Gc FAIR.

PEK-2, to pluck the hair, comb, whence ? Gc FIGHT (? "pull hair").

See **legh-**

PEKU-, wealth, movable property, hence ? cattle (once the commonest form of movable property), whence Gc FEE and FELLOW. From L come PECUNIARY (money) matters, the IMPECUNIOUS person with little or no wealth, and PECULIAR, originally = private (property).

PEKW-, to ripen or L COOK, whence KITCHEN, CUISINE, the KILN in which pottery is "cooked," and BISCUIT, originally = ship's biscuit—soldiers' or sailors' rations "cooked twice" to dry them for storage. The "ripen" sense > L PRECOCIOUS ("early-ripening"), whence—after a long journey through Gk and Arabic—the APRICOT, which ripens earlier than some other fruits.

Gk *peptein*, to ripen or cook, hence digest, > the PEPSIN our stomachs digest protein foods with and the PEPTIC ulcers that sometimes damage them. The "ripen" sense > Gk PUMPKIN, originally a kind of melon eaten only when wholly ripe; the name was transferred to a kind of squash from the New World. Also < the "ripe" sense, via Sanskrit, comes the PUKKA ("ripe," thorough, permanent) sahib of British India.

PEL-1, flour, dust or L POWDER, whence POLLEN, PULVERIZE ("make into powder"), and the idiomatic POULTICE.

PEL-2, L *pallidus*, PALE or PALLID, whence APPALL ("make [someone turn] pale"). Gc FALCON ("the pale [gray] bird") is ? from the same root.

PEL-3, L *plicare*, *plicat-*, Gc to FOLD, whence -FOLD (as in "twofold"); < the L come DUPLICATE ("twofold"), DUPLICITY (see *BLM*), and COMPLICATE ("fold in with"); the L equivalent of -fold > -PLE, as in MULTIPLE (manyfold"), and TRIPLE.

PEL-4, skin, hide, or L PELT. A membrane is a sort of skin (e.g., the "skin" that forms on heated milk), whence Gc FILM.

PEL-5, to sell, whence Gk MONOPOLY ([only] one seller).

PEL-6, L *pellere*, *pelt-*, to thrust, strike, drive, or beat, whence PUSH, and the PULSE that beats in our wrists. L compounds include COMPEL ("drive together"), DISPEL ("drive away"), EXPEL ("drive out"), IMPEL ("push strongly"), PROPEL ("push forward"), and APPEAL ("thrust [a request] toward"). POLISH is a remote relative, < a word = to full ("beat") cloth. From Gc come FELT (wool beaten into layers), which may be used as a FILTER, and the smith's ANVIL ("beaten on" thing).

PEL-7, dish, whence L PELVIS, the bony "dish" that holds our innards.

PELh-1, L *plere*, *plet-*, Gc to FILL, whence FULL and FULFILL. The L verb and various close relatives > PLENTY, ACCOMPLISH and COMPLETE (both = fulfill), COMPLY ("fill" [a request]), COMPLIMENT (fulfill the requirements of courtesy), SUPPLY (originally = to complete), REPLENISH (refill), and the IMPLEMENT with which we fulfill a task. L *plus*, *plur-*, much, more ("fuller"), > PLUS, PLURAL (more than one), and SURPLUS ("more than much"); Gk *polys*, much, many, > POLY- (-mer, -unsaturate).

See
bhergh-2

PELh-2, to spread, flat (see also **plat-**), whence the flat Gc FIELD and FLOOR, and (via Dutch) the African VELDT. L *planus* had many meanings: flat, whence PLANE in nearly all its senses, including the plane that "flattens" wood and the AIRPLANE or AEROPLANE that flies on "flat" wings, as well as the flat geographic PLAIN. Italian *piano*, quiet ("flattened down") > the *piano e forte*, an eighteenth-century keyboard instrument that (unlike the earlier harpsichord) could play both soft and loud notes; it's the direct ancestor of the PIANO.

The "spread out" sense > the spread-out L PALM of the hand—whence the palm tree with its spreading fronds;

another sense, clear ("spread out"), > L EXPLAIN ("make clear")—and "plain" ("clear," unadorned).

Gk *plassein*, to mold ("flatten" material into a mold), > PLASTER, PLASTIC, and the idiomatic PLASMA. Possibly < the same ultimate root is Gk PLANET, a heavenly body that "wanders" (? "spreads out") across the sky, as contrasted with the stars, which are "fixed." Finally, from Slavic *polye*, broad, flat (land), comes the (mostly) flat land of POLAND.

PELh-3, (fortified) citadel, whence Gk *polis*, city, whence METROPOLIS, originally the "mother city" of Gk colonies; See **mater-** also the POLICE who enforce city POLICY—and sometimes city POLITICS.

PENKWE, L *quinque*, Gk *penque*, Sanskrit *panca*, Gc FIVE, whence FIFTH, FIFTEEN, FIFTY, our five FINGERS, and the FIST they make. From L come QUINTET and QUINTESSENCE, the "fifth essence" (see *BLM*); from Gk, the five-sided PENTAGON—and the U.S. Pentagon. From Sanskrit, finally, comes PUNCH—originally, a drink with five ingredients.

PENT-, to tread, go, whence FIND ("go after"); the Gc PATH one treads on was ? borrowed from Iranian, via some steppe people. Various L words center on the sense "way" (where one goes), as with the PONTOONs sometimes used to bridge (make a way across) a river. From *pontifex*, priest ("he who prepares the way"), comes Pontifex Maximus, the "highest priest" (of Rome), now one of the titles of the PONTIFF—whence to PONTIFICATE, "speak as if one were the pope."

PER-1, the root of various prepositions and prefixes with the basic senses of through and Gc FORWARD—whence

FORTH and AFFORD, originally = set forward (if you can afford something, you can "set forward" the money). The root also had many extended senses and developed more; in Gc these included FROM, FAR (whence FARTHER and FURTHER), and BEFORE, whence FORE- (as in -arm), FOREMOST and FIRST ("most before"). FOR originally = before; later against, whence FOR- (as in FORBID, "speak against"), and negation generally, as in FORGET ("lose one's hold on"). Gc FURNISH and FURNITURE are idiomatic.

We find most of these same senses in L. PRO- ("pro-British") = Gc "for"; L PRE- ("prehistoric") = Gc "before"; L *primus* = Gc "first, foremost"—and has begotten many descendants. These include the PREMIER or PRIME minister, PRIMARY, PRIMITIVE, PRIMEVAL (from the first age), and the PRIMATES, our own order of mammals—which is, of course, the foremost. L PER- retains the basic sense of "through" ("percolate"), but also completely ("perfect") or intensively, whence PURCHASE ("chase intensively," as on a shopping expedition).

See **aiw-**

Other L derivatives are distinctive. The "forward" sense > *pronus*, leaning forward, whence PRONE; *prope*, near ("in front of"), > APPROACH ("come near to") and the idiomatic REPROACH; *privus*, alone ("standing out in front"), > PRIVATE, the PRIVY where one goes alone, PRIVILEGE, a "private law," and the idiomatic DEPRIVE. Akin to this sense is *proprius*, one's own, whence PROPERTY, APPROPRIATE ("take to oneself" and various idiomatic senses), and PROPER (originally = one's/it's own; the current sense is idiomatic).

See **leg-1**

More L relatives are *probus*, upright, good, whence the PROBE by which we PROVE (test) the goodness of someone or something—which we may then either APPROVE or try

to IMPROVE; we sometimes REPROVE people we don't ap-
prove of. L *princeps*, "he who takes first place," > PRINCE,   See **kap-**
PRINCIPAL, and PRINCIPLE.

Gk derivatives mostly parallel those in Gc and L, though
fewer of them have passed into English. Thus Gk *protos*,
first, > PROTEIN, once considered the "first" stuff of life
(it must now share that title with DNA). Gk *presbys*, old
man, approximated Gc "forefather"; via VL it > PRIEST
(originally, an "old man"—elder—of the church), and
PRESBYTERIAN, a church ruled by its elders rather than by
bishops or the congregation.

■ Given the many meanings of this root even in I-E times,
and their further elaboration in the daughter languages,
the foregoing account of the family is necessarily much
simplified; for more details, consult the *OEtD* under the
words and prefixes listed above.

PER-2, to lead, pass over, whence the Gc FORD you pass
over on foot and the FJORD or FIRTH where you have to take
a FERRY. A secondary sense, go (FARE) on a journey, > the
WAYFARER—and the fare he or she must sometimes pay.
WELFARE, of course, concerns how well your "journey" is
going (if you're on welfare, not very). Der FÜHRER, "The
Leader," was a retrogression to the original, "lead" sense
in meaning—and retrogressive in many other ways. Gc
FERN is ?? related.

L *portus* was a PORT that vessels passed into or through
and goods were TRANSPORTed through—if they were POR-
TABLE. An improbable but legitimate relative is OPPOR-
TUNE, whose L original = [wind] that drives one toward
port—for storm-beset sailors, an OPPORTUNITY indeed!
Closely related is L *porta*, the entrance or door you pass

through, whence PORTER (originally = doorkeeper or gate-keeper, as in a famous scene from *Macbeth*), and PORCH, a covered entranceway.

PER-3, young animal, whence ? Gc HEIFER (for nonfarmers, it = young cow).

PER-4, to try, hence the risk that often goes with trying something new. The "risk" sense > Gc FEAR and L PERIL; the "try" sense > L EXPERIMENT ("try out"), whence the EXPERIENCE we gain from trying things—and the EXPERT who's amassed a lot of experience. From Gk comes the PIRATE who "takes risks" at sea.

PER-5, to strike, whence L *premere, press-,* to PRESS, whence PRINT (press paper against inked type), COMPRESS (press together), DEPRESS (press down), EXPRESS ("press out"), IMPRESS ("press into"), OPPRESS ("press down upon"), REPRESS ("press back"), and SUPPRESS ("press under").

PER-6, to traffic in, sell, whence the L PRICE one sells at, PRECIOUS ("pricey"), PRAISE (originally = express the worth—"price"—of), APPRAISE (put a price on), APPRECI-ATE ("put the price—or worth—up"), and DEPRECIATE (put it down). Gk *porne* was the prostitute who sold herself or himself, whence PORNOGRAPHY, "whore writing." The "traffic" sense > INTERPRET, "traffic between" two people, as when they speak different tongues.

PERD-, Gc to FART; Gk *perdix,* PARTRIDGE, literally = farter, from the sound of its wings.

PERh-1, to produce, procure, whence L *parare,* try to get, hence equip or PREPARE (get in advance). We often PARE fruit to prepare it for eating; a PARADE was originally a display of military equipment; the Roman EMPEROR (whence IMPERIAL) was originally a commander who prepared his army for battle. The fencer's PARRY is a way of "preparing for" (warding off) the attacker's thrust; a PARA-CHUTE wards off (the effects of) a fall; to REPAIR something "re-prepares" it, and to SEPARATE it "prepares it apart"— whence SEVER and SEVERAL, originally = existing apart.

See **kad-1**

PERh-2, to grant allot—give people their proper L PART, PORTION, or PROPORTION, whence PARCEL—a portion (as in "parcel of land") but now more often a wrapped-up "portion." In L the "allot" sense > equal (allotment or shares), whence PAIR (two "equals"), PEER, COMPARE ("reckon the equality of"), and the PAR that golfers hope to equal. The horseplayer's PARLAY comes < an Italian word = pair of dice, while PARI-MUTUEL is from a French term = wager ("put up an equal sum"). UMPIRE, finally, was the "unpaired" person who had to decide between two "paired off" contestants—as we say, the third man in the ring.

■ The umpire was originally, "a noumpere" ("non-paired"), which was garbled into "an oumpere"; this process, called misdivision, has changed the sound of several English words; compare **netr-**.

PERK-1, various spotted animals such as the Gk PERCH.

PERK-2, to tear or dig, whence the Gc FURROW in dug-up (plowed) land.

PERKWU-, oak, whence Gc FIR.

■ This one is something of a puzzle: the trees are not in the least alike—though a related word in Lombardic (an extinct Gc dialect) does mean oak. But—a hippopotamus isn't much like a horse either (see **ekwo-**).

PES-, L PENIS, whence PENCIL, a "little penis"—originally, a (pointed) brush—whence the brush-shaped Penicillium mold that produces PENICILLIN. ? - tail

PET(h), to rush or fly, whence Gc FEATHER and its L synonym, *pinna*, whence the PEN once made from it. The "rush" sense > L *petere*, *petat-*, go toward, hence seek, whence the PETITION that seeks something, REPEAT ("seek again"), COMPETE ("seek [to win something] with" [someone]), PERPETUAL ("always seeking"), and the APPETITE that leads us to "seek toward" food and other things ("As if increase of appetite had grown by what it fed on"—Shakespeare).

See **ekwo-**

The "rush" sense also > Gk *potamos*, (rushing) river, whence HIPPOPOTAMUS ("river horse"). Gk *piptein*, to fall (? "rush downward"), > the SYMPTOM that "falls upon" a patient.

PETh-, L *pandere*, *pass-*, to spread, stretch out, whence EXPAND and PACE ("stretch the legs"); from a L relative comes PATENT, "spread out," hence obvious or public (the inventor's patent is idiomatic). Gc FATHOM was originally the length of a man's spread arms; Gk PETALS are also spread, as is the Gk *patina*, platter, whence (via VL) PAN.

See **elaiwa**

[**Greek PETRA,** rock, > PETRIFY (turn into rock), PETROLEUM ("rock oil"), and PARSLEY, from a Gk word = rock parsley (presumably a related herb).]

[**Gaulish PETTIA,** PIECE; the word may or may not be related to the ? Celtic source of PETTY and PETITE.]

PEU-, to cut, stamp, or strike, whence L *pavere*, to beat, whence PAVE; Rome's famous paved highways were built on a foundation of "beaten" (pounded) gravel or crushed stone. From the "cut" sense comes L *putare*, literally = cut or prune (trees or vines), whence AMPUTATE ("cut all around"), and ? *puteus*, a well or PIT "cut into" the ground. The verb also had several figurative senses, including think over (? "prune" one's ideas), reckon, whence COMPUTE, COUNT, and ACCOUNT—as well as the COUNTER on which money is counted. To DISPUTE is to "think away from," and your REPUTATION is what people think about you; DEPUTY is idiomatic.

PEUh-, to cleanse or make L PURE, whence the PURGE that supposedly purifies the body—or the body politic—and the PURITANS who seek to "purify" religion and morals; often they EXPURGATE ("purge out") the "impure" parts of books, etc.

PEUK-, PEUG-, L *pungere*, *punct-*, to prick, whence PUNCTURE, the POINTed object that makes one, PUNCTUATE (add "points"—periods, etc.—to), the PUNGENT odor that pricks our noses, and the POIGNANT experience that "pricks" our hearts. A possible relative is L *pugnare*, fight (? "prick") with the fist, whence PUGILIST and PUGNACIOUS; probably < the same source is a Gc verb = to penetrate ("prick") or strike ("bang"), whence FUCK.

PEZD-, to fart (? related to **perd-**), whence FIZZLE (originally = fart silently) and ? FEISTY (? "full of beans").

PhTER-, L and Gk *pater*, Gc FATHER. From L come PATERNAL; the PATRICIAN "born of a [noble] father," who was the PATRON of his dependants; EXPATRIATES outside their fatherland, and the PERPETRATOR who "fathers" a crime. From Gk we get the PATRIOT devoted to the fatherland and the PATRIARCH, "ruling father."

See **arkhein**

P(H)OL-, Gc to FALL; if you FELL a tree you make it fall, and if something BEFALLS you it "falls on" you.

PIK-, L *pix*, PITCH—the sticky pine tar once used to caulk boats.

[**Latin PILA,** PILLAR or pier, made of PILEd-up stones; *pilare*, heap up, > COMPILE, while a secondary sense, plunder (? "heap up booty"), probably > PILLAGE.]

See **peis-1**

■ Neither *AHD* nor *OEtD* accepts this derivation of "pillage"; the first traces it to OF *peille*, rag, whence ? *piller*, tear up, maltreat, plunder; the second suggests an evolution < L *pilum*, javelin (a rather unhandy weapon for a robber!). Since the experts disagree, I feel free to put forward my own theory—which to my eyes looks rather more plausible than theirs.

See **ghers-**

PILO- (possible root), L *pilus*, hair, whence PLUCK (as fleece—compare **pleus-**), PLUSH with its hairy PILE, the DEPILATORY that "dehairs" us, and the HORRIBLE sight that "makes our hair bristle." The CATERPILLAR was supposedly a "hairy cat," but also, I'd say, a "pillaging cat," since that's what the furry insect larvae do to vegetation.

PIPP-, imitative, to peep (as a bird), whence L *pipare*, to chirp, whence the chirping PIGEON and the "chirping" (musical) PIPE, whence pipes of all sorts, including (via German) the FIFE.

■ English "peep" is not from this root, but is rather an imitative "reinvention."

[**Sanskrit PIPPALI,** PEPPER, an early borrowing into L and thence, via Roman merchants, into Gc. The Sanskrit word = the berrylike black pepper of the Orient, but the English word was much later extended to the even more powerful chili pepper of the New World, and later to its "sweet" relative, whence (via Magyar) the PAPRIKA used extensively in Hungarian cookery.]

[**Latin PIUS,** dutiful, devoted, or PIOUS, whence *pietas*, dutifulness, (later) PITY (? because compassion was a Christian's duty).]

PLAB-, Gc to FLAP.

PLAK-1 (related to **pelh-2**), to be flat, whence the flat Gc FLAKE (whence FLAW, originally = flake), FLUKE (fish), FLAGSTONE ("flaked-off stone"), and the equally flat L PLANK. A probable relative is L *placare*, to be PLEASANT (? like the flat, PLACID sea), whence PLEASE, PLEAD ("May it please the Court"), and COMPLACENT, pleased with (oneself).

PLAK-2, to strike, whence L *plangere*, strike one's breast, hence lament or COMPLAIN. Gk PLAGUE strikes communities; APOPLEXY (often called a stroke) strikes individuals. Gc FLING is idiomatic.

PLAT- (another relative of **pelh-2**), to spread, whence Gc FLAT ("spread out"), whence the flat FLOUNDER. Merged with an OE word = floor, it > the "flat" dwelling, laid out on a single floor. To FLATTER originally = caress with the (flat of the) hand—as we'd now say, "stroke."

L *planta*, the (flat) sole of the foot, > PLANT, originally a shoot or seedling around which the earth was "planted"—pressed down with the foot; borrowed into Gaelic, it > CLAN, the "shoots" of a family. From the same L source are the flat PLAN of a city or building, and SUP-PLANT, < a L verb = overthrow (? "tread underfoot").

Gk *plateus*, *plateia*, flat, broad, > the flat PLATE, the geometer's even flatter PLANE, and the broad, spread-out PLAZA, whose French equivalent > PLACE. And a PLATI-TUDE is a "flat" (flavorless) statement.

One of the most intricate etymologies on record begins with a young Greek aristocrat, one Aristocles, whose strength and skill as an amateur wrestler won him the nickname Platon ("Broad Shoulders"). In later life, as the philosopher we know as Plato (427?–347 B.C.), he wrote (among other things) in praise of purely spiritual, nonsexual love—the kind we now call PLATONIC.

[**West Germanic PLEGAN,** to PLEDGE; also ? exercise oneself, whence PLAY (but we may be dealing with two different roots).]

PLEK-, L *plectere*, *plex-*, to PLAIT, weave, entwine, whence COMPLEX things so "entwined with" others that they're often PERPLEXing ("very entwined"). From Gc we get only FLAX ("weaving stuff"). The related L verb *plicare*, *pli-cat-*, to fold, > PLIANT ("foldable"), SUPPLE ("folding under"), SUPPLICATE (on folded knees), APPLY ("bend [oneself] to" a task), EMPLOY (apply someone or something to a purpose), DISPLAY ("unfold"), COMPLICATE ("fold in with"), and IMPLICATE ("fold into").

Possibly related is L *flectere*, *flex-*, to bend or FLEX something, whence DEFLECT ("bend away") and REFLECT ("bend back," as a mirror does light). But the resemblance to *plectere*, *plex-*, though striking, is probably coincidental.

PLE(I)K-, to tear, whence Gc FLAY (tear off the skin), FLECK ("torn off piece of skin"), and ? FLESH torn or cut off a carcass.

PLEU-, Gc to FLOW, whence FLOOD and various loosely related derivatives in Gc and other families. One group centers on Gc FLOATing (? down a flowing stream), whence FLEET and FLOTILLA; Gc FLUTTER is < a term = float to and fro, as ? is Gc FLUSTER; another "floater" is Gk *pneumon*, the balloonlike lung (probably influenced by **pneu-**), whence PNEUMONIA. Another group centers on the idea of Gc FLIGHT (? "float through the air")—FLY (including the insect), FOWL (originally, any bird), and FLEE.

Obviously related is L *pluere*, to rain; not so obvious is its derivative, PLOVER—probably "rain-bringer," since its southbound migrating flocks arrive in the Mediterranean lands when the rainy season begins in early autumn. (This is the most plausible of several explanations.)

PLEUS-, to pluck, which one can do with either Gc FLEECE or L PLUMES. plectrum

■ Fr *plume*, pen, as in *La plume de ma tante*, takes us back to the time—not so long ago—when pens were made of "plumes" (quills).

[Germanic PLOG(W)AZ, PLOW/PLOUGH, a late Gc word borrowed from a non–Indo-European (? North Italic) source.]

PLOU-, Gc FLEA.

[Latin PLUMBUM, lead, whence the chemical symbol for it (PB), the PLUMBER who worked it (until fairly recently, all water pipes were made of lead), and the lead PLUMMET or plumb bob that builders use to made sure a structure is PLUMB. If dropped, a plummet can PLUNGE down onto someone's head.]

■ The L word probably derives from the same source as Gk *molybdos*, heavy, whence the heavy metal molybdenum.

PNEU-, to breathe, whence Gc SNEEZE and Gk *pneuma*, breath, wind, whence PNEUMATIC.

PO(I)-, L *potere* and *bibere*, to drink. From the first verb comes the POTION that may be either POTABLE or POISONous; from the second come BEVERAGE and BEER. Gk SYMPOSIUM literally = drinking together, hence a drinking party, as in Plato's famous dialogue of that name (see *BLM*).

POL-, to touch or Gc FEEL.

See **re-**

[Latin POPULUS, PEOPLE (< Etruscan), whence POPULAR, POPULATE, PUBLIC, and REPUBLIC (< *res publica*, public affairs).]

See **spei-**
See **peisk-**

PORKO-, young pig, whence PORK, PORCUPINE ("spiny pig"), and PORPOISE ("pig fish").

■ Right through the Middle Ages pork and other meats were usually obtained from young animals, which were killed in the fall because of the problems in feeding them during the winter. Also, they were tenderer than their elders!

POTI-, L *potis*, POWERful, able ("having the power" to do something), whence POTENT, POSSESS ("have power over"), and POSSIBLE.

[**Greek PRAK-,** to make or do, whence (via L) PRACTICAL (doable), PRACTICE (doing rather than theorizing), and PRAGMATIC—judging things on practical rather than theoretical grounds.]

PREK-, L *precari*, to ask, entreat, or PRAY; a PRECARIOUS situation is one where prayers may be needed (see *BLM*).

PREU-, to hop, whence Gc FROG and FROLIC ("hop with joy").

PREUS-, to burn or Gc FREEZE, whence FROST. L *prurire*, to burn, hence itch, hence long ("have an itch") for, > the PRURIENT ("itching") interest that some naughty books allegedly appeal to.

■ The dual meaning of the root—burn/freeze—doubtless reflects the well-known fact that very cold things can momentarily feel very hot.

PRI-, to love, whence Gc FRIEND and Frigg, the beloved wife of the god Odin, whose name survives in FRIDAY. More remote is FREE (beloved = not enslaved), whence—after an intricate evolution described in *BLM*—FILIBUSTER.

PU-, to rot or decay, whence Gc FOUL, FILTH, and DEFILE (make foul), and L PUTRID and PUS. Rotten wood is often spongy, which is what Gc FUZZY originally meant.

[**Latin PUBES,** the PUBIC hair, which appears at PUBERTY.]

PUK-2, bushy-haired, whence the bushy-tailed Gc FOX and his mate, the VIXEN (originally "fixen").

PUR-, Gk *pur*, *pyr*, Gc FIRE; the Gk word > PYRO- (as in -maniac) and the PYRE on which bodies were burned.

[**Greek PUXOS,** the BOX tree, whence the box made of its wood.]

P(Y)EL-, tree name, ? the source of L POPLAR.

[**Latin QUAERERE**, **QUAEST-,** to seek, whence the QUERY and QUESTION with which an INQUIREr seeks an answer. We seek things we REQUIRE, and if we can't AC-QUIRE them peacefully we may try to CONQUER them. An INQUEST is an enquiry into an unexpected death, and something EXQUISITE is—sought out.]

RE-1, **RED-,** backward, whence L RE-, RETRO-, and REAR; ARREARS are payments you've fallen behind in.

RE-2, to bestow, endow, whence goods, property, whence L *res*, thing—something REAL rather than imaginary. A REPUBLIC is concerned with "public things."

See
populus

REBH-1, impetuous, violent, whence L RAGE and RABID.

REBH-2, to roof over, whence the Gc RIBS that "roof over" the chest; the ridge of a peaked roof > REEF, an underwater "ridge."

RED-, to scrape, scratch, or gnaw, whence L RODENT, ? Gc RAT, and ? the RASH you scratch at, whence RASCAL—a scabby fellow. More certain relatives are L ERODE and COR-RODE ("gnawed away"); something completly "eroded" is RAZEd or ? ERASEd.

REG-1, to move in a straight line and many related senses, including L DIRECT (in a straight line), whence lead or L RULE. If something is "straight" it's Gc RIGHT or L CORRECT ("straight with"). Other L relatives of the "straight" group are ERECT (straight up), RECTUM (the straight part of the lower bowel), and RAIL, originally a straight piece of wood.

From Gc we get RAKE, with its straight crossbar (for the human rake, see *BLM*), and the RACK made of wooden "rails." Possible Gc relatives in this group are RECKON (? set in "straight" order) and RECKLESS, from an obsolete word = take care (a reckless person doesn't).

The "rule" sense > L REIGN, REGAL, ROYAL, REGIME, REGION (originally = kingdom), REGIMENT (originally = rule; now a body of troops "ruled" by its colonel), and the idiomatic SURGE. Sanskrit contributed RAJAH (king) and MAHARAJAH (great king). Another sense of "rule," princi- See **meg-** ple or regulation, > REGULATE and REGULAR. A distant relative derives from Celtic *rix*, king, which the Germans (who had their own word for king) borrowed to = power-ful, and eventually RICH—which powerful people almost always are (and, of course, vice versa).

REG-2, moist, whence Gc RAIN and ? L IRRIGATE, "put moisture into."

REI-1, to scratch, tear, cut, whence Gc RIFT and L *ripa*, bank cut out by a RIVER, whence ARRIVE—originally = reach the bank or shore. Also Gc are REAP (cut down RIPE grain) and ? things placed in a ROW (? a line scratched in the earth), whence ? ROPE.

REI-3, to flow or Gc RUN (rivers do both).

REIDH-, Gc to RIDE, whence RAID (originally, on horseback); also ? ROAD, whence READY ("prepared to take the road"), and ARRAY, originally = arrange (? for a journey).

REIG-1, to bind, whence Gc RIG a vessel by "binding" its masts with ropes.

REIG-2, to stretch out or Gc REACH, whence ? L RIGID (like a stretched-out rope) and RIGOR.

RENDH-, to tear up or Gc REND, whence the RIND you "tear" off something.

REP-, to snatch, whence L *rapere*, *rapt-*, to seize RAPIDly or violently, whence RAPE and RAVISH. A RAPACIOUS person seizes whatever valuables are around, RAPTURE "seizes" our emotions, and a SURREPTITIOUS action "seizes" something secretly.

REP-1, to creep, whence L REPTILE ("creeping thing").

REP-2, stake or beam, whence Gc RAFTER and the RAFT made of stakes lashed together.

RET-, to run or L ROLL (as a wheel runs), whence ROTARY, ROTATE, ROUND, and ROULETTE—the "little wheel" that's often the cause of big trouble. L CONTROL originally = to check (figures) against a "counter [duplicate] roll" (of parchment). And to L PRUNE a plant involves "cutting around" it.

REU-1, to roar, whence L RAUCOUS, RIOT, and the RUMOR that is "noised abroad," though more often by whispering than roaring.

REU-2, REUh-, to tear out, dig up, smash, whence L RUIN; more dubious relatives are Gc RAG (? "torn-up cloth") and RUG.

REUDH-1, Gc RUDDY or RED, whence reddish RUST and the red-berried ROWAN (mountain ash) tree. From L we get ROUGE, RUBY, RUSSET, and—via *robus*, the red oak—ROBUST ("like an oak").

REUDH-2, to clear land—Gc RID it of unwanted vegetation.

REUh-, to open, hence space, whence Gc ROOM = space ("room enough"); the sense of enclosed space came later. L *rus*, *rur-*, country ("open land"), > RUSTIC and RURAL.

REUG-, to vomit, belch, whence belch smoke, whence Gc REEK (the Scots sometimes call their smoky capital, Edinburgh, "Auld Reekie").

REUP-, REUB-, to snatch, whence Gc RIP; someone whose mate has been "snatched away" is BEREAVED. Another Gc group involves the connection between snatching and stealing ("ripping off"), whence ROB, ROVER (originally = robber), and, improbably, ROBE, originally = clothing snatched as booty. We find the same larcenous sense in LOOT (via Sanskrit).

Snatching often breaks things, whence L *rupere*, *rupt-*, to break, whence RUPTURE, ABRUPT ("broken away," as when someone leaves abruptly), BANKRUPT (a "broke" bank—see *BLM*), DISRUPT (break apart), ERUPT ("break out"), INTERRUPT (break into [a conversation, etc.]), and ROUT—what happens when troops break under attack. CORRUPT is idiomatic.

[**Germanic RISAN,** to RISE, whence ARISE, RAISE, and REAR—what a horse does when it rises on its hind legs.]

RTKO-, bear (animal), whence Gk ARCTIC. The "bear" was the Dipper or Plough, prominent in the northern sky, whence the arctic ("bear") lands of the north (see *BLM*).

RUK-2, Gc ROUGH; L *ruga*, wrinkle, > CORRUGATEd ("wrinkled together") paper or metal.

SA-, L to SATISFY, whence SATURATE ("satisfy" [fill] something with liquid), the ASSETS that satisfy us—if they're big enough—and the idiomatic SATIRE. If you're satisfied you're Gc SATEd, and perhaps SAD (satiation occasionally brings sadness).

SAB-, fluid, juice, whence Gc SAP.

SAG-, Gc to SEEK out, whence RANSACK; if you find what you seek you may SEIZE it—or FORSAKE ("unseize") it; a remote, idiomatic relative is Gc SAKE.

SAI-, suffering, whence Gc SORE and SORRY ("suffering mentally").

SAK-, L *sancire*, *sanct-*, to make SACRED, CONSECRATE, or SANCTIFY, whence SAINT.

SAL-1, L *sal*, Gc SALT, whence SOUSE—meat pickled in brine (the human souse is also "pickled"). From L we get SAUCE, SALSA, SALAD, SAUSAGE, and SALAMI, all originally = salted, as well as SALINE and SALARY, originally a Roman soldier's "salt money" (see *BLM*). And Gc SILT is < an Old Norse word = salt marsh, which may well become silted up with time.

SAL-2, dirty gray, whence Gc SALLOW.

SANO-, L *sanus*, healthy, whence SANE and SANITARY.

SAUS-, dry, whence Gc SEAR. Gk *austeros*, harsh (as long dry spells are), > AUSTERE.

SAWEL-, S(U)WEL-, SU(h)EL-, SU(h)EN-, SUN-, L *sol*, Gk *helios*, Gc SUN, whence SUNDAY (translating L *dies solis*); Gc SOUTH is where most sunlight comes from in the Northern Hemisphere. From L come SOLAR, the

See **sta-**

SOLSTICE when the sun "stands" at its highest or lowest elevation, and the PARASOL that keeps off the sun. From Gk comes HELIUM, the "sun element" (it was first detected in the sun's spectrum and only later found on earth).

SE-1, L *serere*, *sert-*, Gc SOW, whence the SEED that is sown. From L we get SEASON ("sowing time"), INSERT ("sow into"), the SEMEN a man "sows" in a woman, and DISSEMI-NATE ("scatter [like] seeds"—see *BLM*).

SE-2, long, late, whence Gc SINCE ("later," after) and ? SIDE ("lengthwise extension").

SE-3, to bind, tie, whence Gc SINEW, widely used for tying things before people learned to make cordage from vegetable fibers—compare **gherh-**.

SED-1, L *sedere*, *sess-*, Gc SIT, whence SEAT, SET ("sit" something), the SADDLE riders sit on, and the SOOT that SETTLES in or on something. From the L verb come SEDEN-TARY ("sitting" much); the SEDIMENT that "sits" at the bottom of a lake; a SESSION (sitting) of a legislature, and the SIEGE in which an army "sits" around a town to make it surrender. A related L verb, *sedare*, *sedat-*, settle down, > SEDATE and the SEDATIVE that "settles" our nerves.

L compounds from the "sit" sense include PRESIDE ("sit in front," as at a meeting); SUPERSEDE ("seat [oneself] above"), the OBSESSIONS that "sit on" us, POSSESS ("sit See **poti-** potently on"), the DISSIDENT who "sits away" from official opinion, SUBSIDIARY ("sitting under," whence the idiomatic SUBSIDY), and HOSTAGES forced to "sit" until their captors' demands are met. A few seem to stem from the "settle" sense: RESIDE ("settle back," as in a residence),

and SUBSIDE ("settle down"). Gk *kathedra*, a seat, >
CHAIR and CATHEDRAL, referring to a church that is a
bishop's seat or see.

SED-2, to go, whence Gk *hodos*, way, journey. An EXODUS
is a journey out; the theatrical EPISODE came ("made its
way") between two choruses; a PERIOD was a course or
orbit ("way around"), but METHOD is idiomatic (originally = systematic treatment of a disease).

SEGH-, to hold, whence various loosely related Gk expres-
sions. An EPOCH was a pause ("holding back"), hence a
position in time; a SCHEME was the form something holds,
hence a plan. SCHOOL is < another kind of "holding
back": rest or leisure, which might be employed in SCHOL-
ARly pursuits; HECTIC is idiomatic.

■ The connection between school and leisure would startle modern schoolchildren and scholars; it reflects the fact
that in ancient Greece scholarly pursuits, and most
schooling, were leisure-class activities.

SEIB-, to pour out, Gc SIFT (whence SIEVE), or drip (whence
Gc SEEP). The "drip" sense > Gc SOAP—originally, a reddish dye, mixed with resinous drippings from conifers,
that German warriors applied to their hair and/or bodies
as a sort of war paint. The stuff was nothing like soap—
but would have been impossible to remove without it.

SEK-, L *secare*, *secut-*, to cut, whence the SICKLE used to cut
grain, the SECTIONS, SECTORS, and SEGMENTS things are cut
into, and ? the NOTCH cut into something. Compounds
include DISSECT (cut apart), INTERSECT (cut across) and
the idiomatic INSECT ("not cut"). Gc relatives include

both cutting tools (SCYTHE, SAW) and the SKIN cut off a carcass.

SEKW-1, L *sequor*, *secut-*, to follow, whence the SEQUENCE things follow, the SEQUEL that follows a successful book or film, and the SECTS some people follow blindly. SUE originally = follow (whence PURSUE, "follow intensively"), then to pursue someone legally; a SUITOR "pursues" a mate.

Compounds include the CONSEQUENCE that "follows with" something CONSECUTIVELY; EXECUTE ("follow out" a plan or order—though modern EXECUTIVES more often give the orders); PERSECUTE ("pursue" malignantly), PROSECUTE (originally = follow up; now "pursue" a prisoner), and SUBSEQUENT (following after). Closely related are L *secundus*, following, coming next, whence SECOND, and *socius*, ally ("follower"—what most Roman allies were forced to be), whence SOCIETY, people "allied" (ASSOCIATEd) with one another, whence SOCIAL and SOCIABLE; DISSOCIATE = "dis-ally."

More questionably related is L *signum*, identifying mark or SIGN (? < "banner or SIGNAL one follows"), whence the SIGNATURE or SEAL with which documents were signed (during the early Middle Ages, even the upper classes could seldom sign their names); also ASSIGN ("sign over to"), RESIGN ("sign back," hence give up), and DESIGNATE ("mark out"), whence DESIGN.

SEKW-2, Gc to SEE, whence SIGHT.

SEKW-3, Gc to SAY, whence ? SCOLD.

SEL-1, human settlement, ? house, whence (in Gc) room, whence SALON and SALOON.

SEL-2, SELh-, in a good mood, whence L *solari*, to SOLACE or CONSOLE ("put in a good mood"). Gk *hilaros*, gay, > HILARITY and EXHILARATE ("make gay"). Gc SILLY is idiomatic; for an account of its intricate evolution, see *OEtD*.

SEL-3, to take, grasp, whence Gc SELL (originally = give— cause to take) and SALE.

SEL-4, L *salire, saltare*, to leap or jump, whence ASSAIL ("leap at"), EXULT (when your heart "leaps out"), INSULT ("jump onto"), the RESULT that "leaps back" from something, and idiomatic DESULTORY (see *BLM*). Something SALIENT projects ("jumps out"), something SAUTÉED "jumps" in the pan, a SALACIOUS person jumps into bed, and when you SOMERSAULT you jump head over heels. Probably < the same root (via Gaulish) is L SALMON, "the leaper," which it certainly is (compare **laks-**).

SELP-, fat, butter, whence Gc SALVE.

SEM-1, one, whence L SINGLE, whence SIMPLE ("singlefold"). Gc SOME originally = [a certain] one ("some guy came along"); a related sense, "as one," > Gc SAME. L *simul*, at the same (one) time, > SIMULTANEOUS, ASSEMBLE, and ENSEMBLE; L *similis*, of one kind, > SIMILAR and RESEMBLE.

See **plek-**

In Gk the "one" sense > *heteros*, one of two—hence other, whence HETERO-; the "as one" sense > *homos*, same, whence HOMO- (ironically, "homosexual" and

See **do-**

"heterosexual" are almost brothers). More distantly related is Gc SEEM, originally to be fitting or seemly ("making into one"). And from Russian come SOVIET (council, "coming together") and SAMIZDAT, publishing by oneself.

SEM-2, SEMh-, Gc SUMMER.

SEMI-, half, whence L SEMI- (-conscious) and Gk HEMI- (-sphere).

SEN-1, L *senex*, *senil-*, old, whence SENILE, SENIOR (older), SENATE (originally, the Roman council of elders), and terms expressing the respect due one's elders or superiors: SIR and SIRE. Such people were often SURLY in its original sense, lordly; elderly people are still sometimes surly—if treated with insufficient respect.

See **cura**

SEN-2, SENI-, separated, apart, whence Gc ASUNDER and SUNDRY (originally = apart), and L *sine*, without (separated from), whence SINECURE, (a job) "without care" (see *BLM*).

SENDHRO-, "crystalline" (rocklike?) deposit, whence Gc CINDER—originally = slag. (The cinders that Cinderella dealt with were ashes, from an unrelated L word.)

SENGW-, Gc to SINK, whence SAG.

SENGWH-, Gc to SING, whence SONG.

SENK-, to burn, whence Gc SINGE.

SENT-, to head for, go, whence Gc SEND (cause [someone or something] to go). Possibly related is L *sentire*, to feel (? "go mentally"), whence SENTIMENT, RESENT, SENTENCE (originally = meaning, SENSE), DISSENT ("feel away from"), the PRESENTIMENT you feel beforehand, and ? SCENT (originally = track [an animal] by smell).

SEP-, L *sapere*, to taste, whence SAVOR; the L word also = to have taste, hence to be wise, SAGE, or SAVVY.

SEPTM, L *septem*, Gc SEVEN; L SEPTEMBER was the seventh month of the Roman calendar.

SER-1, to protect, whence L *servare*, to keep or PRESERVE, whence CONSERVE ("keep intensively"), RESERVE ("keep back"), whence the RESERVOIR that keeps back water, and OBSERVE, originally = attend to ("keep one's eye on"). A possible Gk relative is the HERO who—in theory—protected the people.

SER-2, to flow, whence SERUM—in L, the whey that flows or is pressed out of curdled milk in cheese making.

SER-3, to line up, whence L *serere*, *sert-*, to arrange or join, as in a SERIES, whence DESERT ("unjoin," abandon), whence the "abandoned" (uninhabited) desert (see below); ASSERT and EXERT are idiomatic. A possible relative is SERMON, ? a "joined" set of statements, hence a discourse.

Also ? related is L *sors*, *sort-*, lot, fortune (? < lots lined up before drawing)—i.e., the SORT of thing you could expect. ASSORT originally = arrange by sorts, your CONSORT shares your lot, and a SORCERER could supposedly foretell your lot. sortilège

■ The modern sense of "desert" (arid region) is relatively new; as late as the nineteenth century the American plains, dry but almost never arid, were known as "the

great American desert," meaning that they were uninhabited—by Europeans.

SERP-1, Gk *harpe*, sickle, whence (after a lengthy evolution) the HARPOON that "harvests" fish or whales as the
sickle harvests grain.

SERP-2, to crawl or creep, whence L SERPENT and Gk
HERPES, the "creeping disease" (even more appropriate
now than when it was coined).

[**Latin SERVUS,** slave, whence SERVE, SERVICE, SERVILE
("slavelike"), SERVITUDE, and DESERVE (originally =
become entitled to, as through faithful service).]

■ The L word may come < the name of some aboriginal
Italian tribe enslaved by the Romans, as Gc SLAVE comes
from the Slavs, long a target of German aggression.

SEUh-1, to give birth, whence Gc SON.

SEUh-2, to take liquid, whence Gc SIP, SOUP, SOP, SUP, and
SUPPER, also ? SUCK and SOAK. From L come SUCTION and
SUCCULENT (full of juice).

SEUT-, to boil or Gc SEETHE, whence SODDEN (originally =
boiled, whence soaked—"boiled too long"), and SUDS—
originally flood or marsh water, which is often "sudsy"
(frothy).

SI-LO, L SILENT.

(S)KAI-, bright, shining, whence (in Gc) the quality that
"shines" from something, whence -HOOD (quality, state,

as in "womanhood"). Sanskrit *citra-*, = (brightly) varie-gated, > the spotted CHEETAH; it also = many-colored, whence CHINTZ.

SKAMB-, KAMB-, to turn, bend, whence L (< Gaulish) *cambiare*, to EXCHANGE, whence CHANGE.

■ A related Gaulish root = crooked, suggesting that the Gauls may have taken a dim view of Roman "exchange" (trade) practices; compare -MONGER under **meng-**.

SKAND-, SKEND-, L *scandere*, to leap, climb, whence ASCEND (climb up), DESCEND (climb down), TRANSCEND ("leap across"), and CONDESCEND ("descend with"), originally = bend or settle down; the modern sense is idiomatic. From the same L verb is SCAN, originally to "measure" verses by "leaping" (moving) the foot up and down; its commonest modern sense (glance over quickly) is idiomatic. L *scala* was the ladder you climb or SCALE, later the musician's "ladder" (scale) of notes. A more remote relative is Gk *skandalon*, trap (? into which an animal or enemy "leaped"), whence the idi-omatic SCANDAL.

SKED-, to split or Gc SCATTER, whence SHATTER and the SHINGLES split from a block of wood.

SKEhI-, to gleam or Gc SHINE, whence SHIMMER. Possible relatives are L *scintilla*, spark ("little gleam"), whence the TINSEL that SCINTILLATES, and STENCIL—originally = to ornament with bright colors; the modern sense is quite recent. Also ? related is Gk *skia*, shadow, whence the "shadow-tailed" SQUIRREL.

See **ors-**

SKEI-, to cut or split, Gk *skhizein*, whence SCHIZO- and SCHISM—a "split" in a church. L relatives all come < *scire*, to know—"tell [split] one thing from another"—whence SCIENCE, CONSCIOUS ("knowing"—aware), and the "inner knowledge" of CONSCIENCE. NICE is < L *nescius*, not knowing, ignorant; its present sense is idiomatic (see *OEtD*).

Gc members of the tribe refer to things cut or split, hence detached ("cut away"), as are SHIT and the tears we SHED. The SHIN was originally a cut-away piece of a carcass, SKIS were made of split boards, and a SHEATH was ? made from a split stick.

■ This root is related to **sek-,** and ?? to **skel-1, skep-, sker-, skeu-,** and **skribh,** which also referred to cutting and/or splitting—and often begot similar derivatives (see next entry). Most experts don't accept these relationships; if they're right, what may have happened is that the SK sound became associated with cutting and "pushed" the senses of several unrelated roots in similar directions, something that happens now and then in language. If the similarities are pure coincidence—well, it's one hell of a coincidence.

SKEL-1, KEL-, L *scalpere/sculpere, sculpt-,* to cut, whence the surgeon's SCALPEL, the pirate's CUTLASS, and the SCULPTURE that's "cut" out of wood or stone. This root, like the last, also = split, and, again, many Gc family members concern cut or split things—the easily split SHALE, the SHELF and SHIELD made of a cut or split board (compare SKI above), and ? the "cut-away" HALF of something.

Other Gc terms center on the husk one splits or cuts away, whence the SCALES of a fish, the SHELL of a mollusk and the SCALP that is the "husk" of the skull. A shell could be used as a bowl for drinking, whence ? the Norse toast SKOAL!, two of them could be used as the pans (scales) of a balance. Yet another Gc derivative is the SKILL of "splitting" things apart—compare SCIENCE under **skei-** above.

SKEL-2, to be under an obligation, whence Gc SHALL; the original sense survives in SHOULD.

SKELh-, to parch, wither, whence Gk *skeletos*, withered corpse, mummy, whence SKELETON.

SKENG-, bent, crooked, whence Gc SHANK (the "bent" leg).

SKEP-, KEP-, the source of many terms concerned with cutting, scraping (whence Gc SHAVE), or hacking (whence Gc HATCHET and HASH—"hacked up" meat). Also Gc is to SHAPE ("cut") something, whence -SHIP (as in "friendship"), the condition or "shape" of something, and LAND-SCAPE, the look or shape of the land. A cut or scratch will form a Gc SCAB, whence Gc SHABBY ("scabby") and L SCABIES ("the scabby disease"). The L CAPON is a "cut" (castrated) cock; the Gk COMMA "cuts" a sentence. SHAFT (of a machine, etc.) is ? related, but more likely comes from* *skabh-*, to prop or support (not included).

SKER-1, KER-, to cut or Gc SHEAR, whence one's SHARE ("cut-off" portion) of something and the PLOWSHARE that cuts into the earth. Also Gc is the SCORE (record) that was cut (scored) on a tally-stick, which > the score of a game (see *BLM*). Cutting something makes it Gc SHORT, whence SHIRT and SKIRT—both of them short compared with a robe; a L CURT reply is a "short" one.

See **legwh-**

L *caro*, *carn-*, (cut off) flesh, > CARNIVOROUS, CARRION, and CARNIVAL. Figurative terms include CARNAL (carnal knowledge = knowledge of the flesh), the CARNATION with its pink (flesh-colored) blossoms, and the INCARNA-TION in which God was allegedly made flesh.

Other family members deal with things that are or can be cut off, such as Gc SCRAPS and Gk *cortex*, bark (of a tree), whence CORTEX, the "bark" (outer layer) of the brain. A Gc group concerns SHARP things, such as swords, used for cutting: a SCABBARD "protects" a sword, while a term = fight with a sword > SKIRMISH. Still other Gc relatives center on SCRAPE (compare **skep-** above), whence SCRUB, and the roughness produced by scraping, whence SHRUBS ("rough vegetation"). SCREW, finally, comes from a L word meaning the female pig that "cuts" (digs or roots in) the earth—in part because a screw resembles a pig's curly tail, but the pedigree is intricate and somewhat scandalous (see *BLM*).

See **bhergh-1**

SKER-2, KER-, to turn, bend, the supposed root of a number of "distantly related" words—but distantly is the operative word. One fairly well-defined group centers on L CURVED ("bent") things—Gc RING, L (< Gk) CROWN and CIRCLE, whence CIRCUM-, and MedL *circare*, go around, whence SEARCH. Gc RIDGE originally = the (bent) spinal column.

Another group concerns things that are curly—L *crispus*, whence the original sense of CRISP, also CREPE; L CREST was originally a tuft (of ? curly hair). Gc SHRINK originally = wrinkle ("curl up")—which often happens to shrunken things. OF *reng*, *reng* (< a Gc word obscurely related to "ring"), a line, row, or RANK, > RANGE, originally = rank; modern senses, including the range some people are home on, are idiomatic, as is RANCH. From the same source are ARRANGE ("put in line") and DERANGE ("put out of line").

SKERB(H)-, to turn, bend (related to last entry), whence Gc RUMPLE (compare SHRINK above), SCORCH ("shrivel"), and ? the SHRIMP with its curved ("bent") body.

(S)KEU-, to cover or Gc HIDE, whence HOARD and various sorts of coverings: the hide that covers an animal, the SCUM that may cover water, the HOSE that covers the legs (or part of them), the SKY (originally = the clouds that sometimes cover it), and HUT—originally, a barracks that "covered" troops. L *obscurus*, dark ("covered"), > OB-SCURE. Less certainly related is L *culus*, backside (? "what you keep covered"), whence the CULOTTES that cover it and RECOIL (draw back), but the L word may come < *skel-3* (not included), crooked, bent, whence bent or curved parts of the body.

SKEUBH-, Gc to SHOVE, whence the SHOVEL used to "shove," SCUFF (shove or SHUFFLE the feet along), the SCUF-FLE in which people shove one another, and ? SCOFF, to "shove" someone with words.

SKEUD-, to chase, throw, or Gc SHOOT, whence SHOT and all the other words in this group. A SHUTTLE was originally a "shot" dart or missile, but now something that "shoots" back and forth. A distant relative is SHUT (< fasten [a door] by "shooting" a bolt); still more distant is SHEET (originally = piece of cloth); the experts agree it's related, but don't explain how.

SKEUP-, cluster or tuft, whence Gc SHEAF.

[**Germanic SKIPAM,** SHIP, whence SKIPPER, SKIFF, and (via Old Norse and OF) EQUIP—originally = fit out a ship, a common occupation among Norse pirates and merchants.]

SKOT-, dark, Gc SHADE, whence SHADOW.

SKREU-, to cut, cutting tool, whence the Gc SHREW (from its sharp snout and/or teeth), whence SHREWD (from its supposed "sharp" temper—see *BLM*). Gc SHRED is a cut-off piece and Gc SCROLL was originally a cut-off strip, especially of parchment. Perhaps related is L *scruta*, rubbish (? rags, "shreds"), whence the SCRUTINY (close examination) that rubbish pickers devoted to it.

SKRIBH-, to cut (also separate, sift), whence L *scribere*, *script-*, to scratch, hence write. The latter sense begot a large family, notably the SCRIBE who writes, the SCRIPT he or she writes or SCRIBBLES in, and SCRIPTURE ("the Writings"). Compounds include ASCRIBE (originally = write in a list), DESCRIBE ("write down"), PRESCRIBE (order in writing, as your doctor does with a prescription), SUBSCRIBE ("write [one's name] under," as on a subscription blank), and TRANSCRIBE ("write across" onto another piece of

See **man-2**   paper or parchment). Others include the MANUSCRIPT written by hand, the POSTSCRIPT written afterward, and the CONSCRIPT whose name was INSCRIBEd on a written list—originally, a list of Roman senators, now, of soldiers.

SKUT-, to shake or Gc SHUDDER.

(S)KW-AL-O-, big fish, whence Gc WHALE—not a fish, of course, but the primitive Germans weren't zoologists.

(S)LAGW-, to seize, whence Gk EPILEPSY, attacks of which are still called seizures.

SLAK-, to strike, whence Gc SLAY, SLAUGHTER, ONSLAUGHT, SLEDGE(hammer), and SLY—originally = clever, "able to strike."

SLEB-, to be weak or Gc SLEEP.

SLEG-, to be L LANGUID or Gc SLACK; L *laxus*, loose > LAX and RELAX ("slack off"). In OF the "slack" sense > leave or RELEASE, whence the LEASE by which one (temporarily) releases property to another, and the DELAY that leaves things until later. RELAY is idiomatic; it originally = fresh hounds released to take up the chase.

SLEIDH-, Gc to SLIDE, whence the sliding SLED, SLEIGH, and SLEDGE.

SLENGWH-, to slide, whence Gc SLINK ("slide along"); also throw (make [something] "slide") or Gc SLING.

[Germanic SLEU- (a "hypothetical" root), is the supposed source of SLEET and SLUSH, but also ? of SLUMBER and the SLUGGISH or LOGY garden SLUG (whose shape may have inspired the lead slug that "slugs" the recipient).]

■ The experts don't explain how all these words might be related. Since the root's supposed descendants include two quite different ideas (sleet/slush and slumber/sluggish/logy), we may well be dealing with two separate roots.

SLEUBH-, to slide or slip, whence the Gc SLEEVE you slip your arm into, slippery SLOP (whence SLOPPY—see *BLM*), and the SLOOP that "slides" through the water. When you L LUBRICATE something you make it slide easily.

SLI-, bluish, whence L LIVID and Serbo-Croatian SLIVOVITZ, brewed from (blue) plums.

SLOUG-, help, service, whence (after much change in meaning) Gaelic *sluagh*, army, whence a SLEW ("army") of people and SLOGAN, originally = war cry.

SME-, to smear—which, however, comes from a different source (see **[s]mer-3**). The only certain English descendant is SMITE, originally = to smear, pollute. Possible but unlikely relatives are Gc MEASLES and L MICRO-.

SMEG-, to taste, whence Gc SMACK (originally, the lips).

SMEI-, to laugh or Gc SMILE, whence SMIRK. A very dubious relative is L *mirari*, to wonder or MARVEL at, whence MIRACLE, ADMIRE—and the MIRROR we admire ourselves in.

(S)MEIT(h)-, to throw, whence ? L *mittere*, *miss*-, to throw, send off, let go. The "throw" sense > MISSILE and EMIT ("throw out"); the "send" sense > MESSAGE, MISSIVE, and the MISSION on which someone is sent, as well as a number of compounds. These include REMIT (send back), DISMISS (send away), TRANSMIT ("send across"), PROMISE ("send forth" [an assurance]), COMPROMISE ("promise together," hence reach agreement), and ADMIT ("send in," as to a meeting; the sense of "concede the truth of" is idiomatic).

In some L terms the "send" sense > put, place, whence SUBMIT ("put [oneself] under"). MESS was originally a portion of food put (served) out, as in Esau's "mess of pottage," whence the military mess; the modern "messy" sense may reflect the troops' opinion of their rations. Idiomatic derivatives include PERMIT and COMMIT, entrust ("put") with ("We now commit their bodies to the deep")—the criminal sense is modern; an officer is entrusted with his COMMISSION. Also idiomatic is the religious MASS; it may derive from a phrase such as L *Ite*, *missa est*, "Go thou, it is the dismissal" (i.e., the service is ended).

(S)MER-1, L to REMEMBER, whence MEMORY, REMINISCE ("call back to mind"), COMMEMORATE ("remember" someone or something), and MEMORANDUM ("thing to be remembered"). From Gc we have MOURN, "remember sorrowfully."

(S)MER-2, to get a share of something, whence L *merere*, *merit-*, get a share, hence deserve, whence MERIT. Gk *meros*, share, part, > the chemist's POLYMER—a molecule consisting of many (identical) parts.

(S)MER-3, Gc to SMEAR.

SMERD-, pain, whence Gc SMART (a "smart" person can make you smart).

SMEUG-, Gc to SMOKE.

SMI-, to cut, work with a sharp tool, whence SMITH—apparently a generalized term for craftsman that later acquired its specialized sense. The notion that the word derives from the "smiting" of metal, though plausible, is false.

(S)NAU-, to (let) flow, whence suckle, whence the L NURSE who NOURISHes a baby with NUTRITIOUS NUTRIENTS.

(S)NE-, to spin or sew, whence Gc NEEDLE.

(S)NEhU-, tendon, sinew (related to the previous root; sinews were what people originally sewed with). L NERVE originally = sinew; its modern sense dates from the eighteenth century. The Gk equivalent (also originally = sinew) > NEUROSIS, "nerve disease."

SNEG-, to creep, a creeping thing, such as a Gc SNAKE or SNAIL.

SNEIGWH-, Gc SNOW.

SNER-, root of various noises, including SNEER, SNARL, and SNORE, whence the SNORKEL through which a diesel submarine (later, a swimmer) SNORTS air.

(S)NER-, to wind, twist, whence a twisted cord, noose, or Gc SNARE; Gc NARROW (? "cordlike") is ?? related. If your muscles are twisted they may become cramped or even numb, whence the Gk NARCOTIC that (sometimes) numbs your senses.

■ A narcotic, as its name implies, was originally an opiate or other drug that numbed you. For historical reasons, it now encompasses almost any "recreational" drug except alcohol and nicotine, many of which certainly don't numb you (they do worse!).

SNEUBH-, L *nubare*, to marry, whence NUPTIAL and NUBILE ("of marriageable age").

SNEUDH-, mist or cloud, L *nubes*, whence NUANCES of meaning or feeling, like the shades of color we see in clouds.

[Germanic SNU-, imitative root of words having to do with the nose: SNOUT, SNOT, SNIFF(LE), SNUFF, SNIVEL, SNUB ("turn up one's nose at"), and SNOOP ("stick one's nose into"). More distantly related is a group centered on biting, ? < the "nose" (muzzle) of a dog: SNATCH, SNACK, ? SNAP, and ? SNIP. (The last two may well be later, imitative formations.)]

SO-, this, that, whence Gc SHE ("that [female] person").

SOL-, SOLh-, L *sollus*, whole, whence L *sollicitare*, stir, agitate ("put the whole thing in motion"), whence SOLICIT, and the British SOLICITOR—who, like attorneys elsewhere, may well stir things up. Also < L are SOLID ("whole"), whence CONSOLIDATE ("make into a whole together"), SAVE ("make whole or healthy"), SAFE, and SAGE ("the healing herb"). A SALUTE was originally a greeting ("Good health!"), but SOLEMN is idiomatic. See **kel-3**

SPE-1, to thrive or L PROSPER; L *speres*, hopes (of future "prosperity") > DESPAIR (no hope). Gc SPEED originally = success; its modern sense is idiomatic.

SPE-2, long, flat piece of wood, whence Gc SPOON and SPADE (both originally wooden), and Gk SPATULA, whence (via Italian *spada*, broadsword) the spades on cards—originally swords, as they still are in the tarot pack.

SPEI-, sharp point, whence Gc SPIKE, SPIRE, the SPIT used for roasting, and the SPOKE of a wheel. From L are SPINE and PORCUPINE. See **porko-**

SPEIGH-, Gk *splen*, SPLEEN.

(S)PEIK-, bird's name, magpie, woodpecker—L *picus*, whence *piccare*, "peck at," prick, whence ? PICK, PIQUE ("prick," annoy), and PICKET, originally a pointed stake (as in "picket fence"), then a cavalry patrol (with its horses tied to stakes), then a "patrolling" striker.

SPEK-, L *specere*, *spect-*, to observe, look at. A SPECIMEN or SPECTACLE is something you look at, and perhaps SPECU-LATE about its varied ASPECTS. If you're CIRCUMSPECT, you "look around" carefully; if you EXPECT something you "look out" for it, and if you INSPECT it you "look into" it. If it's CONSPICUOUS you "look intensively" at it, but a DESPISED or DESPICABLE person is one you look down on. If you SUSPECT something you "look under" it (? to see what's going on); RESPECT (literally "look back at") is idiomatic.

A PROSPECT is what you look at in front of you; a PERSPICA-CIOUS person can look through things to achieve PERSPEC-TIVE (which also has many idiomatic senses). A SPECIES is a SPECIAL form ("what you look at") of something; in L it could also = merchandise or groceries—SPECIFICally, SPICES.

Gk *skepesthai*, to examine, consider ("look at closely"), > the SKEPTIC who examines (other people's) ideas very closely. Gk *skopos*, watcher, > MICROSCOPE (small watcher), TELESCOPE (far watcher), PERISCOPE (around watcher), and HOROSCOPE (hour watch—determining the aspect of the heavens at a particular time). From the same source is *episkopos*, the BISHOP who "watches over" churches, especially those of EPISCOPAL denominations (governed by their bishops). The Gc "watcher" eventu-ally > the SPY, engaged in ESPIONAGE.

SPEL-1, to split, break off, whence Gc SPILL and ? L *spolium*, hide stripped ("split") from a carcass, later armor stripped from a dead foe—the SPOILS of war—which had most likely been somewhat spoiled by combat.

spall

SPEL-2, L *splendere*, shine (also glow), whence SPLENDID ("shining") and RESPLENDENT.

SPEL-3, to say aloud, recite, as a witch reciting a SPELL, a messenger proclaiming news (whence GOSPEL, the "good message"), the pitchman or barker giving his SPIEL, or anyone reading (SPELLing) out something.

(S)PEN-, to draw, stretch, or Gc SPIN ("draw out a thread"), whence the web-spinning SPIDER, and SPAN, the distance that something "stretches" over. In L the root > three verbs, with overlapping meanings: to hang (? "stretch" a rope), cause to hang, and weigh (? "hang" on a balance). Their many descendants include the PENDANT that hangs or is hung—SUSPENDed ("hanging down")—from something, the SUSPENSE story that "leaves you hanging" from scene to scene, and the SUSPENDERS from which American pants and British socks hang. Something that DEPENDs figuratively hangs from something else, and the APPENDIX to a book "hangs on" the main text.

The "weighing" sense > PENSIVE ("weighing" ideas), whence the PANSY, supposed to resemble a pensive face; when you COMPENSATE, you're "weighing together"— figuratively adding weight to one or the other side of a balance. Related L words in this group > POUND, PONDER ("weigh" an idea), and PONDEROUS ("heavy," whence the modern sense of overheavy, clumsy).

SPEND-, to make an offering, perform a ritual, whence L *spondere, spons-*, make a solemn promise, whence the SPOUSE who's made such a promise, and the SPONSOR who, at a baptism, promises to be RESPONSIBLE for the infant's moral upbringing. If you make someone such a promise, they're supposed to RESPOND ("promise back"); if they don't, you may become idiomatically DESPONDENT. And if if you promise of your own accord it's SPONTANEOUS.

SPER-1, pole or Gc SPEAR, whence SPARERIBS—roasted on a "spear" (spit).

SPER-2, to turn, twist, whence Gk SPIRAL.

SPER-3, bird's name, especially the Gc SPARROW.

SPER-4, to strew or Gc SPREAD, whence SPRAWL, SPURT, and SPROUT ("spurt up" as a sprouting plant does). Gk *sporas*, scattered ("strewn"), > SPORADIC; *sperma*, seed scattered across the fields, > SPERM, the male "seed."

■ The Greeks, patriarchal to a man, believed that babies grew entirely from the male seed; the mother was merely the "field" in which they grew. The sperm whale acquired its name because a waxy oil found in its head was thought to be its sperm; the stuff is called spermaceti, "sperm of the whale." *Moby Dick* includes a vivid description of how spermaceti was extracted from a reservoir in the animal's head.

SPERh-, ankle, whence the SPUR strapped to it and SPURN— "give [someone] the ankle."

SPERGH-, to move, hasten, or Gc SPRING—whence water that springs from a spring and the spring season when vegetation springs up.

(S)PEUD-, to push, repulse, whence L REPUDIATE and RE- PULSE ("push back," as we do with repulsive things). The related L *pudere*, to feel shame (? "find oneself repul- sive"), > IMPUDENT—"shameless."

(S)PING-, bird's name, especially the Gc FINCH, one of a large group of songbirds—whence the FINK who "sings" to the cops.

[**Latin SPIRARE,** to breathe, whence INSPIRE (breathe in, literally or figuratively), EXPIRE (breathe out, temporar- ily or permanently—"breathe one's last"), RESPIRE (breathe back and forth, as we do in respiration), PERSPIRE ("breathe through" [the skin]), and CONSPIRE ("breathe together," hence agree [to break the law]). SPIRIT reflects the ancient connection between breath and soul—com- pare **anh-**.]

SPLEI-, Gc to SPLIT, whence SPLICE ("split" two ropes to join them together), SPLINTER and SPLINT ("split-off" pieces of wood), and ? FLINT, which for tens of thousands of years was split and flaked into tools.

(S)POI-MO-, Gc FOAM; L PUMICE has a foamy texture.

SPREG-, Gc to SPEAK, whence SPEECH.

(S)PREG-, to jerk, scatter, or Gc SPRINKLE, whence FRECKLES "sprinkled" on the skin. L *spargere*, *spars-*, to strew or scatter, > SPARSE ("scattered"), DISPERSE ("scatter away"), and INTERSPERSE ("scatter between").

SP(Y)EU-, Gc to SPIT or SPEW, whence the spitting SPUTTER and the spewing SPOUT.

SREBH-, to suck, whence Gc SLURP, and L ABSORB ("suck in").

SREU-, Gk *rhein*, to flow, whence the flowing Gc STREAM and the Gk RHYTHM and RHYME that mark the "flow" of verse.

■ We find the same root (probably via Celtic) in the flowing Rhine and Rhone.

SRIG-, L *frigus*, cold, whence FRIGID and REFRIGERATE.

STA-, L *stare*, *stat-*, Gc STAND, whence UNDERSTAND, originally = stand under, whence comprehend (? "have a good hold on") and STANDARD (originally, a rallying place where warriors came to stand). A Gc STOOL stands on its legs and a plant stands on its STEM.

Also Gc are STEED, originally a stallion standing at STUD; a STEER was ? once a stud bull—but the builder's stud originally = a standing post. STEERing a ship (as opposed to rowing it) was done standing at the STERN ("steering place") on the STARBOARD side, where the steering oar was mounted.

The L branch of the family is both larger and more diversified, with the basic "stand" idea proliferating into cause to stand, hence set up, erect, stop (bring to a standstill), and even the height or STATURE to which things stand. To complicate things even further, in some English words the L root has shrunk to -ST.

From the basic sense we get STAY ("stand" in a particular place), STABLE (standing firm and, through a different route, the stable where horses stand), the standing POST (compare STUD above), and the STATE or STATUS in which things stand—the STAGE they're at (whence the stage where performers stand).

Compounds include the PROSTITUTE who "stands forward" in the street but is not CONSTANT ("standing firm"), because he or she COSTS ("stands at a price"); the CIRCUMSTANCES that "stand around" something (see *BLM*); DISTANT ("standing away"), and INSTANT ("standing right at hand"—the modern sense, a very short time, is idiomatic). SUBSTANCE is the basic essence that "stands under" a thing's outward appearance, an OBSTACLE stands in your way, an ARMISTICE is a "standstill" of armies, and an OBSTINATE person "stands on" his or her opinion.

See **ar-**

The "cause to stand" (stop) sense has > only ARREST, but the "set up" sense has begotten many children: the STATUE set up in a public place, the STATUTES set up to ESTABLISH "law and order," the SUBSTITUTE "set up" instead of someone or something, and DESTINY— what is "set up" to happen. To RESTORE something = "set it up again," to STORE something is to set it away, and to CONTRAST two things is to "set them against" each other.

Also < L, via a different route, are INSIST ("stand upon"), DESIST ("stand away" [from doing something]), PERSIST ("stand firmly"), RESIST ("stand against"), EXIST ("stand out," hence be visible, hence be), and the idiomatic ASSIST. From Gk we get STASIS, a STATIC standstill; the EC-

STASY that puts our emotions "out of place" (not where they usually "stand"); SYSTEM (how things "stand together"), and the PROSTATE that "stands before" the bladder.

STAG- (possible root), to seep or drip, whence L *stagnum*, swamp, pond, whence STAGNANT and ?? TANK (artificial pond or reservoir; the military term originated as a "cover name" during World War I).

■ "Tank" originated in India as *tankh*, ? borrowed < Portuguese *tanque* = pond, < the L word above, or ? derived < Sanskrit *tadaga*, pond, < the same I-E root. Most likely, however, it was borrowed < one of the indigenous languages of India, where storage tanks for water were being constructed centuries before the I-Es arrived. In most of India the rains are highly seasonal, so that tanks were essential for any developed civilization.

STAK-, to stand, whence the Gc STAY that props or braces something—makes it "stand"—and STEEL, the metal that "stands firm."

[Germanic STAM-, to push, stutter, or Gc STAMMER (? "push out" words with difficulty), whence STUMBLE, as the stammering tongue does.]

[Germanic STAUP-, cooking pot, > STOVE.] *étuve*

■ Another descendant, the obsolete "stoup" (pot, drinking vessel), crops up in a famous line from *Hamlet*: "Get thee to Yaughan and fetch me a stoup of liquor!"

STEBH-, a post, hence to support, place or press firmly on, fasten. The "post/support" sense > Gc STAFF in all its senses, from the one that supports a traveler to the one that "supports" a general. The "press firmly" sense > Gc STEP, STAMP (whence the STAMPEDE of stamping cattle), and ? STUMP. The "fasten" sense > the Gc STOOP (small porch) "fastened" to the front of a house, and the STAPLE we fasten things with ("staple" as in crops is idiomatic).

STEG-, pole, stick, whence Gc STAKE, the STOCKADE made from stakes, and the STACK of grain or hay originally built around a stake. Also Gc are to STAGGER (? stumble over a stick), and (via Old Italian) ATTACK (? < "strike with a stick"), which >, via OF, the idiomatic ATTACH.

(S)TEG-, L *tegere*, to cover, whence the TILE that covers or PROTECTS a house, and DETECT, "uncover" (something hidden). From Gc are the THATCH that covers a house and the DECK that covers a ship, as well as deck = cover with ornaments, as in "Deck the halls." Possibly related is THUG (literally "deceiver"), originally a member of a murderous Hindu sect exterminated by the British; the word may derive from Sanskrit *sthagayati*, he covers, hence conceals.

STEGH-, to stick, prick, or Gc STING; also pointed ("prickly"), whence the Gc STAG with pointed antlers.

STEI-, Gc STONE, whence the beer drinker's STEIN, originally made of stoneware.

STEIG-, (related to **stegh-**), Gc to STICK or prick, pointed—whence a (pointed) stick of wood. Also Gc are the STITCHes that "stick" pieces of material together, the

STEAK roasted on a stick, and the idiomatic TICKET. L INSTI-
GATE = to prod on (as with a pointed stick); possible
members of the family include L DISTINGUISH, EXTIN-
GUISH, and INSTINCT, but they have no clear relationship
either to the root or to one another. Another alleged family member is TIGER, ? from a Persian word = arrow, referring to its supposedly arrowlike stripes.

See **rei-1**

STEIGH-, to stride, step, or rise (step up), whence Gc
STAIR and STIRRUP, originally = mounting rope—a loop of
rope thrown across a horse's back to help the rider step
into the saddle; the word was later transferred to wooden
and metal stirrups.

STEIP-, to stick or compress, whence Gc STIFF ("compressed," rigid). L *stipare*, compress, pack, > the STEVE-
DORE who packs cargo into a ship, and CONSTIPATE, originally = pack close together; its intestinal sense came
later.

STEL-, to put or stand Gc STILL, as does a STALLION IN-
STALLed in a STALL—whence FORESTALL, "make still in advance"; also Gc is the STALK on which a plant stands. L
stolidus described the "firm-standing," STOLID person—
sometimes rather stupid (*stultus*), whence STULTIFY. Possible relatives are Gc STILT (? < "firm-standing stick")
and ?? STOUT, supposedly < a Gc root = strut ("as if
walking on stilts"), but the connection is tenuous.

STELh-, to extend, whence L *latus*, broad, wide ("extended"), whence DILATE ("make wide") and LATITUDE,
"broadness" (its geographical sense is idiomatic).

(S)TENh-, L *tonare*, Gc to THUNDER, whence Thor or Thu-
nor, the Gc thunder-god, whose day was THURSDAY. From

the L come TORNADO (originally, a violent thunderstorm) and DETONATE, "explode like thunder." And if you're ASTONISHed or STUNned, you're figuratively thunderstruck (see *BLM*).

STER-1, Gc STIFF, as STARCHed cloth is and as the STORK stands. A STERN person is "stiff" (firm); so is a STARK ("hard") fact, while to STRUT is to walk stiffly (also, a stiff support). STARVE originally = to die (become a stiff), and the REDSTART is named for its stiff red tail, but START and STARTLE are idiomatic. All these are Gc. L *torpere*, to be stiff, > TORPID, and the TORPEDO (fish) whose electric discharge can stiffen you, whence the naval weapon.

STER-2, STERh-, to spread, whence the Gc STRAW often STREWn in stables. L *struere, struc-*, to pile up, hence CONSTRUCT, > STRUCTURE, DESTROY ("deconstruct"), OBSTRUCT ("pile up against"), and the idiomatic INSTRUCT; more loosely related are INDUSTRY (in its original sense of diligence) and STREET, originally one of the great "constructed" (paved) Roman roads (the word was an early borrowing into Gc). Gk *strator*, a "spread-out" multitude, hence army, > the *strategos* who led it —devised its STRATEGY.   See **ag-**

STER-3, L *stella*, Gk *aster*, Gc STAR. From the L come STELLAR and CONSTELLATION ("stars together" [in a group]); from the Gk, ASTRO- (-nomy, -logy, etc.) and DISASTER (an "ill-starred" occurrence—see *BLM*), as well as the star-shaped ASTER and ASTERISK.

STER-4, Gc to STEAL, whence STEALTH and STALK ("move stealthily").

STER-5, barren, whence L STERILE.

(S)TER-N-, (related to **ster-1**), the name of various Gc THORNY plants.

(S)TEU-, to push, stick, knock, or beat, but with many other loosely related derivatives. A STOKER pushes coal into a furnace, a STEPchild sometimes was (and is) "pushed out," a STUB sticks out, to STOOP is to "push oneself" down, while STUTTER comes < a word = to force ("push"), hence "force oneself to speak"—as the stutterer indeed must do. All these are Gc, as are the idiomatic STEEP (precipitous), whence STEEPLE, and STOCK (originally = tree trunk), in all its senses, most of them idiomatic.

The family's L branch is equally diverse; it includes *stupere*, to be stunned (? "knocked on the head"), whence STUPID and the STUPENDOUS things that STUPEFY us, and *studere*, to be diligent ("push forward"), which > STUDY and STUDENT. The "beat" sense > *tudicula*, a mill for crushing ("beating") olives, whence eventually TOIL, and *tundere*, beat, thrust, whence PIERCE ("thrust through"). Finally, Gk *typos*, a blow, hence the image or impression (e.g., of a coin) made by a blow, > TYPE in all its senses.

STEU(h)-, (possible root), to condense, cluster, whence Gk *stuppe*, the tow used to STUFF or STOP up the seams of a boat.

STh-MEN-, various body parts, such as the Gk STOMACH.

STORO-, Gc STARLING.

■ The root is ?? connected with or influenced by **ster-3**, star: in winter the bird's black plumage is speckled with white "stars."

STREB(H), Gk *strephein*, to turn, wind, whence CATAS-TROPHE—originally, the denouement of a drama in which the action takes a sudden turn and winds down. The denouements of many Elizabethan tragedies (e.g., the last scene of *Hamlet*, in which almost everyone is killed) helped give the term its modern sense.

STREIG-, to rub, press, or Gc STROKE, whence STRIKE (originally = stroke) and STREAK (a "stroke" of color). L *stringere*, *strict-*, draw tight, press together, > STRICT, RE-STRICT, the ASTRINGENT that tightens the skin, and STRAIN—"draw tight." PRESTIGE, from a L verb = to blind, is idiomatic; it originally = conjuring trick (see *BLM*).

STRENK- (possible root), tight (whence Gk STRANGLE) or narrow, whence Gc STRING, and ? STRONG and STRENGTH, < a Gc root = severe (? "narrow").

STREP-, to make a noise, whence the noisy, L OBSTREPER-OUS person.

SU-, L *sus*, Gk *hys*, Gc SWINE, whence SOW. HOG comes < Celtic **sukk-*, which also = pig's snout, hence the plow-share that "roots up" the soil—whence ? SOCKET. The L word > *suculus*, little pig, whence SOIL (things) ("make a pig of oneself"); the Gk word > HYENA, another animal with supposedly dirty habits.

SURO-, sharp-tasting—salty, bitter or Gc SOUR, whence SAUERKRAUT.

SWAD-, pleasant or Gc SWEET. L *suadere*, advise ("recommend as pleasant"), > PERSUADE and DISSUADE ("advise

against"); L *suavis*, sweet, agreeable, > SUAVE and AS-
SUAGE ("make more agreeable").

(S)WAGH-, to resound or Gc ECHO.

SWARD-, to laugh, whence Gk *sardanios*, sneering,
whence SARDONIC. The word was influenced by the name
of Sardinia—see *BLM*.

S(W)E-, reflexive pronoun, whence Gc (-)SELF, SIBLING ("related to oneself"), and GOSSIP—originally = godfather or
godmother, later the chum with whom one gossips. L *sui*,
See **kah-id-** of oneself, > SUICIDE; *sed*, *se*, apart, without ("by oneself"), > SE-, for whose derivatives (SECEDE, SECRET, etc.)
see the "Index of English Words" at the end of this book.

Also ? related is L *solus*, by oneself, alone, whence SOLI-
TARY, SOLITUDE, SOLE (only), the SOLO performed alone, the
SOLILOQUY delivered by an actor alone on stage, SULLEN
(what solitary people often are), and DESOLATE ("left
alone"). Another group concerns "what is one's own,"
hence distinctive—L CUSTOM and Gk ETHIC, ETHNIC, IDIOM
(the distinctive traits of a language), and the idiomatic
IDIOT.

SWEI-, to bend, turn, whence Gc SWOOP, SWIFT ("quick-
turning"—as the swift indeed is), the turning SWIVEL, and
the flexible, bending SWITCH—whence the switch that
turns electricity on or off. SWAP is sometimes assigned to
this root, but is more likely unrelated.

SWEID-1, to shine, whence ? L *sidus*, star, whence CON-
SIDER ("examine the stars") and the idiomatic DESIRE.

SWEID-2, Gc SWEAT.

S(W)EKS, L *sex*, Gc SIX; the L word > SEMESTER—originally = six months.   See **me-2**

SWEL-1, to eat or drink, whence Gc SWALLOW.

SWEL-2, to shine or burn, whence the Gc SULTRY weather
in which we SWELTER.

SWEL-3, post, board, whence Gc SILL.

SWEM-, to move or Gc SWIM, whence ? SOUND (the depth
of water), and the sounds mariners sometimes sound.

SWEN-, L *sonare*, *sonat-*, Gc to SOUND, whence the
"sounding" SWAN. From the L we get RESOUND ("sound
again"), the CONSONANT that "sounds with" a vowel, DIS-
SONANT ("sounding against"), and the SONATA that is
"sounded" (played) rather than sung, as is the cantata.

■ The swan would have been the (European) whooper
swan, rather than its relative, the mute swan, which (as
its name indicates) makes very few sounds.

SWENG(W)-, to turn, toss, or Gc SWING, whence ? SWAY
and SWAG, whose original sense survives in the "swag"
(bundle) that an Australian SWAGMAN (tramp) swings
over his shoulder. SWANK is ? related, through various
English dialect words concerned with vigorous ("swing-
ing") actions.

SWENTO-, strong, healthy, whence Gc SOUND.

SWEP-1, to sleep, whence L INSOMNIA (not sleeping) and
Gk HYPNOSIS, a sort of sleep. A related L word = deep

sleep > the SOPORIFIC book or speaker that puts you into one.

SWEP-2, to sling, throw, L *sipare*, whence DISSIPATE ("throw apart"); ?? related is the Gc SWAB that sailors "sling" around the deck.

SWER-1, to speak, talk, whence Gc SWEAR and ANSWER ("speak back").

SWER-2, to whisper or buzz, like a Gc SWARM of bees; also ? SWIRL and ?? L ABSURD, from *surdus*, deaf (see *BLM*).

SWER-3, to cut, pierce, whence Gc SWORD.

SWER-4, to lift; heavy, whence L SERIOUS ("heavy").

SWERBH-, to wipe off, turn (connection obscure), whence Gc SWERVE.

SWERGH-, to worry, be sick, whence Gc SORROW.

SWESOR-, L *soror*, Gc SISTER; the L word > SORORITY ("sisterhood"), while a related term > COUSIN.

S(W)OKWO-, resin, juice, whence Gk OPIUM, made from the sticky juice of the opium poppy.

SWOMBHO-, spongy, whence Gc SWAMP, with its spongy, water-soaked soil.

SWORDO-, black, whence Gc SWARTHY, or dirty, whence L SORDID.

SYU-, to bind or Gc SEW, whence SEAM. From L come the SUTURES with which the high-priced surgeon sews us up—and the high-priced seamstress's COUTURE.

TA-, to melt, dissolve, whence Gc THAW.

TAG-1, to handle or touch (not related), whence L *tangere*, *tact-*, to touch, whence TANGIBLE ("touchable"), the TANGENT that just touches a circle, TACT (originally = sense of touch), TASTE (originally = examine by touch), CONTACT ("touch with"), INTACT ("untouched"), and ATTAIN ("touch toward," hence get to). Closely related is L *taxare*, to touch ("run the hands through"), hence assess, whence the TAXES assessed on us and the TAXI meter that measures the "tax" we must pay the cab driver. L *integer*, whole ("untouched"), > ENTIRE and INTEGER (whole number), but also = morally "whole," whence INTEGRITY.   See **me-2**

TAG-2, to set in order, whence Gk *tattein*, to arrange, whence TACTICS (military "arrangements") and SYNTAX—how the elements of a language are "arranged."

[Germanic TAK-, to TAKE, whence MISTAKE, "take amiss."]   See **mei-1**

[Germanic TAP(P)-, the supposed source of words dealing with several (very) loosely related ideas. One,

241

"(to) plug," > the TAP that "plugs" a cask—and through which beer, wine, or water flows; a TAMPON is another kind of plug. A second sense, to strike lightly, > another kind of tap; a third sense, "projecting object," > TIP, TOP, and TUFT (of hair), whence TOUPEE. TAPE is a possible but unlikely relative.]

■ As with several other hypothetical roots, the "loose" relationship makes any relationship questionable. The "plug" and "projecting object" senses are ?? cousins, but "tap" = strike lightly is more likely imitative.

TAURO-, L *taurus*, bull, whence the TOREADOR who kills it and the constellation TAURUS.

[Germanic TAW-, to make, prepare, whence the TOOLS we use to make things.]

TEGU-, Gc THICK.

TEKS-, L *texere*, *text-*, to weave or fabricate, whence TEXTILE, TISSUE (originally, a thin woven fabric), and the TEXTURE ("weaving") of fabrics and (later) other things. Figurative descendants include TEXT (words "woven" into a document), CONTEXT (what something is "woven together" with), and the PRETEXT "fabricated beforehand"; SUBTLE is idiomatic. Gk *texton*, builder, > ARCHITECT, "master builder"; *tekhne*, craft, skill, > TECHNOLOGY, TECHNICAL, and POLYTECHNIC ("many crafts").

See **arkhein**

See **pelh-1**

TEKW-, to run, flee, whence Gk (via Iranian) *toxa*, (bow and) arrow ("thing that flies"), whence—via a phrase = poison (an) arrow—TOXIC.

■ The evolution may have been influenced by the Gk cult of Apollo, who was sometimes depicted as holding in one hand the cup of healing and in the other the "toxic" arrows of death.

TEL-, ground, floor, board, whence ? L *titulus*, signboard, whence the TITLE that is the "signboard" of a book—or (in some countries) of a person.

TELh-, to lift, support, hence weigh, whence derivatives concerning payment (for weighed-out goods). The "lift/ support" sense > "carry/bear", whence L *tolerare*, TOLER- ATE, and *latus*, carried, borne, whence LEGISLATOR ("law bearer"), ELATE ("carry out" [of oneself]), TRANSLATE ("carry across"—now usually from one language to an- other), RELATE ("carry back" a story, etc.), and SUPERLA- TIVE ("carried above").   See **legh-**

The same sense > the Gk demigod Atlas, who supported the world on his shoulders, whence the ATLAS that holds the whole world, as well as the ATLANTIC Ocean—and the Atlas Mountains. The "weigh/pay" sense > L RETALIATE ("pay back"), the Gk TOLL you pay, and Gk TALENT, origi- nally a measure of weight—see *BLM*.

TEM-, TEMh-, Gk *temnein*, to cut, whence -TOMY (cut- ting), as in ANATOMY ("cutting back" the tissues, hence the structures thus revealed), and -ECTOMY (cutting out, as in appendectomy). An ATOM was "uncuttable"— though now, alas, we know better. L *templum*, shrine ("place cut out"—i.e., reserved), > both the religious TEMPLE and CONTEMPLATE, view with attention, as from such an "elevated" place.

TEN-, L *tendere*, *tent-*, to stretch, is the parent of a large family. The basic sense > L TENSE, TEND ("stretch to- ward"), and the "stretched" TENDON and TENT. Compounds include ATTEND ("stretch [oneself] toward"), whence tend = take care of; CONTEND ("stretch [oneself] with," hence strive); DISTEND ("stretch apart"); EXTEND (stretch out); INTEND ("stretch [the mind] into"); DÉTENTE, an "unstretching" of strained relations that relieves international tensions, and PRETEND, originally = put ("stretch") oneself forward, whence the pretender who puts forward a false claim to something, whence the modern, deceptive sense.

Another branch of the family concerns things that are "stretched out," hence Gc THIN, L *tenuis*, whence TENUOUS, ATTENUATE ("make thinner"), and EXTENUATE—"thin out" an offense. More remote is Gk *tonos*, (stretched) string, whence TONE, whence the TONIC that supposedly improves the "tone" of the body—though not, one suspects, when mixed with gin. Finally, thin things are often delicate or L TENDER—as are plant TENDRILS.

See **man-2**

A third branch derives from L *tenere*, to hold (? "keep stretched out"), keep, or MAINTAIN ("hold in the hand"), whence TENACIOUS (holding fast), the TENANT who holds something from the landlord, the TENOR who originally "held" the melody in a male choir, the TENURE by which academicians hold on to their jobs, and the TENABLE opinion that can (reasonably) be held.

Compounds in this group include ABSTAIN ("hold [oneself] away from"), DETAIN (hold back), RETAIN ("hold back" [for oneself]), CONTAIN ("hold with[in limits]"), CONTINUE ("keep holding" = keep going), OBTAIN ("hold toward" [oneself]), SUSTAIN ("hold [up] from beneath"); ENTERTAIN (originally = hold in a certain state), See **locus** and the idiomatic PERTAIN. A LIEUTENANT "holds the place" of a higher officer.

TENG-, to soak, whence Gc DUNK and L *tingere*, *tinct-*, to soak, hence soak in dye, whence TINT, TINGE, STAIN, and TAINT.

TENK-2, to become firm, curdle, thicken, whence Gc TIGHT, which originally = dense (thick), now firmly fixed. A possible relative is TANGLE, < an Old Norse word = seaweed (? "thick mass").

TEP-, to be warm, whence L TEPID.

TER-, peg, post, whence boundary marker, goal. L *terminus*, boundary marker, hence limit, end, > TERMINUS, TERMINATE, TERM, DETERMINE ("bring to an end"), and EXTERMINATE, originally = expel ("put beyond the boundary").

TERh-1, to rub or L TURN, whence derivatives concerning twisting and Gc DRILLing. Others deal with rubbing grain to remove the husks, whence Gc THRESHing—sometimes by the tread of oxen, whence the Gc THRESHOLD we tread on. The "rubbing" group includes L *terere*, *trit-*, rub away, hence wear out, whence the TRITE, worn-out expression, ATTRITION that wears things away—to their DETRIMENT ("wearing away"), and CONTRITE ("very worn out" [in spirit]).

The "turn/twist" group includes L *tornus*, lathe (for turning wood or metal), whence RETURN ("turn back"), DETOUR ("turn away" [from the usual route]), and CONTOUR, from the "turning" of a pen or pencil making a drawing. Gc THREAD is made of twisted yarn, Gc THROWing involves twisting the body, and TRAUMA is from a Gk word = hole (as if made by a twisted drill). TRUANT is a possible but very unlikely relative.

TERh-2, to cross over, overcome, pass Gc THROUGH (whence THOROUGH). L *trans*, across, > TRANS- (-Atlantic, etc.). The "pass through" sense > L TRANSIENT, "passing through" but not staying; related senses are "pierce" (as a drill does), the original sense of Gc THRILL, and "hole," whence Gc NOSTRIL ("nose hole"). A possible but unlikely relative is L *truncus*, deprived of branches or limbs, mutilated (? "overcome"), whence TRUNK (of a tree or the body), TRUNCATE, and TRENCH, originally a track cut through a forest.

TERKW-(related to terh-1), to twist, whence L TORQUE (twisting force on, e.g., a shaft), TORTUOUS, TORMENT (originally = "twist" someone on the rack), the TORCH once made of a twisted length of tow, CONTORT, DISTORT ("twist away" from its proper shape or sense), and EXTORT ("twist out" [of someone]—by twisting their arm, you might say). Possibly related are L TORTURE and Gc THWART (< twisted = crosswise).

TERS-, to dry, whence Gc THIRST and L *torrere*, to dry, parch, or burn, whence TOAST (always parched; sometimes burned), TORRID, and TORRENT, a "boiling" stream. Another branch of the family derives from L *terra*, earth ("dry land"), whence the TERRACE of banked-up earth, TERRAIN (how the land lies), TERRESTRIAL (sometimes combined with extra-), TERRITORY, and the TERRIER bred to dig animals from the earth. INTER, of course, = put something in the earth; the MEDITERRANEAN is "in the middle of the land" (see your atlas), and something SUBTERRANEAN is underground.

See
medhyo-

TEU-, to pay attention to, whence L *tueri*, look at, watch, guard (guards are supposed to pay attention), whence

TUTOR, the TUITION (originally = guardianship) a tutor gives (also what you pay for it), and the idiomatic INTUITION—though, by coincidence, it amounts to a sort of "inner tutor."

TEU(h)-, L *tumere*, to swell, be swollen, whence TUMOR; L *tuber*, ("swollen") lump, > both TUBER and TRUFFLE. Gc THIGH is the "swollen" part of the leg, the THUMB is the "swollen finger" (whence THIMBLE), and a THOUSAND is a "swollen hundred." Possible relatives are Gk TOMB (? "swollen" mound of earth) and ?? BUTTER—originally = cow cheese (? in a swollen lump).   See **dekm-**

TEUTA-, tribe, whence the ancient TEUTONS (< Gaulish via L), the modern Gc DUTCH—and the citizens of *Deutchland*. Possibly related is L *totus*, all (? "the whole tribe"), whence TOTAL.

TIT-, TIK-, KIT-, to tickle (not related), whence L TITILLATE.

[West Germanic TITTA, TIT or TEAT (pronounced identically, with a short I).]

TKE-, to gain control or power over, whence ? Persian *shah*, king, whence (via the game of chess) CHECKMATE ("the king is dead"—see *BLM*) and CHECK in all its senses; SHAH is a recent borrowing.

TKEI-, to settle, dwell, be at Gc HOME (whence HAMLET— "little hometown"), also HAUNT (dwell in = frequent). L *situs*, location, > SITE and SITUATION.

TO-, demonstrative pronoun; its English descendants are all Gc: THIS, THAT, THESE, THOSE; later, THE, THEY, THEIR, and THEM. Like other pronoun roots (compare **i-**), it also > various other parts of speech: THEN (at that time), THERE (in that place), THUS (in this manner), THOUGH, and THAN.

TOLKW-, L *loqui*, to speak, talk (unrelated), whence LO-QUACIOUS (talkative), the CIRCUMLOCUTION that "talks around" a subject, the SOLILOQUY of an actor speaking alone, and the VENTRILOQUIST who seems to "talk through his belly"—that is, not with his mouth.

TONG-, to feel or Gc THINK, whence THOUGHT and THANK (originally = thought, then kindly thought).

TRAGH-, L *trahere*, *tract-*, to pull, draw, drag, whence the TRACTOR that pulls (exerts TRACTION) on a plow or trailer, the TRAIN pulled by a locomotive, the TRACE or TRAIL left by something dragged along, and the TRACT of land originally marked out by lines actually drawn on the earth. Closely related is L *tractare*, to drag, hence handle, manage (whence TRACTABLE animals or people); other senses include deal with, whence TREAT, and negotiate ("make a deal"), whence TREATY.

Compounds include ATTRACT (draw to), CONTRACT (draw together), DETRACT ("draw [something] away from"), DISTRACT (draw [one's attention] away), EXTRACT (draw out), RETRACT ("draw back"), and SUBTRACT ("draw down"). And a PORTRAIT PORTRAYS ("draws") someone.

TREI-, L *tres*, Gc THREE, whence THIRTY, THIRTEEN, and THIRD; the L word > TRIPLE, TRIO, the three-"toothed"

TRIDENT, and the Christian TRINITY. Another L group See **dent-**
stems from *testis*, witness, the "third man" present at an
agreement who could TESTIFY to its terms, whence also
TESTIMONY, TESTAMENT (a witnessed will), and—TESTICLES,
the "little witnesses" that ATTEST to a man's virility (see
BLM). The related L *testari*, bear witness, > PROTEST
("witness forth"), DETEST (originally = denounce—"bear
witness against"), and CONTEST ("call witnesses"
[against]).

TREM-, L *tremere*, to TREMBLE, whence the TREMOR of the
quaking ("trembling") earth and TREMENDOUS—"enough
to make you tremble."

TREP-1 (? related to last root), to tremble, whence the
INTREPID person who doesn't.

TREP-2, to turn, whence Gk TROPIC, from the Tropics of
Cancer and Capricorn, where the sun is directly overhead
at the "turns" of the year—the summer and winter sol-
stices; the tropics lies between these two imaginary lines.
CONTRIVE is ? < L *tropus*, figure ("turn") of speech;
RETRIEVE (< OF "find again") is either idiomatic or unrelated.

TRES- (? related to **trem-** and **trep-1**), to tremble,
whence L *terrere*, to frighten (cause to tremble), whence
TERROR, TERRIBLE, TERRIFIC, and DETER ("frighten away").

TREUD-, to squeeze, hence (in several families) push,
exert force, whence Gc THRUST and THREAT. L *trudere*,
thrust, push, > INTRUDE ("push in"), EXTRUDE ("push
out"), and PROTRUDE ("push forward").

TROZDO-, L *turdus*, Gc THRUSH. The L word is the improbable but attested source of the idiomatic STURDY (see *OEtD*).

TU-, second-person singular pronoun, whence Gc THOU, THEE, THY, and THINE.

TWENGH-, to press in on, whence Gc TWINGE (originally = pinch) and THONG (originally = constricting band).

TWER-, to turn, whence Gc STIR, or whirl, whence Gc STORM. L *turba*, tumult (a "stirred-up" situation), > TROUBLE, DISTURB, PERTURB, and TURBID—as troubled or stirred-up waters often are. L *turbo*, spinning top, eventually > the spinning TURBINE.

[Germanic TWIK-, to pinch off, whence TWEAK and TWITCH.]

UD-, up, Gc OUT, whence UTMOST ("outermost"), OUTLAW (outside the law), and UTTER in both its senses: "speak out" and "more out" ("far out"), as in "utter nonsense." BUT and ABOUT come < an Old English word = outside, and when you CAROUSE you're going all out.

See **tem-**

UDERO-, abdomen, stomach, or L UTERUS, Gk *hysteros*, whence HYSTERECTOMY (cutting out the uterus) and HYSTERIA, once considered a disorder of the uterus (see *BLM*).

UKWS-EN-, bull or Gc OX.

UL-, Gc to HOWL, whence the "howling" OWL.

[Latin UOLCAE, Celtic tribal name, thought to resemble the source of a Gc term = foreigner, whence WELSH (applied by the English to the British "foreigners" from whom they seized England), and WALNUT, "foreign nut." Gc FOLK is ? from a similar, non-Germanic tribal name (see *OMNT*).]

UPER, L *super*, Gk *hyper*, Gc OVER. The L term also = above, whence SUPER- (-man, -human, etc.), SUPERIOR ("more above"), SUPERB, SIRLOIN ("above the loin"), the SOVEREIGN who reigned SUPREME over his or her people, SOMERSAULT (jump head over heels), and the SOPRANO voice that sings above all the rest. L *summus* (< **supmus*), topmost ("most above"), > SUMMIT and SUM, the "topmost" (total) amount—now the "bottom line." The Gk word is, of course, the source of HYPER- (-active, etc.).

See **lendh-1**

See **sel-4**

UPO, under, up from under, over, whence Gc UP, UPROAR (originally = uprising), ABOVE, and OPEN ("set up"); OFTEN is ? related. Also Gc are the EAVES set above the wall of a house, whence EAVESDROP—see *BLM*. L *sub*, under, > SUB- (-marine, etc.) and SUPPLE ([with knees] "folded under"); a Celtic word = servant ("underling") > (via MedL) VALET and the VASSAL who served his (or her) lord. Gk *hypo*, under, > HYPO-, as in the HYPODERMIC that injects things under the skin.

See **plek-**

See **der-2**

US-, thorn, point, whence ? Gc ODD, from Old Norse *odda*, deciding vote, umpire—the "odd" (third) man in a contest. (The relationship—if real—may derive from the third "point" of a triangle.)

[**Latin VIRERE,** to be green or VERDANT.]

WAB-, to cry, scream, whence Gc WEEP.

WADH-1, to pledge, whence Gc WED and ENGAGE (both = pledge to do something). WAGES and WAGERS are different kinds of pledges, while a MORTGAGE is a pledge that

See **mer-2**   survives the pledger's death.

WADH-2, L *vadere*, to go, whence VAMOOSE, EVADE ("go away from"), INVADE ("go into"), and PERVADE ("go through"). Other relatives, in both Gc and L, acquired the special sense of "step [go] through the water," whence Gc WADE. *vade mecum*

WAG-, L *vagina*, sheath, whence the L VAGINA that sheathes a man's "sword," and VANILLA, whose dried, beanlike fruit looks vaguely like a leather sheath.

WAI, alas (exclamation), whence Gc WOE ("Woe is me!") and WAIL. *L. Vae; Ger. Weh*

252

WAK-, L *vacca*, cow, whence Spanish *vaquero*, cowherd (BUCKAROO in English), and *vaccinia*, cowpox, whence VACCINE.

■ The great medical pioneer Edward Jenner (1749–1823) discovered that inoculating people with material from the skin lesions of cowpox (vaccinia), an annoying but benign disease, would protect them against the much more serious smallpox. The word "vaccine" was eventually transferred to all other immunizing agents, though none of them had anything to do with cows. Jenner's discovery ultimately led to the complete wiping out of smallpox in the 1970s.

WAL-, L *valere*, to be strong, whence VALIANT (originally = stalwart), VALOR, VALID ("strongly true"), INVALID (= either not valid or, medically, "not strong"), AVAIL ("be strong enough"), PREVAIL ("have greater strength"), and CONVALESCE ("grow stronger"). The L verb could also = to have VALUE, whence EQUIVALENT ("having equal value"). From Gc we get WIELD, originally = rule, act effectively ("strongly").

WALSO-, L *uallum*, *vallum*, post; later, a stake, then a palisade of stakes, whence WALL. An INTERVAL was originally the space between two palisades.

WE-1, Gc WE.

WE-2, to blow, whence Gc WIND, WEATHER, the WINDOW they blow through, and the bird's WING that "blows" (fans) the air. L *ventus*, wind, > VENT and VENTILATE.

WEBH-, Gc to WEAVE, whence WEB (originally = cloth). The root also = move quickly (as a weaver's hands do), whence WOBBLE, the quick-moving WEEVIL, and ? WAVE (e.g., the hand). A possible Gc derivative = honeycomb (? "woven" by bees), whence WAFFLE (presumably from its honeycomb texture) and WAFER.

WED-1, Gc WATER or WET, whence WASH, WINTER ("wet season"), and the water-dwelling OTTER. Gk *hydor*, *hydr-*, water, > HYDRANT and HYDRO- (-electric, etc.). L *unda*, wave (in the water), > UNDULATE (move like a wave), INUNDATE (push "waves" into), and the figurative SURROUND ("overflow") and ABOUND, whence ABUNDANT (present in "overflowing" quantities—see *BLM*). WHISKEY comes < (where else?) Scots and Irish Gaelic *uisgebeatha*, "water of life" (!); VODKA ("little water") comes < (where else?) Russian.

■ The notion of distilled spirits as a kind of water seems to have occurred independently in many lands—doubtless because unaged spirits look like water (though, in the southern moonshiner's phrase, they "kick like a mule"). Thus "whiskey" is matched by French *eau de vie* = water of life (brandy), and Scandinavian *akavit* (a kind of flavored vodka) comes < L *aqua vitae*, water of life. In Spanish, spirits are often called—more accurately—*aguardiente* ("burning water").

WED-2, to speak, whence Gk *aeidein*, to sing ("speak" musically), whence MELODY (? "sweet song"), COMEDY ("singing revel"), TRAGEDY (first element obscure), and PARODY ("mocking song").

■ In Greece, as in most other places, poetry was originally sung or chanted; Gk comic and tragic drama grew out of songs and dances at religious festivals.

WEG-1, to weave a web, whence L VEIL and REVEAL ("draw back the veil").

WEG-2, to be strong, lively, whence L VIGOR, VELOCITY, and VEGETABLE ("growing vigorously"). In both Gc and L the sense of "lively" > Gc AWAKE, whence WAKE, WATCH ("be awake"), and WAIT (originally = watch as an enemy, "lie in wait"). L *vigil*, awake, > the REVEILLE that wakes up soldiers and VIGILANT, watchful ("awake"), whence the idiomatic VIGILANTE.

WEGH-, to go, transport in a L VEHICLE—eventually a Gc WAGON. Other derivatives in both Gc and L concern the road or Gc WAY one goes, whence ANYWAY (in northern England, "any road") and ALWAYS ("by all roads"); from L we have VOYAGE, VIA (by way of), and the VIADUCT that "leads" a road over a valley, etc.

See **deuk-**

Compounds include CONVEY (originally = to escort, "travel with," whence CONVOY), DEVIATE ("travel away from"), DEVIOUS ("away from the direct [straight] way"), OBVIOUS ("lying in the road"—"you could trip over it"), PREVIOUS ("going beforehand"), and the idiomatic TRIVIAL (see *OEtD*). From the same root are L VEX ("set in motion," agitate) and CONVEX ("carried together" [to a point]), and Gc WEIGH ("carry" in a scale); more distantly related are Gc WAG (move back and forth, ? as in a jolting vehicle), whence WIGGLE.

■ Though to us a vehicle implies wheels, the original vehicle was probably a sledge; the I-Es almost certainly knew nothing of wheels.

WEGW-, wet, whence L HUMID and HUMOR—originally, one of the body's fluids; its modern sense is idiomatic (see

See
ukws-en-

BLM). Some have assigned OX to this root, but the connection is tenuous.

WEGWH-, EUGWH-, to preach, speak solemnly, whence L *vovere*, to vow, whence the DEVOTED or DEVOUT person who has "vowed" to be or do something. A secondary sense of the L word, wish, > VOTE—formally express one's "wish."

WEI-1, WEIh-, to turn, twist, whence supple, "twisting" things such as Gc WIRE and L *vitis*, vine, whence VISE—originally, a spiral staircase, then a spiraling screw, then the screw-fastened clamp used to hold wood or metal.

WEI-2, to go after something; if you go after it vigorously, you may Gc GAIN it.

WEI-3, to wither, whence Gc WIZENED.

WEI-4, fault, guilt, L VICE, whence VICIOUS.

WEID-, L *videre*, *vis-*, to see or look, whence VIEW, VISION, VISTA, and VOYEUR. Compounds include ADVISE ("tell [someone] what you see"), EVIDENT ("making itself seen"), PROVIDE (originally = foresee), REVIEW ("see again"), SUPERVISE and SURVEY (both = oversee), the IN-TERVIEW in which two people "see each other," and the idiomatic ENVY ("look [maliciously] on"). Gc relatives in this group include GUIDE ("look after") and GUISE (how something "looks"), whence the DISGUISE that alters it; from Gk we get IDEA (originally = appearance) and IDEO- (as in IDEALOGY).

Another group derives from the obvious relationship of seeing and knowing or understanding ("I see!"): Gc WISE (whence the idiomatic -WISE), WISDOM, WIT, UNWITTING ("not having seen"), and WITNESS—someone who has firsthand knowledge of something. And Gk *histor*, wise, knowing (originally *widtor*), > both HISTORY and STORY.

WEIDH-, to separate or L DIVIDE ("separate apart"); a Gc WIDOW is separated from her husband by death.

WEIh-, (vital) force, whence L *violare*, to use force on, whence VIOLATE and VIOLENT.

WEIK-1, clan, but in many derivatives the sense has shrunk to household or house, as in L *villa*, country house, farm, whence the villein (serf) who worked it—a "low" fellow who > a VILLAIN—and the VILLAGE or VICIN-ITY he lived in. Gk *oikos*, house, > ECONOMY—originally, household management (home economics), and ECOLOGY, the study of the biological "households" in which all plants and animals (including us) live. Gk *paroikos*, "dwelling alongside," > the PARISH of believers who dwell in the same village or vicinity.

WEIK-2, found in L and Gc words concerning magic and religion, > Gc WITCH (whence BEWITCH) and GUILE, and ? L VICTIM—originally, an animal used in a religious sacri-fice.

WEIK-3, to be like, whence Gk *eikon*, image, whence the religious IKON and the ICONOCLAST who is an "image breaker" (see *BLM*).

WEIK-4, WEIG-, to bend or wind, as Gc WICKERwork does. Things that are easily bent may be Gc WEAK, but Gc WEEK ("turn, change"—originally ? > the changing phases of the moon) is idiomatic, as is L VICE- (-president, etc.).

WEIK-5, to fight or conquer, L *vincere*, *vict-*, whence both the INVINCIBLE (unconquerable) VICTOR and the vincible VANQUISHed. To CONVINCE is to "conquer" in argument, while EVICT is > a L verb = obtain by conquest—something like what an evicting landlord does.

WEIP-, to turn, vacillate, tremble, whence L VIBRATE. In Gc the "vacillate" sense > move back and forth, whence WIPE and WHIP.

WEIS-, to flow, whence Gc OOZE (mud) and L VISCOUS. Dubiously related are several words involving the idea of "strong-smelling" (? like mud), whence the smelly Gc WEASEL and L BISON, or "unpleasant," whence L VIRUS (originally = poison).

■ The L animal was not, of course, the American bison but its close European relative, the wisant. I don't know whether American bison are strong-smelling, but weasels certainly are.

See **ne**

WEKTI-, thing, creature, whence Gc AUGHT (anything) and the negative NAUGHT (nothing), whence NAUGHTY (originally = poor—"having naught").

WEKW-, to speak, > L *vox*, *voc-*, VOICE, whence VOCAL, VOWEL, and EQUIVOCAL ("with equal voices"). L *vocare*, *vocat-*, to call, > the VOCATION to which we are "called," the ADVOCATE who "calls out" his argument, the reply he EVOKES ("calls forth") or PROVOKES ("calls forward"), and REVOKE ("call back"; the bridge player's sense is idiomatic). The Gk EPIC was originally "called out" (sung).

WEL-1, to wish or Gc WILL, whence WELL ("going according to one's will") and the WEALTH that brings well-being. L *volo*, I wish, > VOLITION ("willpower"), VOLUNTARY (willing), BENEVOLENT (well-willing), and MALEVOLENT (ill-willing). Obscurely related (if at all) are Gc GALLOP and WALLOP.

WEL-2, to turn or roll, whence various rolling and curved (hence enclosing) objects. From Gc we get the WILLOW, with curved/flexible branches; WELL, originally a spring from which water "rolled" (bubbled); WALLOW (roll in mud); the WALTZ with its "rolling" motion, and ?? WALK. The Gk HELIX (originally, *welix*) turns on itself.

From L we get the VALVE we turn; the VAULT with its curved, enclosing ceiling, and the VOLUME that originally = a rolled-up piece of writing, now a book (its idiomatic senses include the volume control you turn up or down on a radio or TV). Also L is ? the VALLEY "enclosed" by hills. L compounds include EVOLVE ("unroll"), INVOLVE ("roll up in," hence implicate), and REVOLVE ("turn back or around"), whence the REVOLT or REVOLUTION that seeks to "turn around" a government.

WEL-4, L *vellere*, to tear, pull, whence the CONVULSION that "tears" at the sufferer, and REVULSION ("pulling back"). L *vullis*, shaggy (? "pulled or torn") hair, wool (see next root), > VELVET, with its "shaggy" nap.

WELh-1, Gc WOOL; later (via Celtic) the woolen cloth called FLANNEL.

WELh-2, to strike, wound, whence L VULNERABLE ("woundable").

WELT-, forest, also Gc WILD, whence WILDERNESS ("place of wild beasts").

WEMh-, L *vomere*, *vomit-*, Gk *emein*, to L VOMIT, whence the Gk EMETIC that makes you do it.

WEN-1, to Gc WISH, desire, or strive for, whence Gc WIN. In L the "strive for" sense > *venari*, to hunt, whence VENISON; the "desire" sense > *venus*, love, whence the goddess and planet VENUS, the VENEREAL disease acquired by pursuing love unselectively, and VENOM—originally, a love potion (!). And if we love someone or something sufficiently, we may VENERATE them or it.

WEN-2, to beat or Gc WOUND.

WENDH-, to turn, weave, or Gc WIND, whence the WIND-LASS on which ropes are wound. The "turn/weave" senses > WANDER ("weave back and forth"), also ? the Vandals ("wanderers"), whose destructive incursions into the declining Roman Empire are commemorated in VANDAL.

WENG-, to bend, turn. When we Gc WINK we "turn down" our eyelids; when we WINCE we "bend aside," and ropes are "bent" (rolled) on a turning WINCH.

■ It's interesting—though probably coincidental—that these similar roots should have > words for two very similar mechanisms—winch and windlass.

WEP-, bad, Gc EVIL.

[Germanic WEPNAM, WEAPON.]

WER-1, raised spot, such as a Gc WART. L *varius*, spotty, speckled, hence changeable, > VARIOUS, VARY, and VARIETY.

WER-2, to raise, hold suspended, whence ? Gk ARTERY (the connection, though generally accepted, is obscure). Also ?? related is Gk/L *aer*, AIR, whence AERIAL, AERO-, and MALARIA ("bad air," once thought to be the cause of the disease).

WER-3, the presumed base of a group of similar roots centering on the idea of turning, in some cases also bending, winding, or twisting. The "turning" sense > the Gc suffix -WARD, as in TOWARD ("turned to") and INWARD ("turned in"). WORTH, STALWART, and WEIRD (originally = fate) are ? related to these, but the connection is unclear.

More certainly related are L *vertere*, to turn, and several other similar verbs, whence the VERSATILE (originally = changeable, "turning") person, VERSION (originally = translation, a "turning" from one language into another), VERSUS ("turned against"), the VERTEBRAE that the body turns on, and VERSE, originally a line of writing, from the furrows left by the turning plow-ox. Also the idiomatic CONVERSE, originally = dwell ("move around [a place]"); now hold a conversation with.

Compounds in this group include PROSE ("turned forward" [straightforward] discourse), ADVERSE ("turned against"), AVERT ("turn [something] away"), DIVERT and DIVERGE ("turn from"), ANNIVERSARY ("turn of a year"), CONTROVERSY (when people are "turned against" one another), CONVERT (change or "turn" someone or something), CONVERGE ("turn together"), INVERT (turn upside down), as well as the "turned-out" EXTROVERT and the "turned-in" INTROVERT. A PERVERT has allegedly "turned altogether" from truth or propriety, REVERT = "turn back," SUBVERT = overturn, and the UNIVERSE is "everything turned into one."

The "bend/wind" group includes Gc WRAP ("wind up [in something]"), and the WREATH that is "wound around" (in a circle); the "twist" group includes Gc WRENCH, WRITHE, WARP, WRING, WRINKLE, WRONG ("twisted"), the bendable (and twistable) WRIST, the WRATH that "twists" (torments) us, and the WORRY that figuratively strangles us ("twists the neck"). A special kind of twisting > Gc WRESTLE and WRANGLE (originally = wrestle); yet another > Gc WRIGGLE and WORM, whose L equivalent, *vermis*, > VERMICELLI ("little worms") and VERMIN. These last, however, were influenced by **kwrmi-**.

WER-4, to perceive, watch out for, hence be Gc WARY or AWARE, whence BEWARE and WARN. WARDENS, GUARDS, and STEWARDS watch out for various things, while a WARD-ROBE "guards" your clothes. And a REWARD was the fee someone got for guarding something. (All Gc.)

WER-5, L *operire*, *cooperire*, to COVER, whence COVERT ("covered"—and often covered up). L *aperire*, to uncover or open, > OVERT ("in the open"), the APERITIF that "opens" a meal, and the OVERTURE that opens an opera, as well as the open APERTURE and idiomatic PERT. In Gc the "cover" sense > "protect," whence the GARAGE that protects vehicles and the GARRISON that protects military conquests; a second sense, "equip," > GARMENT and GAR-NISH, while a third, "authorize" (? "cover someone's rear"), > WARRANT and GUARANTEE.

WER-6, WERh-, to speak, whence Gc WORD and L VERB (originally = any word), whence ADVERB ("at [modifying] a verb") and the idiomatic Gk IRONY ("speaking tongue-in-cheek)."

WER-7, to be wet, whence Gk URINE.

WERG-, to do, whence Gc WORK and WROUGHT (wrought iron is "worked"—hammered). Gk *ergon*, work, > the ENERGY it requires, METALLURGY (metalworking), SURGERY ("hand-working"—see **ghesor-**), and the idiomatic ALLERGY ("working of other [foreign] things"). Gk *organon*, device, mechanism (for doing something), > ORGAN—both the mechanism used to make music and the various mechanisms of the body. ORGY (originally = "secret rites") is idiomatic.

WERO-, L *verus*, true, whence VERY (truly, verily), VERIFY ("make [sure it's] true"), and a jury's "true-saying" VERDICT. SEVERE and PERSEVERE are probably not related to this root, though they are to each other. See **deik-**

WERS-1, to confuse, mix up, whence Gc WORSE ("more mixed up"), WORST—and WURST, "mixed up" meat (sausage). Gc WAR (whence GUERRILLA, originally = little war) is also "mixed up"—to say the least.

WES-1, to buy, whence L VEND (if somebody's buying, somebody's selling), and the VENAL official who "vends" himself to the highest bidder.

WES-2, wet, whence Gc to OOZE (seep); compare **weis-**.

WES-3, to stay (overnight), dwell, hence be, whence Gc WAS and WERE; if you stayed overnight in a place, you were there.

WES-4, to clothe, whence Gc WEAR; L *vestis*, garment, > VEST, INVEST (originally, "clothe" with authority; the modern sense is idiomatic), DIVEST (take off, as a garment), and TRAVESTY, "cross-dressing" (? < a man dressed as a woman or vice versa).

WES-PERO-, night, evening, whence Gc WEST—where the evening sun sets. *Hesperus : evening star*
Vesper : evening prayer

WET-1, to blow, inspire (? receive the breath of a god), whence the "inspired" Gc god Woden, whence WEDNESDAY. L *vannus* was a winnowing FAN that blew away the chaff from threshed grain; Gk *atmos* = breath or vapor, whence ATMOSPHERE. *Atman, mahatma : soul*

WET-2, year, whence L VETERAN ("having many years") and VEAL, the meat of a (yearling) calf.

WI-, in half, apart, whence Gc WIDE ("far apart") and the idiomatic WITH.

WIDHU-, tree, whence Gc WOOD—both a collection of trees and the material they yield.

WI-RO-, L *vir*, man, whence VIRILE and VIRTUE ("manly traits"). The Gc equivalent, **wer-*, is all but extinct in English; its only descendant is WEREWOLF, "man-wolf." Gc WORLD originally = human existence, the "age of mankind." *virtù*

WLEIK-, to run, flow, whence L LIQUID and LIQUOR.

WLKWO-, Gc WOLF.

WOGWH-NI-, plowshare, whence Gc WEDGE (the plow-
share "wedges" the soil apart).

[Mediterranean W(O)IN-, L *uinum*, *vinum*, WINE,
whence the VINE that yields it and the VINEGAR made from   See **ak-**
it.]

WOKSO-, Gc WAX.

WOPSA, Gc WASP.

- In some British dialects, wasps are still called "wopses."

WRAD-, branch, also Gc ROOT, L *radix*, *radic-*, whence
RADISH, the RADICAL proposal that supposedly goes to the
root of a problem (see *BLM*), and ERADICATE—root out.

- Note that "root" = dig up is from a different, though
? related, source—see **wrod-2**.

WREG-, to track down, push, shove or drive, whence L
URGE. From Gc we get WRETCH (originally, a "pushed out"
exile) and WRECK (? "drive ashore").

rhododaktulos
[Mediterranean WROD-, L ROSE; Gk RHODODENDRON,   See **deru-**
= "rosy tree." Persian *gulab*, rose water (used as a flavor-
ing in the Middle East), > JULEP.]

WROD-2, to gnaw or Gc ROOT (related to or influenced by
wrad-).

WROG-, to burgeon, swell with strength, whence Gk OR-   *bhel-2*
GASM—from the man's point of view, of course. *cf*

WRUGHYO-, Gc RYE.

[**Germanic WYF,** female person, WOMAN (< OE
wyfman—see **man-1**), whence WIFE. The original
sense survives in HOUSEWIFE, "female person of the
house."]

YA-, to be aroused, whence Gk JEALOUSY and ZEAL—two
different kinds of arousal.

YE-, L *jacere*, *jact-*, to throw; a closely related L verb = to
lie ("be thrown") down. The "throw" group includes the
"thrown" JET of, say, water, INJECT ("throw into"), EJECT
and EJACULATE ("throw out"), PROJECT ("throw forward,"
like a projectile), REJECT ("throw back"), OBJECT ("throw
in front of"), and DEJECTED ("thrown down"—downcast).
The "lie down" group > ABJECT ("lying down" [on one's
belly]), ADJACENT (lying next to), and the ADJECTIVE that
"lies next to" a noun.

YEG-, ice, whence Gc ICICLE—but "ice" is < **eis-2**.

YEK-, to speak, whence L *jocus*, JOKE, whence JOCULAR and
the idiomatic JUGGLE and JEWEL. In VL, joke > game, sport,
See **perh-2**   whence JEOPARDY, a "divided game" whose result was uncertain (see *BLM*).

YEKWR-, liver, whence Gk HEPATITIS., *hepatica*
                                        = liverwort

YER-, season or Gc YEAR. Gk *hora* = season, but also time
of day, whence HOUR and HOROSCOPE.   See **spek-**

YES-, to boil or bubble, whence the Gc YEAST that makes
dough and fermented liquids bubble.

YEU-, vital force, youthful vigor, whence Gc YOUTH and
YOUNG. L *iuvenis*, young, > JUNIOR ("younger"), JUVE-
NILE, and REJUVENATE (make young again).

YEUh-, to blend or mix food, whence L JUICE—which, by
sheer coincidence, is now often made in a blender.

YEUG-, L *jungere, junct-,* to JOIN, whence JUNCTION,
JUNTA (people "joined together"—usually for no good),
ADJOIN ("be joined [next] to"), and the CONJUGAL couple
joined together. Another group of words, found in several
families, derives from the Gc YOKE that joined draft oxen.
L *jugulum* ("little yoke"), the collarbone that "yokes"
the shoulderbone to the breastbone, > the adjacent JUGU-
LAR vein; L SUBJUGATE = "bring under the yoke" (see
BLM); to CONJUGATE originally = to yoke, later, to "yoke
together" the various forms of a verb (I go, thou goest, he
goes, etc.). ADJUST is idiomatic.

YEWES-, L *jus, jur-,* law, whence L JUST ("lawful," fair),
JUSTICE, JUSTIFY ("make lawful"), INJURY (something
"unlawful"); also the JUDGE who gives out the law
within a certain JURISDICTION, and PREJUDICE—prejudging.   See **deik-**
A related L word = to swear a religious or legal oath,
whence the JURY sworn to render a true verdict, ABJURE
("swear off"), PERJURE (break one's oath), and the idiomatic CONJURE.

YOS-, to gird, whence Gk *zone*, girdle, whence the ZONES of latitude (temperate, tropic) that girdle the earth.

YU-1, Gc YOU.

YU-2, an exultant, L JUBILANT outcry.

INDEX OF ENGLISH WORDS

A **OI-NO-**
A- (L prefix) **AD-**
AB- **(A)PO-**
A.M. **MEDHYO-**
ABANDON **BHA-2**
ABASE **BASSUS**
ABASH **BAT-**
ABATE **BATTUERE**
ABBREVIATE **MREGH-U-**
ABCESS **KED-**
ABDICATE **DEIK-**
ABERRATION **ERS-1**
ABHOR **GHERS-**
ABIDE **BHEIDH-**
ABILITY **GHABH-**
ABJECT **YE-**
ABJURE **YEWES-**
ABLE **GHABH-**
ABORT **ER-1**
ABOUND **WED-1**
ABOUT **UD-**
ABOVE **UPO**
ABRIDGE **MREGH-U-**
ABRUPT **REUP-**
ABSENT **ES-**
ABSOLUTE **LEU-1**
ABSORB **SREBH-**
ABSTAIN **TEN-**
ABSURD **SWER-2**
ABUNDANT **WED-1**

ABUT **BHAU-**
ACCEDE **KED-**
ACCELERATE **KEL-3**
ACCENT **KAN-**
ACCEPT **KAP-**
ACCESS **KED-**
ACCIDENT **KAD-**
ACCLAIM **KELh-2**
ACCOMMODATE **MED-**
ACCOMPLISH **PELh-1**
ACCORD **KERD-**
ACCOST **KOST-**
ACCOUNT **PEIL-**
ACCUMULATE **KEUh-2**
ACCURATE **CURA**
ACERBIC **AK-**
ACHE **AG-ES-**
ACID **AK-**
ACNE **AK-**
ACORN **OG-**
ACOUSTIC **KEU-1**
ACQUIESCE **KWEIh-2**
ACQUIRE **QUAERERE**
ACRE **AGRO-**
ACRID **AK-**
ACROBAT **AK-, GWA-**
ACT **AG-**
ACTION **AG-**
ACTIVE **AG-**
AD- **AD-**
ADAGE **EG-**
ADAMANT **DEMh-**
ADAPT **AP-**
ADD **DO-**

ALTERNATE **AL-1**
ALTERNATIVE **AL-1**
ALTITUDE **AL-2**
ALTO **AL-2**
ALTRUISM **AL-1**
ALWAYS **WEGH-**
AM **ES-**
AMATEUR **AMMA**
AMBASSADOR **AG-**
AMBIDEXTROUS **(AM)BHO-, DEKS-**
AMBIENCE **EI-1**
AMBITION **EI-1**
AMBUSH **BUSK-**
AMEND **MEND-**
AMETHYST **MEDHU-**
AMICABLE **AMMA**
AMID **MEDHYO-**
AMISS **MEI-1**
AMMUNITION **MEI-2**
AMNESIA **MEN-1**
AMNESTY **MEN-1**
AMOEBA **MEI-1**
AMONG **MAG-**
AMOUNT **MEN-2**
AMPHIBIOUS **(AM)BHO-, GWEI-**
AMPLE **AMPLUS**
AMPLIFY **AMPLUS**
AMPUTATE **PEU-**
AN **OI-NO-**
ANALYSIS **LEU-1**
ANATOMY **TEM(h)-**
ANCESTOR **KED-**
ANCHOR **ANG-**
ANCIENT **ANT-**
AND **EN**
ANECDOTE **DO-**
ANESTHETIC **AU-2**
ANGEL **ANGELOS**
ANGER **ANGH-**

ANGINA **ANGH-**
ANGLE **ANG-**
ANGLER **ANG-**
ANGUISH **ANGH-**
ANIMAL **ANh-**
ANIMATE **ANh-**
ANIMOSITY **ANh-**
ANKLE **ANG-**
ANNEX **NED-**
ANNIHILATE **NE**
ANNIVERSARY **AT-, WER-3**
ANNOUNCE **NEU-1**
ANNOY **OD-2**
ANNUAL **AT-**
ANNUITY **AT-**
ANNUL **NE**
ANOINT **ONGW-**
ANONYMOUS **NO-MEN-**
ANSWER **SWER-1**
ANT **MAI-1**
ANTAGONIST **AG-**
ANTARCTIC **ANT-, RTKO-**
ANTE **ANT-**
ANTHEM **BHA-2**
ANTHROPOLOGY **WER-2**
ANTI- **ANT-**
ANTICIPATE **KAP-**
ANTIDOTE **DO-**
ANTIPASTO **PA-**
ANTONYM **NO-MEN-**
ANUS **ANO-**
ANVIL **PEL-6**
ANXIOUS **ANGH-**
ANY **OI-NO-**
APERITIF **WER-5**
APERTURE **WER-5**
APOLOGY **LEG-1**
APOPLEXY **PLAK-2**
APPALL **PEL-2**
APPEAL **PEL-6**
APPEASE **PAG-**

ASTRO- **STER-3**
ASUNDER **SEN-2**
AT **AD-**
ATHEIST **DHES-**
ATLANTIC **TELh-**
ATLAS **TELh-**
ATMOSPHERE **WET-1**
ATOM- **TEM(h)-**
ATONE **OI-NO-**
ATRIUM **ATER-**
ATROCIOUS **ATER-**
ATTACH **STEG-**
ATTACK **STEG-**
ATTAIN **TAG-1**
ATTEND **TEN-**
ATTENUATE **TEN-**
ATTEST **TREI-**
ATTIRE **SA-**
ATTRACT **TRAGH-**
ATTRITION **TERh-1**
AUCTION **AUG-**
AUDIBLE **AU-2**
AUDIENCE **AU-2**
AUDIO- **AU-2**
AUDIT **AU-2**
AUDITORIUM **AU-2**
AUGER **NOBH-**
AUGHT **WEKTI-**
AUGMENT **AUG-**
AUK **EL-2**
AUNT **AMMA**
AURORA **AUS-1**
AUSPICES **AWI-**
AUSTERE **SAUS-**
AUTHOR **AUG-**
AUTHORITY **AUG-**
AUTOMATIC **MEN-1**
AUTONOMOUS **NEM-**
AUTOPSY **OKW-**
AVAIL **WAL-**
AVENUE **GWA-**

AVERT **WER-3**
AVIARY **AWI-**
AVIATOR **AWI-**
AWARE **WEG-2**
AWAKE **WER-4**
AWE **AGH-1**
AWKWARD **(A)PO-**
AX **AGWESI-**
AXIS **AKS-**
AXLE **AKS-**
AZALEA **AS-**

BABBLE **BABA-**
BABY **BABA-**
BACILLUS **BAK-**
BACK **BAKKON**
BACON **BAKKON**
BACTERIA **BAK-**
BAD **BHAD-**
BAGEL **BHEUG-3**
BAIRN **BHER-1**
BAKE **BHE-**
BALCONY **BHELG-**
BALE **BHEL-2**
BALL (round object)
   BHEL-2
BALL (dance) **GWELh-1**
BALLAD **GWELh-1**
BALLET **GWELh-1**
BALLOON **BHEL-2**
BALLOT **BHEL-2**
BAN **BHA-2**
BANAL **BHA-2**
BAND **BHENDH-**
BANDANNA **BHENDH-**
BANDIT **BHA-2**

BETRAY **DO-**
BETROTH **DERU-**
BETTER **BHAD-**
BETWEEN **DWO-**
BEVEL **BAT-**
BEVERAGE **PO(I)-**
BEWARE **WER-4**
BEWITCH **WEIK-2**
BICYCLE **KWEL-1**
BID **BHEUDH-, GWHEDH-**
BIER **BHER-1**
BILINGUAL **DNGHU-**
BILL (birds) **BHEI-2**
BILL (money, etc.) **BEU-1**
BILLOW **BHELGH-**
BIND **BHENDH-**
BINN **BHENDH-**
BIRCH **BHERhG**
BIRTH **BHER-1**
BISCUIT **PEKW-**
BISHOP **SPEK-**
BISON **WEIS-**
BIT (piece) **BHEID-**
BITE **BHEID-**
BLACK **BHEL-1**
BLADDER **BHLE-2**
BLADE **BHEL-3**
BLAME **BHA-2**
BLARE **BHLE-1**
BLASPHEMY **BHA-2**
BLAST **BHLE-2**
BLATHER **BHLE-2**
BLAZE **BHEL-1**
BLEACH **BHEL-1**
BLEAK **BHEL-1**
BLEAT **BHLE-1**
BLEMISH **BHEL-1**
BLEND **BHEL-1**
BLIND **BHEL-1**
BLISTER **BHLEI-**
BLOND(E) **BHEL-1**

BLOOM **BHEL-3**
BLOW **BHLE-2**
BLUE **BHEL-1**
BLUSH **BHEL-1**
BOAR **BHER-**
BOARD **BHERDH-**
BOAST **BEU-**
BOAT **BHEID-**
BOG **BHEUG-3**
BOIL **BEU-**
BOLD **BHEL-2**
BOLE **BHEL-2**
BOLLIX **BHEL-2**
BOLLOCKS **BHEL-2**
BOLSHEVIK **BEL-**
BOLSTER **BHELGH-**
BOLT **BHELD-**
BOMB **BAMB-**
BONANZA **DEU-2**
BONBON **DEU-2**
BOND (finance) **BHENDH-**
BONDAGE **BHEU(h)-**
BONUS **DEU-2**
BOOBY **BABA-**
BOODLE **BHEU-**
BOOK **BHAGO-**
BOON (companion) **DEU-2**
BOON (gift) **BHA-2**
BOOTH **BHEU-**
BORDELLO **BHERDH-**
BORDER **BHERDH-**
BORE (drill) **BHER-2**
BOROUGH **BHERGH-2**
BORROW **BHERGH-1**
BOSOM **BEU-**
BOTH **(AM)BHO-**
BOTTOM **BHUDH-**
BOUGH **BHAGU-**
BOULDER **BHEL-2**
BOUND (leap) **BAMB-**
BOUND (going) **BHEU-**

BOUNTY **DEU-2**
BOUQUET **BUSK-**
BOURGEOIS **BHERGH-2**
BOW **BHEUG-3**
BOWEL **GWET-3**
BOWER **BHEU-**
BOWL **BHEL-2**
BOWLING **BEU-1**
BOX **PUXOS**
BRAIN **MREGH-M(N)O-**
BRAMBLE **BHREM-**
BRAND **GWHER-**
BRANDISH **GWHER-**
BRANDY **GWHER-**
BRASS **FERRUM**
BRASSIERE **MREGH-U-**
BREACH **BHREG-**
BREAD **BHREU-2**
BREAK **BHREG-**
BREAKFAST **PAST-**
BREAST **BHREUS-1**
BREATH **GWHRE-**
BREECH **BRAK-**
BREED **BHREU-2**
BREW **BHREU-2**
BRIDE **BRUDHIZ**
BRIDEGROOM **DHGHEM-**
BRIDGE **BHRU-**
BRIEF **MREGH-U-**
BRIGHT **BHERhG**
BRIM **BHREM-**
BRING **BHER-1**
BRISTLE **BHAR-**
BRITTLE **BHREU-1**
BRONCHITIS **GWERh-3**
BROOD **BHREU-2**
BROOM **BHREM-**
BROTHER **BHRATER-**
BROW **BHRU-**
BROWN **BHER-3**
BROWSE **BHREUS-1**

BRUISE **BHREUS-2**
BRUNET(TE) **BHER-3**
BRUTAL **GWERh-1**
BRUTE **GWERh-1**
BUCK (male animal)
BHUGO-
BUCKAROO **WAK-**
BUCKLE **BEU-1**
BUCKWHEAT **BHAGO-**
BUCOLIC **GWOU-**
BUDGE **BEU-1**
BUDGET **BHELGH-**
BUILD **BHEU-**
BULGE **BHELGH-**
BULK **BHEL-2**
BULL **BHEL-2**
BULLETIN **BEU-1**
BULLY **BUOLE**
BULWARK **BHEL-2**
BUNDLE **BHENDH-**
BUNGLE **BHEG-**
BURDEN **BHER-1**
BURG **BHERGH-2**
BURGHER **BHERGH-2**
BURGLAR **BHERGH-2**
BURN **GWHER-**
BURR **BHAR-**
BURST **BHRES-**
BURY **BHERGH-1**
BUS **OP-1**
BUSH **BUSK-**
BUT **UD-**
BUTCHER **BHUGO-**
BUTT **BHAU-**
BUTTER **GWOU-, TEU(h)-**
BUTTOCK **BHAU-**
BUTTON **BHAU-**
BUTTRESS **BHAU-**
BUXOM **BHEUG-3**
BY **(A)MBHI-**
BYTE **BHEID-**

CAB **KAPRO-**
CABLE **KAP-**
CADENCE **KAD-**
CADET **KAPUT**
CAGE **KEUh-2**
CAKE **KAK-2**
CALAMITY **KEL-1**
CALDRON **KELh-1**
CALENDAR **KELh-2**
CALIBER **PED-1**
CALL **GAL-2**
CALLOUS **KAL-2**
CALLOW **GAL-1**
CALLUS **KAL-2**
CALM **KEU-3**
CALORIE **KELh-1**
CALUMNY **KEL-7**
CAMERA **KAMER-**
CAN (be able) **GNO-**
CANAL **KANNA**
CANCEL **CARCER**
CANCER **KAR-1**
CANDID **KAND-**
CANDIDATE **KAND-**
CANDLE **KAND-**
CANE **KANNA**
CANINE **KWON-**
CANNABIS **KANNABIS**
CANNON **KANNA**
CANTEEN **KANTO-**
CANTOR **KAN-**
CANVAS **KANNABIS**
CANYON **KANNA**
CAPE **KAPUT**
CAPER **KAPRO-**
CAPITAL **KAPUT**
CAPON **(S)KEP-**

CAPSULE **KAP-**
CAPTAIN **KAPUT**
CAPTION **KAP-**
CAPTIVATE **KAP-**
CAPTIVE **KAP-**
CAPTURE **KAP-**
CAR **KERS-**
CARAT **KER-1**
CARBON **KER-4**
CARE **GAR-**
CAREER **KERS-**
CARESS **KA-**
CARGO **KERS-**
CARICATURE **KERS-**
CARIES **KER-5**
CARNAL **SKER-1**
CARNATION **SKER-1**
CARNIVAL **SKER-1,**
  LEGWH-
CARNIVOROUS **SKER-1**
CAROL **AULO-**
CAROUSE **UD-**
CARPENTER **KERS-**
CARPET **KERP-**
CARRIAGE **KERS-**
CARRION **SKER-1**
CARROT **KER-1**
CARRY **KERS-**
CART **GER-2, KERS-**
CARVE **GERBH-**
CASCADE **KAD-**
CASE (container) **KAP-**
CASE (instance) **KAD-**
CASEMENT **KAD-**
CASH **KAP-**
CASTE **KES-2**
CASTLE **KES-2**
CASTRATE **KES-2**
CATACLYSM **KLEU-2**
CATALOGUE **LEG-1**
CATASTROPHE **STREB(H)-**

-CIDE **KAh-ID-**
CINCH **KENK-1**
CINDER **SENDHRO-**
CINEMA **KEI-3**
CIRCLE **(S)KER-**
CIRCUIT **(S)KER-, EI-1**
CIRCUM- **(S)KER-**
CIRCUMLOCUTION **(S)KER-, TOLKW-**
CIRCUMSPECT **(S)KER-, SPEK-**
CIRCUMSTANCE **(S)KER-, STA-**
CISTERN **KISTA**
CITIZEN **KEI-1**
CITY **KEI-1**
CIVIC **KEI-1**
CIVIL **KEI-1**
CIVILIAN **KEI-1**
CIVILIZE **KEI-1**
CLAIM **KELh-2**
CLATTER **GAL-2**
CLAM **GEL-1**
CLAMMY **GEL-1**
CLAMOR **KELh-2**
CLAMP **GEL-1**
CLAN **PLAT-**
CLANDESTINE **KEL-2**
CLANG **KLEG-**
CLASS **KELh-2**
CLATTER **GAL-2**
CLAW **GEL-1**
CLAY **GEL-1**
CLEAN **GEL-2**
CLEAR **KELh-2**
CLEAVE **GLEUBH-**
CLENCH **GEL-1**
CLERGY **KEL-1**
CLEAT **GEL-**
CLERK **KEL-1**
CLEVER **GLEUBH-**

CLIENT **KLEI-**
CLIMATE **KLEI-**
CLIMAX **KLEI-**
CLIMB **GEL-1**
CLINCH **GEL-1**
CLING **GEL-1**
CLINIC **KLEI-**
CLIP (fasten) **GEL-1**
CLOD **GEL-1**
CLONE **KEL-1**
CLOSE **KLEU-3**
CLOT **GEL-1**
CLOUD **GEL-1**
CLOUT **GEL-1**
CLOVE (garlic) **GLEUBH-**
CLOVE (spice) **KLEU-3**
CLUB **GEL-1**
CLUE **GEL-1**
CLUMP **GEL-1**
CLUTCH **GEL-**
CO- **KOM**
COAGULATE **AG-**
COAL **G(E)U-LO-**
COAST **KOST-**
COCK (rooster) **KU-**
COCKLE **KONK(H)O-**
CODEINE **KEUh-2**
COERCE **AREK-**
COHABIT **GHABH-**
COHERE **GHAIS-**
COITUS **EI-1**
COLANDER **KAGH-**
COLD **GEL-3**
COLESLAW **KAUL-**
COLLABORATE **LEB-1**
COLLAPSE **LEB-1**
COLLAR **KWEL-1**
COLLEAGUE **LEG-1**
COLONEL **KEL-5**
COLONY **KWEL-1**
COLUMN **KEL-5**

CRUEL **KREUh-**
CRULLER **GER-2**
CRUMB **GER-2**
CRUMPLE **GER-2**
CRUST **KREUS-**
CRUSTACEAN **KREUS-**
CRUTCH **GER-2**
CRYPT **KRAU-**
CRYPTIC **KRAU-**
CRYPTO- **KRAU-**
CRYSTAL **KREUS-**
CUBBY **KU-**
CUBE **KEU-2**
CUBICLE **KEU-2**
CUDGEL **KU-**
CUISINE **PEKW-**
CULMINATE **KEL-5**
CULOTTES **(S)KEU-**
CULT **KWEL-1**
CULTIVATE **KWEL-1**
CULTURE **KWEL-1**
CUMULUS **KEUh-2**
CUNNING **GNO-**
CUNT **KU-**
CUP **KEU-2**
CUPID **KWEP-**
CURATOR **CURA**
CURB **(S)KER-**
CURD **GREUT-**
CURIOUS **CURA**
CURL **GER-2**
CURRENT **KERS-**
CURSOR **KERS-**
CURT **SKER-1**
CURVE **(S)KER-**
CUSHION **KOKSA**
CUSTOM **S(W)E-**
CUTLASS **SKEL-1**
CUTLET **KOST-**
CUTTLEFISH **KU-**
CYCLE **KWEL-1**

CYCLONE **KWEL-1**
CYMBAL **KEU-2**
CYNIC **KWON-**

DAINTY **DEK-1**
DAIRY **DHEIGH-**
DAISY **AGH-2, OKW-**
DALE **DHEL-**
DAMAGE **DAP-**
DAMN **DAP-**
DANDELION **DENT-**
DANE **DAN-**
DANGER **DEM(h)-**
DARE **DHERS-**
DARK **DHER-1**
DATA **DO-**
DATE **DO-**
DAUGHTER **DHUGhTER-**
DAWN **AGH-2**
DAY(BREAK) **AGH-2**
DE- **DWO-**
DEACON **KEN-1**
DEAD **DHEU-3**
DEAF **DHEU-1**
DEAL **DAIL-**
DEAN **DEKM-**
DEATH **DHEU-3**
DEBASE **BASSUS**
DEBATE **BATTUERE**
DEBAUCH **BHELG-**
DEBILITATE **BEL-**
DEBRIS **BHREI-**
DEBT **GHABH-**
DECADE **DEKM-**
DECADENT **KAD-1**
DECAPITATE **KAPUT**

DRAGON **DERK-**
DRAIN **DREUG-**
DRAMA **DERh**
DRAPE **DER-2**
DRASTIC **DERh**
DRAW **DHRAGH-**
DREAM **DHREUGH-**
DREARY **DHREU-**
DREGS **DHER-1**
DRENCH **DHRAGH-**
DRIFT **DHREIBH-**
DRILL **TERh-1**
DRINK **DHRAGH-**
DRIP **DHREU-**
DRIVE **DHREIBH-**
DRIVEL **DHER-1**
DRIZZLE **DHREU-**
DROMEDARY **DER-1**
DROOP **DHREU-**
DROP **DHREU-**
DROUGHT **DREUG-**
DROWN **DHRAGH-**
DROWSE **DHREU-**
DRUNK **DHRAGH-**
DRY **DREUG-**
DUBIOUS **DWO-**
DUCT **DEUK-**
DUE **GHABH-**
DUEL **DUELLUM**
DUET **DWO-**
DUKE **DEUK-**
DULL **DHEU-1**
DUMB **DHEU-1**
DUMP **DUB-**
DUNE **DHUNO-**
DUNG **DUNGA**
DUNGEON **DEM(h)-**
DUNK **TENG-**
DUPLICATE **DWO-, PEL-2**
DUPLICITY **DWO-, PEL-2**
DURABLE **DEUh-**

DURATION **DEUh-**
DURING **DEUh-**
DUSK **DHEU-1**
DUST **DHEU-1**
DUTCH **TEUTA-**
DUTY **GHABH-**
DWINDLE **DHEU-3**
DYNAMIC **DEU-2**
DYNAMITE **DEU-2**
DYNAMO **DEU-2**
DYNASTY **DEU-2**

E- **EGHS**
EACH **LIK-**
EAGER **AK-**
EAR **OUS-**
EARLY **AYER-**
EARN **ESEN-**
EARNEST **ER-1**
EARTH **ER-2**
EASEL **ASINUS**
EAST **AUS-1**
EASTER **AUS-1**
EAT **ED-**
EAVES **UPO**
EAVESDROP **UPO**
EBB **(A)PO-**
EBULLIENT **B(H)EU-**
ECCENTRIC **KENT-**
ECHO **(S)WAGH-**
ECLAIR **KELh-2**
ECLIPSE **LEIKW-**
ECOLOGY **WEIK-1**
ECONOMY **WEIK-1**
ECSTASY **STA-**
-ECTOMY **TEM-**

EDEMA **OID-**
EDGE **AK-**
EDIBLE **ED-**
EDIT(ION) **DO-**
EDUCATE **DEUK-**
EFFACE **DHE-**
EFFECT **DHE-**
EFFERVESCENT **BHREU-2**
EFFETE **DHE(I)-**
EFFICIENT **DHE-**
EFFORT **BHERGH-2**
EGG (birds) **AWI-**
EGG (someone on) **AK-**
EGOIST **EG**
EGREGIOUS **GER-1**
EIDER **ETI-**
EIGHT **OKTO(U)**
EITHER **KWO-**
EJACULATE **YE-**
EJECT **YE-**
ELAPSE **LEB-1**
ELATE **TELh-**
ELBOW **EL-1**
ELDER (older) **AL-3**
ELEVATE **LEGWH-**
ELEVEN **OI-NO-**
ELIXIR **KSERO-**
ELK **EL-2**
ELM **EL-2**
ELONGATE **DEL-1**
ELOPE **KLOU-**
ELSE **AL-1**
ELUCIDATE **LEUK-**
ELUDE **LEID-**
EMACIATE **MAK-**
EMANCIPATE **MAN-2**
EMASCULATE **MAS**
EMBELLISH **DEU-2**
EMBER **EUS-**
EMBRACE **MREGH-U-**
EMERGE **MEZG-1**

EMETIC **WEMh-**
EMIGRATE **MEI-1**
EMINENT **MEN-2**
EMIT **(S)MEIT(h)-**
EMOTION **MEUh-**
EMPEROR **PERh-1**
EMPHASIS **BHA-1**
EMPHATIC **BHA-1**
EMPLOY **PLEK-**
EMPTY **MED-**
EN- **EN**
ENAMOR **AMMA**
ENCHANT **KAN-**
ENCLOSE **KLEU-3**
ENCOUNTER **KOM**
ENCROACH **GER-2**
ENCYCLOPEDIA **PAU-**
ENDORSE **DORSUM**
ENDOW **DO-**
ENDURE **DERU-**
ENEMY **AMMA**
ENERGY **WERG-**
ENFORCE **BHERGH-2**
ENGAGE **WADH-1**
ENGINE **GENh-**
ENGRAVE **GHREBH-2**
ENHANCE **AL-2**
ENJOY **GAU-**
ENNUI **OD-2**
ENOUGH **NEK-2**
ENSEMBLE **SEM-1**
ENSURE **CURA**
ENTER **EN**
ENTERPRISE **GHE(N)D-**
ENTERTAIN **TEN-**
ENTHUSIASM **DHES-**
ENTIRE **TAG-1**
ENTREPRENEUR **GHE(N)D-**
ENUMERATE **NEM-**
ENVY **WEID-**
EPIC **WEKW-**

EXPURGATE **PEUh-**
EXQUISITE **QUAERERE**
EXTEND **TEN-**
EXTENUATE **TEN-**
EXTERIOR **EGHS**
EXTERMINATE **TER-**
EXTERNAL **EGHS**
EXTINGUISH **STEIG-**
EXTORT **TERKW-**
EXTRA- **EGHS**
EXTRACT **TRAGH-**
EXTREME **EGHS**
EXTROVERT **WER-3**
EXTRUDE **TREUD-**
EXUBERANT **EUhDH-**
EXULT **SEL-4**
EYE **OKW-**
EYELET **OKW-**

FABLE **BHA-2**
FABRIC **DHABH-**
FABRICATE **DHABH-**
FABULOUS **BHA-2**
FACADE **DHE-**
FACE **DHE-**
FACILE **DHE-**
FACILITY **DHE-**
FACT **DHE-**
FACTION **DHE-**
FACTOR(Y) **DHE-**
FAINT **DHE(I)-**
FAIR (festival) **DHES-**
FAIR (just, pretty) **PEK-1**
FAITH **BHEIDH-**
FALCON **PEL-2**
FALL **P(H)OL-**

FAME **BHA-2**
FAMOUS **BHA-2**
FAN **WET-1**
FANATIC **DHES-**
FANG **PAG-**
FANTASY **BHA-1**
FAR **PER-1**
FARE **PER-2**
FARM **DHER-2**
FARRIER **FERRUM**
FART **PERD-**
FARTHER **PER-1**
FASHION **DHE-**
FAST (all senses) **PAST-**
FASTEN **PAST-**
FAT **PELh-**
FATE **BHA-2**
FATHER **PhTER-**
FATHOM **PET(h)-**
FAVA (bean) **BHA-BHA-**
FAVOR **GHOW-E-**
FEAR **PER-4**
FEASIBLE **DHE-**
FEAST **DHES-**
FEAT **DHE-**
FEATHER **PET(h)-**
FEATURE **DHE-**
FEDERAL **BHEIDH-**
FEE **PEKU-**
FEEBLE **BHLE-1**
FEED **PA-**
FEEL **POL-**
FEIGN **DHE(I)-**
FEISTY **PEZD-**
FELL (cut down) **P(H)OL-**
FELLATIO **DHE(I)-**
FELLOW **PEKU-, LEGH-**
FELT (fabric) **PEL-6**
FEMALE **DHE(I)-**
FEMININE **DHE(I)-**
FENCE **GWHEN-1**

FLING **PLAK-2**
FLINT **SPLEI-**
FLOAT **PLEU-**
FLOG **BHLAG-**
FLOOD **PLEU-**
FLOOR **PELh-2**
FLORID **BHEL-3**
FLORIST **BHEL-3**
FLOTILLA **PLEU-**
FLOUNDER (fish) **PLAT-**
FLOUR **BHEL-3**
FLOURISH **BHEL-3**
FLOW **PLEU-**
FLOWER **BHEL-3**
FLUCTUATE **BHLEU-**
FLUENT **BHLEU-**
FLUID **BHLEU-**
FLUKE (fish) **PLAK-1**
FLUSH **BHLEU-**
FLUSTER **PLEU-**
FLUTTER **PLEU-**
FLY **PLEU-**
FOAL **PAU-**
FOAM **(S)POI-MO-**
FODDER **PA-**
FOE **PEIG-2**
FOIL (metal) **BHEL-3**
FOLD **PEL-3**
-FOLD **PEL-3**
FOLIAGE **BHEL-3**
FOLK **UOLCAE**
FOOD **PA-**
FOOL **BHEL-2**
FOOT **PED-1**
FOR **PER-1**
FOR- **PER-1**
FORAGE **PA-**
FORBEAR **BHER-1**
FORBID **BHEUDH-,**
FORCE **BHERGH-2**
FORD **PER-2**

FORE- **PER-1**
FORECLOSE **DHWER-**
FOREGO **GHE-**
FOREIGN **DHWER-**
FOREMOST **PER-1**
FOREST **DHWER-**
FORESTALL **STEL-**
FOREVER **AIW-**
FORFEIT **DHE-**
FORGE **DHABH-**
FORGET **GHE(N)D-**
FORGIVE **GHABH-**
FORGO **GHE-**
FORLORN **LEU-1**
FORM **MERPH-**
FORMAL **MERPH-**
FORMULA **MERPH-**
FORNICATE **GWHER-**
FORSAKE **SAG-**
FORT(RESS) **BHERGH-2**
FORTE **BHERGH-2**
FORTH **PER-1**
FORTIFY **BHERGH-2**
FORTITUDE **BHERGH-2**
FORTY **KWETWER-**
FOSSIL **BHEDH-**
FOSTER **PA-**
FOUL **PU-**
FOUND (establish)
BHUDH-
FOUNDRY **GHEU-**
FOUNDATION **BHUDH-**
FOUNTAIN **DHEN-**
FOUR(TEEN) **KWETWER-**
FOURTH **KWETWER-**
FOWL **PLEU-**
FOX **PUK-2**
FRACTION **BHREG-**
FRACTURE **BHREG-**
FRAGILE **BHREG-**
FRAGRANT **BHRAG-**

FRAIL **BHREG-**
FRANCE **FRANKON-**
FRANK **FRANKON-**
FRATERNAL **BHRATER-**
FRATERNITY **BHRATER-**
FRECKLE **(S)PREG-**
FREE **PRI-**
FREEZE **PREUS**
FREIGHT **EIK-**
FRENCH **FRANKON-**
FRENETIC **GWHREN-**
FRENZY **GWHREN-**
FREQUENT **BREKW-**
FRET (vex) **ED-**
FRIDAY **PRI-**
FRIEND **PRI-**
FRIGID **SRIG-**
FRITTER (dissipate) **PED-2**
FROLIC **LIK-**
FROM **PER-1**
FROST **PREUS-**
FRUIT **BHRUG-**
FRY **BHER-4**
FUCK **PEUK-**
FUGITIVE **BHEUG-1**
FÜHRER **PER-2**
FULFILL **PELh-1**
FULL **PELh-1**
FUME **DHEU-1**
FUNCTION **BHEUG-2**
FUND **BHUDH-**
FUNDAMENTAL **BHUDH-**
FUNNEL **GHEU-**
FUR **PA-**
FURLOUGH **LEUBH-**
FURNACE **GWHER-**
FURNISH **PER-1**
FURNITURE **PER-1**
FURROW **PERK-2**
FURTHER **PER-1**
FURTIVE **BHER-1**

FUSE **GHEU-**
FUTILE **GHEU-**
FUTURE **BHEU-**
FUZZY **PU-**
-FY **DHE-**

GABLE **GHEBH-EL-**
GAIN **WEI-2**
GAINSAY **GAGINA**
GAIT **GHE-**
GALAXY **MELG-**
GALL **GHEL-2**
GALLOP **WEL-2, KLOU-**
GALLOWS **GHALGH-**
GAMBIT **KAMP-**
GAMBOL **KAMP-**
-GAMY **GEMh-**
GANDER **GHANS-**
GANNET **GHANS-**
GAOL **KEUh-2**
GAP **GHAI-**
GAPE **GHAI-**
GARB **GARWIAN**
GARAGE **WER-5**
GARBLE **KREI-**
GARDEN **GHER-1**
GARLIC **GHAISO-**
GARMENT **WER-5**
GARNISH **WER-5**
GARRISON **WER-5**
GARRULOUS **GAR-**
GAS **GHEU-**
GASH **GHER-4**
GASP **GHAI-**
GATHER **GHEDH-**
GAUDY **GAR-**

CRACKLE **GERE-2**
GRADE **GHREDH-**
GRAFFITO **GERBH-**
GRAIN **GREN-NO-**
GRAMMAR **GERBH-**
GRANITE **GREN-NO-**
GRANT **KERD-**
GRAPE **GER-2**
GRAPH(IC) **GERBH-**
GRAPHITE **GERBH-**
GRAPNEL **GER-2**
GRAPPLE **GER-2**
GRASP **GHREBH-1**
GRASS **GHRE-**
GRATE (scrape) **GRAT-**
GRATE (fireplace) **KERT-**
GRATEFUL **GWERh-2**
GRATIFY **GWERh-2**
GRATING **KERT-**
GRATITUDE **GWERh-2**
GRATUITY **GWERh-2**
GRAVE (burial) **GHREBH-2**
GRAVE (serious) **GWERh-1**
GRAVEL **GHREU-**
GRAVITY **GWERh-1**
GRAY **GHER-3**
GREAT **GHREU-**
GREEDY **GHER-5**
GREEN **GHRE-**
GREET **GHER-2**
GREGARIOUS **GER-1**
GRENADE **GREN-NO-**
GRID **KERT-**
GRIDDLE **KERT-**
GRIEF **GWERh-1**
GRIM **GHREM-**
GRIMACE **GHREM-**
GRIME **GHREI-**
GRIND **GHRENDH-**
GRIP **GHREIB-**
GRIPPE **GHREIB-**

GRISLY **GHREI-**
GRIT **GHREU-**
GROCER **GWRES-**
GROOVE **GHREBH-2**
GROPE **GHREIB-**
GROSS **GWRES-**
GROW **GHRE-**
GRUDGE **GRU-**
GRUESOME **GHREU-**
GRUFF **KREUP-**
GRUMBLE **GHREM-**
GRUNT **GRU-**
GRUESOME **GHREU-**
GUARANTEE **WER-5**
GUARD **WER-4**
GUERRILLA **WERS-1**
GUESS **GHE(N)D-**
GUEST **GHOS-TI-**
GUIDE **WEID-**
GUILE **WEIK-2**
GUISE **WEID-**
GULF **KWELP-**
GULLET **GWEL-3**
GUM (teeth) **GHEU-**
GUSH **GHEU-**
GUST **GHEU-**
GUSTO **GEUS-**
GUT **GHEU-1**
GYMNASIUM **NOGW-**
GYMNAST **NOGW-**
GYNECOLOGY **GWEN-**

HABIT **GHABH-**
HABITAT **GHABH-**
HACK (chop) **KEG-**
HAFT **KAP-**

HAIL (ice) **KAGHLO-**
HALE **KAILO-**
HALF **SKEL-1**
HALL **KEL-2**
HALLOW **KAILO-**
HALLUCINATE **ALU-**
HALT **KEL-3**
HALTER **KELP-**
HAM **KONhMO-**
HAMLET **TKEI-**
HAMMER **AK-**
HANDKERCHIEF **KAPUT-**
HANG **KONK-**
HANKER **KONK-**
HAPLESS **KOB-**
HAPPEN **KOB-**
HAPPY **KOB-**
HARBINGER **KORO-**
HARBOR **KORO-**
HARD(Y) **KAR-1**
HARE **KAS-**
HARM **KORMO-**
HARMONY **AR-**
HARPOON **SERP-1**
HARRY **KORO-**
HARVEST **KERP-**
HASH **(S)KEP-**
HAT **KADH-**
HATCHET **(S)KEP-**
HATE **KAD-**
HAUL **KELh-2**
HAUNT **TKEI-**
HAVE **KAP-**
HAWK **KAP-**
HAWKER **KEU-2**
HAWTHORN **KAGH-**
HAY **KAU-2**
HAZEL **KOSELO-**
HE **KO-**
HEAD **KAPUT**
HEALTH **KAILO-**

HEAP **KEU-2**
HEAR **KEU-1**
HEART(Y) **KERD-**
HEARTH **KER-4**
HEAT **KAI-**
HEATH **KAITO-**
HEATHEN **KAITO-**
HEAVE **KAP-**
HEAVEN **AK-**
HEAVY **KAP-**
HECKLE **KEG-**
HECTIC **SEGH-**
HEDGE **KAGH-**
HEEL (foot) **KENK-3**
HEEL (tilt) **KEL-4**
HEIFER **PER-3**
HEIGHT **KEU-2**
HEINOUS **KAD-2**
HEIR **GHE-**
HELIUM **SAWEL-**
HELIX **WEL-2**
HELL **KEL-2**
HELM (boat) **KELP-**
HELMET **KEL-2**
HELP **KELB-**
HELVE **KELP-**
HEM (sewing) **KEM-2**
HEMI- **SEMI-**
HEMP **KANNABIS**
HEN **KAN-**
HEPATITIS **YEKWR-**
HER **KO-**
HERALD **KORO-**
HERD **KERDH-**
HERE **KO-**
HEREDITY **GHE-**
HERITAGE **GHE-**
HERMIT **ERh-2**
HERNIA **GHERh-**
HERO **SER-1**
HERPES **SERP-2**

HYDRO- **WED-1**
HYENA **SU-**
HYGIENE **GWEI(h)-**
HYPER- **UPER**
HYPNOSIS **SWEP-1**
HYPO- **UPO**
HYPODERMIC **DER-2**
HYPOCRITE **KREI-**
HYSTERECTOMY **UDERO-**
HYSTERIA **UDERO-**

I **EG**
ICONOCLAST **WEIK-**
ID **I-**
ICE **EIS-2**
ICICLE **YEG-**
IDEA **WEID-**
IDENTICAL **I-**
IDENTIFY **I-**
IDEO- **WEID-**
IDIOM **S(W)E-**
IDIOT **S(W)E-**
IF **I-**
INGENIOUS **GEN(h)-**
IGNEOUS **EGNI-**
IGNITE **EGNI-**
IGNOMINY **NO-MEN-**
IGNORANT **GNO-**
IGNORE **GNO-**
IKON **WEIK-**
ILLITERATE **DEPH-**
ILLUMINATE **LEUK-**
ILLUSION **LEID-**
ILLUSTRATE **LEUK-**
IM- **EN**
IMMACULATE **MACULA**

IMMENSE **ME-2**
IMMERSE **MEZG-1**
IMMIGRATE **MEI-1**
IMMINENT **MEN-2**
IMMUNE **MEI-1**
IMPAIR **PED-1**
IMPEACH **PED-1**
IMPECCABLE **PED-1**
IMPECUNIOUS **PEKU-**
IMPEDE **PED-1**
IMPEL **PEL-6**
IMPERIAL **PERh-1**
IMPLEMENT **PELh-1**
IMPLICATE **PLEK-**
IMPOSE **(A)PO-**
IMPOUND **BEND-**
IMPREGNABLE **GHE(N)D-**
IMPRESS **PER-5**
IMPROVE **PER-1**
IMPUDENT **(S)PEUD-**
IMPUNITY **KWEI-1**
IN **EN-**
IN- **EN**
INCANTATION **KAN-**
INCARCERATE **CARCER**
INCARNATE **SKER-1**
INCENDIARY **KAND-**
INCENSE **KAND-**
INCH **OI-NO-**
INCIDENT **KAD-**
INCINERATE **KENI-**
INCISION **KAh-ID-**
INCITE **KEI-3**
INCLINE **KLEI-**
INCLUDE **KLEU-3**
INCREASE **KER-3**
INCUBATE **KEU-2**
INCUMBENT **KEU-2**
INDEMNITY **DAP-**
INDENT **DENT-**
INDEX **DEIK-**

LEEK **LEUG-1**
LEGAL **LEG-1**
LEGEND **LEG-1**
LEGIBLE **LEG-1**
LEGISLATOR **LEG-1, TELh-**
LEGITIMATE **LEG-1**
LEND **LEIKW-**
LENGTH **DEL-1**
LENT (religious) **DEL-1**
LESS **LEIS-2**
LET **LE-2**
LETTER **DEPH-**
LETTUCE **MELG-**
LEVEL **LITHRA**
LEVER **LEGWH-**
LIBERAL **LEUDH-2**
LIBERATE **LEUDH-2**
LIBERTINE **LEUDH-2**
LIBERTY **LEUDH-2**
LIBIDO **LEUBH-**
LICK **LEIGH-**
LICORICE **DLK-U-**
LID **KLEI-**
LIE (falsehood) **LEUGH-**
LIE (recline) **LEGH-**
LIEF **LEUBH-**
LIEN **LEIG-1**
LIEUTENANT **LOCUS, TEN-**
LIFE **LEIP-**
LIGHT (illumination)
  LEUK-
LIGHT (weight) **LEGWH-**
LIKE **LIK-**
LIKELY **LIK-**
LIKENESS **LIK-**
LIMP **LEB-1**
LINDEN **LENTO-**
LINE **LINO-**
LINEN **LINO-**
LINGER **DEL-1**
LINGERIE **LINO-**
LINGO **DNGHU-**

LINGUIST **DNGHU-**
LINIMENT **LEI-**
LINING **LINO-**
LINK **KLEI-**
LINOLEUM **LINO-**
LINSEED **LINO-**
LINT **LINO-**
LIP **LEB-2**
LIQUID **WLEIK-**
LIQUOR **WLEIK-**
LIST **LEIZD-**
LISTEN **KLEU-1**
LITER **LITHRA**
LITERAL **DEPH-**
LITERARY **DEPH-**
LITERATE **DEPH-**
LITHE **LENTO-**
LITRE **LITHRA**
LITTLE **LEUD-**
LIVE **LEIP-**
LIVELY **LEIP-**
LIVER **LEIP-**
LIVID **SLI-**
LOAD **LEIT-2**
LOAM **LEI-**
LOAN **LEIKW-**
LOATHE **LEIT-1**
LOBBY **LEUP-**
LOCAL **LOCUS**
LOCATE **LOCUS**
LOCH **LAKU-**
LOCK **LEUG-1**
LODGE **LEUP-**
LOFT **LEUP-**
LOGIC **LEG-1**
LOGY **SLEU-**
-LOGY **LEG-1**
LOIN **LENDH-1**
LONE **OI-NO-**
LONELY **OI-NO-**
LONG **DEL-1**
LOON (bird) **LA-**

LOOSE **LEU-1**
LOOT **REUP-**
LOPE **KLOU-**
LOQUACIOUS **TOLKW-**
LOSE **LEU-1**
LOSS **LEU-1**
LOT **KLEU-3**
LOTION **LEU(h)-**
LOTTERY **KLEU-3**
LOUD **KLEU-1**
LOUSE **LUS-**
LOVE **LEUBH-**
LOW **LEGH-**
LOX **LAKS-**
LOYAL **LEG-1**
LUBRICATE **SLEUBH-**
LUCID **LEUK-**
LUDICROUS **LEID-**
LULL **LA-**
LUMBAGO **LENDH-1**
LUMBER (gait) **LEM-1**
LUMINOUS **LEUK-**
LUMP **LEB-1**
LUNAR **LEUK-**
LUNATIC **LEUK-**
LUNG **LEGWH-**
LUNGE **DEL-1**
LUST **LAS-**
LUSTER **LEUK-**
LUXURY **LEUG-1**
-LY **LIK-**
LYE **LEU(h)-**

MACHINE **MAGH-1**
MACHO **MAS**
MAD **MEI-1**
MADAM **DEM(h)-**

MADONNA **DEM(h)-**
MAESTRO **MEG-**
MAGIC **MAGH-1**
MAGISTRATE **MEG-**
MAGNANIMOUS **MEG-,**
   ANh-
MAGNIFICENT **MEG-**
MAGNIFY **MEG-**
MAHARAJAH **MEG-**
MAID(EN) **MAGHU-**
MAIL **MOLKO-**
MAIM **MAI-1**
MAIN **MAGH-1**
MAINTAIN **MAN-2, TEN-**
MAJESTY **MEG-**
MAJOR **MEG-**
MAJORITY **MEG-**
MAKE **MAG-**
MAL- **MEL-5**
MALADY **MEL-5**
MALE **MAS**
MALEFACTOR **MEL-5, DHE-**
MALEVOLENT **MEL-5, WEL-2**
MALICE **MEL-5**
MALIGN **MEL-5, GEN(h)-**
MALLET **MELh**
MALT **MEL-1**
MAM(M)A **MA-2**
MAMMAL **MA-2**
MAN **MAN-1**
MANAGE **MAN-2**
MANE **MON-**
MANEUVER **MAN-2, OP-1**
MANGER **MENDH-2**
MANGLE **MAI-1**
MANIA **MEN-1**
MANICURE **MAN-2, CURA**
MANIFEST **MAN-2**
MANIPULATE **MAN-2**
MANNER **MAN-2**
MANOR **MEN-3**
MANSION **MEN-3**

MEGA- **MEG-**
MELANCHOLY **MEL-3,**
   GHEL-2
MÉLANGE **MEIK-**
MELODRAMA **MEL-3**
MELODY **MEL-1, WED-2**
MELON **MELON**
MELT **MEL-1**
MEMBER **MEMS-**
MEMORANDUM **(S)MER-1**
MEMORY **(S)MER-1**
MENACE **MEN-2**
MENARCHE **ME-2,**
   ARKHEIN
MEND **MEND-**
MENDACIOUS **MEND-**
MENOPAUSE **ME-2, PAUS-**
MENSTRUATE **ME-2**
MENTAL **MEN-1**
MENU **MEI-2**
MERCENARY **MERK-**
MERCHANDISE **MERK-**
MERCHANT **MERK-**
MERCURY **MERK-**
MERCY **MERK-**
MERE (lake, pond) **MORI-**
MERE (only) **MER-1**
MERGE **MEZG-1**
MERIDIAN **MEDHYO-**
MERIT **(S)MER-2**
MERRY **MREGH-U-**
MESH **MEZG-2**
MESS **(S)MEIT(h)-**
MESSAGE **(S)MEIT(h)-**
METALLURGY **WERG-**
-METER **ME-2**
METER **ME-2**
METHOD **SED-2**
METRE **ME-2**
METRO **MATER-**

METROPOLIS **MATER-,**
   PELh-3
MICRO- **SME-**
MICROBE **SME-, GWEI-**
MICROSCOPE **SME-, SPEK-**
MIDDLE **MEDHYO-**
MIDGE **MU-2**
MIGHT (strength) **MAGH-1**
MIGRATE **MEI-1**
MILD **MEL-1**
MILE **GHESLO-**
MILLENNIUM **GHESLO-, AT-**
MILK **MELG-**
MILL **MELh**
MILLI- **GHESLO-**
MIME **MIMOS**
MIMIC **MIMOS**
MINCE **MEI-2**
MIND **MEN-1**
MINE ("of me") **ME-1**
MINESTRONE **MEI-2**
MINGLE **MAG-**
MINISTER **MEI-2**
MINNOW **MEN-4**
MINOR **MEI-2**
MINT (coinage) **MEN-1**
MINUS **MEI-2**
MINUTE **MEI-2**
MIRACLE **SMEI-**
MIRE **MEU-**
MIRROR **SMEI-**
MIRTH **MREGH-U-**
MIS- **MEI-1, MEI-2**
MISCELLANEOUS **MEIK-**
MISCHIEF **KAPUT**
MISCREANT **KERD-**
MISER **MISER**
MISERABLE **MISER**
MISERY **MISER**
MISHAP **KOB-**
MISNOMER **NO-MEN-**

MISS (not hit) **MEI-1**
MISS (woman) **MEG-**
MISSILE **(S)MEIT(h)-**
MISSION **(S)MEIT(h)-**
MISSIVE **(S)MEIT(h)-**
MISSUS **MEG-**
MIST **MEIGH-**
MISTAKE **MEI-1**
MISTER **MEG-**
MISTRESS **MEG-**
MITE **MAI-1**
MITIGATE **MEI-**
MIX **MEIK-**
MIXTURE **MEIK-**
MOAN **MEI-NO-**
MOB **MEUh-**
MOBILE **MEUh-**
MODE **MED-**
MODEL **MED-**
MODERATE **MED-**
MODERN **MED-**
MODEST **MED-**
MODIFY **MED-, DHE-**
MOIST **MEUG-**
MOLAR **MELh**
MOLASSES **MELIT-**
MOLD (shape) **MED-**
MOLE (spot) **MAI-2**
MOLEST **MO-**
MOLLUSK **MEL-1**
MOLT **MEI-1**
MOM(MA) **MA-2**
MOMENT **MEUh-**
MOMENTUM **MEUh-**
MONARCHY **MEN-4, ARKHEIN**
MONASTERY **MEN-4**
MONDAY **ME-2**
MONEY **MEN-1**
-MONGER **MENG-**
MONGREL **MAG-**

MONK **MEN-4**
MONO- **MEN-4**
MONOPOLY **MEN-4, PEL-5**
MONSTER **MEN-1**
MONTH **ME-2**
MONUMENT **MEN-1**
MOOCH **MEUG-1**
MOOD **MED-**
MOON **ME-2**
MOOR (boat) **MER-3**
MOOR (wasteland) **MA-3**
MOP **MAPPA**
MORASS **MORI-**
MORBID **MER-2**
MORE **ME-3**
MORIBUND **MER-2**
MORNING **MER-1**
MORON **MO(U)RO-**
MORSEL **MER-2**
MORTAL **MER-2**
MORTAR **MER-2**
MORTGAGE **MER-2, WADH-1**
MORTIFY **MER-2**
MOSQUITO **MU-2**
MOSS **MEU-**
MOST **ME-3**
MOTH **MATH-**
MOTHER **MATER-**
MOTION **MEUh-**
MOTIVE **MEUh-**
MOTOR **MEUh-**
MOUNT(AIN) **MEN-2**
MOURN **(S)MER-1**
MOULD **MED-**
MOUSE **MUS-**
MOUTH **MEN-2**
MOW **ME-4**
MUCH **MEG-**
MUCILAGE **MEUG-**
MUCUS **MEUG-**

MUGGY **MEUG-**
MULTIPLE **MEL-4, PEL-3**
MULTITUDE **MEL-4**
MUM (mother) **MA-2**
MUM (silent) **MU-1**
MUMBLE **MU-1**
MUMPS **MU-1**
MUNICIPAL **MEI-1, KAP-**
MUNIFICENT **MEI-1**
MUNITION **MEI-2**
MURAL **MEI-2**
MURDER **MER-2**
MURK **MER-1**
MURMUR **MORMOR-**
MUSCLE **MUS-**
MUSEUM **MEN-1**
MUSIC **MEN-1**
MUSKET **MU-2**
MUST **MED-**
MUSTACHE **MENDH-2**
MUSTARD **MEU-**
MUTATE **MEI-1**
MUTE **MU-1**
MUTILATE **MUT-**
MUTTER **MU-1**
MUTTON **MEL-1**
MUTUAL **MEI-1**
MUZZLE **MUSUM**
MY(SELF) **ME-1**
MYSTERY **MU-1**
MYSTIC **MU-1**

NAG (annoy) **GHEN-**
NAIL **NOGH-**
NAIVE **GEN(h)-**
NAKED **NOGW-**

NAME **NO-MEN-**
NANNY **NANA**
NAP (sleep) **KEN-2**
NAPKIN **MAPPA**
NARCOTIC **(S)NER-**
NARRATE **GNO-**
NARROW **(S)NER-**
NASAL **NAS-**
NATION **GEN(h)-**
NATIVE **GEN(h)-**
NATURE **GEN(h)-**
NAUGHT(Y) **NE, WEKTI-**
NAUSEA **NAU-2**
-NAUT **NAU-2**
NAUTICAL **NAU-2**
NAVAL **NAU-2**
NAVEL **NOBH-**
NAVIGATE **NAU-2, AG-**
NAVY **NAU-2**
NEAR **NEHW-IZ**
NEAT **NEI-**
NEBULA **NEBH-**
NEBULOUS **NEBH-**
NECESSARY **KED-**
NECK **KEN-5**
NECTAR **NEK-1**
NEED **NAU-1**
NEEDLE **(S)NE-**
NEGATE **NE**
NEGATIVE **NE**
NEGLECT **NE**
NEGLIGEE **NE**
NEGOTIATE **NE**
NEGRO **NEGW-RO-**
NEIGHBOR **NEHW-IZ,**
 BHEU-
NEITHER **NE, KWO-**
NEMESIS **NEM-**
NEO- **NEWO-**
NEON **NEWO-**
NEPHEW **NEPOT-**

NUN **NANA**
NUPTIAL **SNEUBH-**
NURSE **(S)NAU-**
NUT **KEN-4**
NUTRIENT **(S)NAU-**
NUTRITIOUS **(S)NAU-**
NUZZLE **NAS-**

OAR **AIRO**
OAT **OID-**
OATH **OITO-**
OBESE **ED-**
OBEY **AU-2**
OBITUARY **EI-1**
OBJECT (oppose) **YE-**
OBLIGE **LEIG-1**
OBLITERATE **DEPH-**
OBLIVION **LEI-**
OBLONG **DEL-1**
OBNOXIOUS **NEK-1**
OBSERVE **SER-1**
OBSESS **SED-1**
OBSTACLE **STA-**
OBSTINATE **STE-**
OBSTREPEROUS **STREP-**
OBSTRUCT **STER-2**
OBSCURE **(S)KEU-**
OBTAIN **TEN-**
OBVIOUS **WEGH-**
OCCASION **KAD-**
OCCULT **KEL-2**
OCCUR **KERS-**
OCTAVE **OKTO(U)**
OCTOBER **OKTO(U)**
OCTOPUS **OKTO(U), PED-1**
ODD **US-**

ODOR **OD-1**
OF **(A)PO-**
OFF **(A)PO-**
OFFER **BHER-1**
OFFICE **DHE-**
OFTEN **UPO**
OIL **ELAIA**
OINTMENT **ONGW-**
OLD **AL-2**
OLIVE **ELAIA**
OMNIBUS **OP-1**
ON **AN-1**
ONCE **OI-NO-**
ONE **OI-NO-**
ONEROUS **EN-ES-**
ONLY **OI-NO-**
ONSLAUGHT **SLAK-**
ONUS **EN-ES-**
OOZE (noun) **WEIS-**
OOZE (verb) **WES-2**
OPEN **UPO**
OPERA **OP-1**
OPERATE **OP-1**
OPHTHALMO- **OKW-**
-OPIA **OKW-**
OPINION **OP-2**
OPIUM **S(W)OKWO-**
OPPORTUNE **PER-2**
OPPORTUNITY **PER-2**
OPPOSE **(A)PO-**
OPPRESS **PER-5**
OPTIC **OKW-**
OPTION **OP-2**
OPUS **OP-1**
ORAL **OS-**
ORATION **OR-**
ORATOR **OR-**
ORCHARD **GHER-1**
ORCHESTRA **ERGH-**
ORCHID **ERGH-**
ORDEAL **DAIL-**

QUADRILLE **KWETWER-**
QUAGMIRE **MEU-**
QUAINT **GNO-**
QUALITY **KWO-**
QUANTITY **KWO-**
QUARANTINE **KWETWER-**
QUARREL **KWES-**
QUARRY (stone)
   KWETWER-
QUART(ER) **KWETWER-**
QUAY **KAGH-**
QUEEN **GWEN-**
QUELL **GWEL-1**
QUERULOUS **KWES-**
QUERY **QUAERERE**
QUESTION **QUAERERE**
QUICHE **KAK-**
QUICK **GWEI-**
QUIET **KWEIh-2**
QUINTESSENCE **PENKWE**
QUINTET **PENKWE**
QUORUM **KWO-**
QUOTA **KWO-**
QUOTE **KWO-**

RABID **REBH-**
RACE (contest) **ERS-1**
RACK **REG-1**
RAUCOUS **REU-1**
RADICAL **WRAD-**
RADISH **WRAD-**
RAFT(ER) **REP-2**
RAG **REU-2**

RAGE **REBH-1**
RAID **REIDH-**
RAIN **REG-2**
RAIL **REG-1**
RAISE **REG-2**
RAJAH **REG-1**
RAKE **REG-1**
RALLY **LEIG-1**
RANCH **(S)KER-**
RANGE **(S)KER-**
RANK (position) **(S)KER-**
RANKLE **DERK-**
RANSACK **SAG-**
RANSOM **EM-**
RAPACIOUS **REP-**
RAPE **REP-**
RAPID **REP-**
RAPTURE **REP-**
RARE (meat) **KERh-**
RARE (uncommon) **ERh-2**
RASCAL **RED-**
RASH (skin) **RED-**
RAT **RED-**
RATE **AR-**
RATHER **KRET-**
RATION **AR-**
RATIONAL **AR-**
RAVEN **KER-2**
RAVISH **REP-**
RAW **KREUh-**
RAZE **RED-**
RE- **RE-1**
READ **AR-**
REACH **REIG-2**
READY **REIDH-**
REAL **RE-2**
REAP **REI-1**
REAR (back) **RE-1**
REAR (horse, etc.) **RISAN**
REASON **AR-**
REBEL **DUELLUM**
REBOUND **BAMB-**

REBUT **BHAU-**
RECEDE **KED-**
RECEIPT **KAP-**
RECEIVE **KAP-**
RECENT **KEN-3**
RECKLESS **REG-**
RECKON **REG-**
RECIPE **KAP-**
RECLAIM **KELh-2**
RECLINE **KLEI-**
RECOGNIZE **GNO-**
RECOIL **(S)KEU-**
RECOMMEND **MAN-2**
RECORD **KERD-**
RECOURSE **KERS-**
RECRUIT **KER-3**
RECTUM **REG-1**
RECUR **KERS-**
REDEEM **EM-**
RED **REUDH-1**
REDSTART **STER-1**
REDUCE **DEUK-**
REED **KREUT-**
REEF **REBH-2**
REEK **REUG-**
REEL(ING) **KREK-1**
REFER **BHER-1**
REFLECT **PLEK-**
REFRACT **BHREG-**
REFRAIN (song) **BHREG-**
REFRAIN (not do)
    GHRENDH-
REFRIGERATE **SRIG-**
REFUGE **BHEUG-1**
REFUND **GHEU-**
REFUSE **GHEU-**
REGAL **REG-1**
REGIME **REG-1**
REGIMENT **REG-1**
REGULATE **REG-1**
REGULAR **REG-1**
REGION **REG-1**

REGISTER **GERERE**
REGRESS **GHREDH-**
REIGN **REG-1**
REIMBURSE **BURSA**
REINDEER **KER-1**
REINFORCE **BHERGH-2**
REJECT **YE-**
REJOICE **GAU-**
REJUVENATE **YEU-**
RELAPSE **LEB-1**
RELATE **TELh-**
RELAX **SLEG-**
RELENT **LENTO-**
RELEASE **SLEG-**
RELIEVE **LEGWH-**
RELINQUISH **LEIKW-**
RELUCTANT **LEUG-1**
RELY **LEIG-1**
REMEDY **MED-**
REMEMBER **(S)MER-1**
REMIND **MEN-1**
REMINISCE **MEN-1**
REMIT **(S)MEIT(h)-**
REMORSE **MER-2**
REMOTE **MEUh-**
REMOVE **MEUh-**
REMUNERATE **MEI-1**
RENAISSANCE **GEN(h)-**
REND **RENDH-**
RENDER **DO-**
RENEGADE **NE**
RENEGE **NE**
RENEW **NEU-1**
RENOUNCE **NEU-1**
RENOVATE **NEWO-**
RENOWN **NO-MEN-**
RENT **DO-**
REPAIR (fix) **PERh-1**
REPAST **PA-**
REPEAT **PET(h)-**
REPLENISH **PELh-1**
REPOSE **PAUS-**

ROOT (dig up) **WROD-**
ROOT (of plant) **WRAD-**
ROPE **REI-1**
ROSE (flower) **WROD-**
ROSEMARY **ERS-2**
ROTARY **RET-**
ROTATE **RET-**
ROUGE **REUDh-**
ROUGH **RUKh-**
ROUND **RET-**
ROULETTE **RET-**
ROW (arrangement) **REI-1**
ROW (boat) **ERh-1**
ROWAN **REUDH-1**
ROYAL **REG-1**
RUBY **REUDH-1**
RUDDER **ERh-1**
RUDDY **REUDH-1**
RUFFLE **KREUP-**
RUIN **REU-2**
RULE **REG-1**
RUMPLE **(S)KERBH-**
RUMOR **REU-1**
RUN **REI-3**
RUPTURE **REUP-**
RURAL **REUh-**
RUSSET **REUDH-1**
RUST **REUDH-1**
RUSTIC **REUh-**
RYE **WRUGHYO-**

SACRED **SAK-**
SACRIFICE **SAK-, DHE-**
SACRILEGE **SAK-, LEG-1**
SAD **SA-**
SADDLE **SED-1**
SAFE **SOL-**

SAG **SENGW-**
SAGE (herb) **SOL-**
SAGE (wise) **SEP-**
SAINT **SAK-**
SAKE **SAG-**
SALACIOUS **SEL-4**
SALAD **SAL-1**
SALAMI **SAL-1**
SALARY **SAL-1**
SALE **SEL-3**
SALIENT **SEL-4**
SALINE **SAL-1**
SALLOW **SAL-2**
SALMON **SEL-4**
SALON **SEL-1**
SALOON **SEL-1**
SALSA **SAL-1**
SALT **SAL-1**
SALUTE **SOL-**
SALVE **SELP-**
SAME **SEM-1**
SAMIZDAT **SEM-1, DO-**
SAMPLE **EM-**
SANCTIFY **SAK-**
SAND **BHES-1**
SANE **SANO-**
SANITARY **SANO-**
SAP (plants) **SAB-**
SARDONIC **SWARD-**
SATE **SA-**
SATIRE **SA-**
SATISFY **SA-**
SATURATE **SA-**
SAUCE **SAL-1**
SAUERKRAUT **SURO-**
SAUSAGE **SAL-1**
SAUTÉ **SEL-4**
SAVE **SOL-**
SAVOR **SEP-**
SAVVY **SEP-**
SAW (tool) **SEK-**
SAY **SEKW-3**

SHUFFLE **SKEUBH-**
SHUT **SKEUD-**
SHUTTLE **SKEUD-**
SIBLING **S(W)E-**
SICKLE **SEK-**
SIDE **SE-2**
SIEGE **SED-1**
SIEVE **SEIB-**
SIFT **SEIB-**
SIGHT **SEKW-2**
SIGN **SEKW-1**
SIGNAL **SEKW-1**
SIGNATURE **SEKW-1**
SILENT **SI-LO-**
SILL **SWEL-3**
SILLY **SEL-2**
SILT **SAL-1**
SIMILAR **SEM-1**
SIMPLE **SEM-1**
SIMULTANEOUS **SEM-1**
SIN **ES-**
SINCE **SE-2**
SINCERE **KER-3**
SINECURE **SEN-2, CURA**
SINEW **SE-3**
SING **SENGWH-**
SINGE **SENK-**
SINGLE **SEM-1**
SINK **SENGW-**
SIP **SEUh-2**
SIR(E) **SEN-1**
SIRLOIN **UPER, LENDH-1**
SISTER **SWESOR-**
SIT **SED-1**
SITE **TKEI-**
SITUATION **TKEI-**
SIX **S(W)EKS**
SKELETON **SKELh-**
SKEPTIC **SPEK-**
SKI **SKEI-**
SKIFF **SKIPAM**

SKILL **SKEL-1**
SKIN **SEK-**
SKIPPER **SKIPAM**
SKIRMISH **SKER-1**
SHIRT **SKER-1**
SKOAL **SKEL-1**
SKY **(S)KEU-**
SLACK **SLEG-**
SLAM **LEB-1**
SLAP **LEB-1**
SLAUGHTER **SLAK-**
SLAVE **SERVUS**
SLAY **SLAK-**
SLED **SLEIDH-**
SLEDGE (vehicle) **SLEIDH-**
SLEDGE (hammer) **SLAK-**
SLEEP **SLEB-**
SLEET **SLEU-**
SLEEVE **SLEUBH-**
SLEIGH **SLEIDH-**
SLEW (many) **SLOUG-**
SLICK **LEI-**
SLIDE **SLEIDH-**
SLIGHT **LEI-**
SLIME **LEI-**
SLING **SLENGWH-**
SLIP **LEI-**
SLIPPERY **LEI-**
SLIVOVITZ **SLI-**
SLOB **LEB-1**
SLOGAN **SLOUG-, GAR-**
SLOOP **SLEUBH-**
SLOP(PY) **SLEUBH-**
SLUG **SLEU-**
SLUGGISH **SLEU-**
SLUMBER **SLEU-**
SLUMP **LEB-1**
SLURP **SREBH-**
SLUSH **SLEU-**
SLY **SLAK-**
SMACK **SMEG-**

SMALL **MELO-**
SMART **SMERD-**
SMEAR **(S)MER-3**
SMILE **SMEI-**
SMIRK **SMEI-**
SMITH **SMI-**
SMOCK **MEUG-**
*SMOKE **SMEUG-**
SMORGASBORD **BHERDH-**
SMUG **MEUG-2**
SMUGGLE **MEUG-2**
SHACK **SNU-**
SNAIL **SNEG-**
SNAKE **SNEG-**
SNAP **SNU-**
SNARE **(S)NER-**
SNARL (dog) **SNER-**
SNATCH **SNU-**
SNEER **SNER-**
SNEEZE **PNEU-**
SNIFF(LE) **SNU-**
SNIP **SNU-**
SNIVEL **SNU-**
SNOOP **SNU-**
SNORE **SNER-**
SNORKEL **SNER-**
SNORT **SNER-**
SNOT **SNU-**
SNOUT **SNU-**
SNOW **SNEIGWH-**
SNUB **SNU-**
SNUFF **SNU-**
SOAK **SEUh-2**
SOAP **SEIB-**
SOBER **EGWH-**
SOCIABLE **SEKW-1**
SOCIAL **SEKW-1**
SOCIETY **SEKW-1**
SOCKET **SU-**
SODDEN **SEUT-**
SOIL **SU-**

SOLACE **SEL-2**
SOLAR **SAWEL-**
SOLE (foot) **SEL-1**
SOLE (only) **S(W)E-**
SOLEMN **SOL-**
SOLICIT **SOL-**
SOLICITOR **SOL-**
SOLID **SOL-**
SOLILOQUY **TOLKW-**
SOLITARY **S(W)E-**
SOLITUDE **S(W)E-**
SOLO **S(W)E-**
SOLSTICE **SAWEL-, STA-**
SOLUBLE **LEU-1**
SOLUTION **LEU-1**
SOLVE **LEU-1**
SOME **SEM-1**
SOMERSAULT **UPER, SEL-4**
SON **SEUh-1**
SONATA **SWEN-**
SONG **SENGWH-**
SOOT **SED-1**
SOOTHE **ES-**
SOP **SEUh-2**
SOPORIFIC **SWEP-1**
SOPRANO **UPER**
SORCERER **SER-2**
SORDID **SWORDO-**
SORE **SAI-**
SORORITY **SWESOR-**
SORROW **SWERGH-**
SORRY **SAI-**
SORT **SER-2**
SOUFFLÉ **BHLE-2**
SOUND (hearing) **SWEN-**
SOUND (undamaged)
 SWENTO-
SOUND (water) **SWEM-**
SOUP **SEUh-2**
SOUR **SURO-**
SOUSE **SAL-1**

SOUTH **SAWEL-**
SOUVENIR **GWA-**
SOVEREIGN **UPER**
SOVIET **SEM-1**
SOW (pig) **SU-**
SOW (seed) **SE-1**
SPADE **SPE-2**
SPAN **(S)PEN-**
SPARERIBS **SPER-1**
SPARROW **SPER-3**
SPARSE **(S)PREG-**
SPATULA **SPE-2**
SPEAK **SPREG-**
SPEAR **SPER-1**
SPECIAL **SPEK-**
SPECIES **SPEK-**
SPECIFIC **SPEK-**
SPECIMEN **SPEK-**
SPECTACLE **SPEK-**
SPECULATE **SPEK-**
SPEECH **SPREG-**
SPEED **SPE-1**
SPELL **SPEL-3**
SPERM **SPER-4**
SPEW **SP(Y)EU-**
SPICE **SPEK-**
SPIDER **(S)PEN-**
SPIEL **SPEL-3**
SPIKE **SPEI-**
SPILL **SPEL-1**
SPIN **(S)PEN-**
SPINE **SPEI-**
SPIRAL **SPER-2**
SPIRE **SPEI-**
SPIRIT **SPIRARE**
SPIT (expectorate)
  SP(Y)EU-
SPIT (for roasting) **SPEI-**
SPLEEN **SPEIGH-**
SPLENDID **SPEL-2**
SPLICE **SPLEI-**

SPLINT **SPLEI-**
SPLINTER **SPLEI-**
SPLIT **SPLEI-**
SPOIL **SPEL-1**
SPOKE (wheel) **SPEI-**
SPONSOR **SPEND-**
SPONTANEOUS **SPEND-**
SPOON **SPE-2**
SPORADIC **SPER-4**
SPOUSE **SPEND-**
SPOUT **SP(Y)EU-**
SPRAWL **SPER-4**
SPREAD **SPER-4**
SPREE **GHE(N)D-**
SPRING **SPERGH-**
SPRINKLE **(S)PREG-**
SPROUT **SPER-4**
SPUR **SPERh-**
SPURN **SPERh-**
SPURT **SPER-4**
SPUTTER **SP(Y)EU-**
SPY **SPEK-**
SQUAD **KWETWER-**
SQUARE **KWETWER-**
SQUASH (mash) **KWET-**
SQUAT **AG-**
SQUIRREL **SKEhI-, ORS-**
STACK **STEG-**
STAFF **STEBH-**
STAG **STEGH-**
STAGE **STA-**
STAGGER **STEG-**
STAGNANT **STAG-**
STAIN **TENG-**
STAIR **STEIGH-**
STAKE (post) **STEG-**
STALK (move stealthily)
  STER-4
STALK (stem) **STEL-**
STALL **STEL-**
STALLION **STEL-**

STALWART **WER-3**
STAMMER **STAM-**
STAMP **STEBH-**
STAMPEDE **STEBH-**
STAND(ARD) **STA-**
STAPLE **STEBH-**
STAR **STER-3**
STARBOARD **STA-,**
  BHERDH-
STARCH **STER-1**
STARK **STER-1**
STARLING **STORO-**
START **STER-1**
STARTLE **STER-1**
STARVE **STER-1**
STASIS **STA-**
STATE **STA-**
STATIC **STA-**
STATUE **STA-**
STATURE **STA-**
STATUS **STA-**
STATUTE **STA-**
STAY (remain) **STA-**
STAY (support) **STAK-**
STEADFAST **PAST-**
STEAK **STEIG-**
STEAL **STER-4**
STEALTH **STER-4**
STEED **STA-**
STEEL **STAK-**
STEEP (precipitous)
  (S)TEU-
STEEPLE **(S)TEU-**
STEER (all senses) **STA-**
STEIN **STEI-**
STELLAR **STER-3**
STEM (plants) **STA-**
STENCIL **SKEh-**
STEP **STEBH-**
STEP- **(S)TEU-**
STERILE **STER-5**

STERN (severe) **STER-1**
STERN (ship) **STA-**
STEVEDORE **STEIP-**
STEWARD **WER-4**
STICK **STEIG-**
STIFF **STEIP-**
STILL (quiet) **STEL-**
STING **STEGH-**
STIR **TWER-1**
STIRRUP **STEIGH-**
STITCH **STEIG-**
STOCK **(S)TEU-**
STOKER **(S)TEU-**
STOLID **STEL-**
STOMACH **STh-MEN-**
STONE **STEI-**
STOOL **STA-**
STOOP (bend) **(S)TEU-**
STOOP (porch) **STEBH-**
STOP **STEU(h)-**
STORE **STA-**
STORK **STER-1**
STORM **TWER-1**
STORY (tale) **WEID-**
STOUT **STEL-**
STOVE **STAUP-**
STRAIN (stress) **STREIG-**
STRANGE(R) **EGHS**
STRANGLE **STRENK-**
STRATEGY **STER-2, AG-**
STRAW **STER-2**
STREAK **STREIG-**
STREAM **SREU-**
STREET **STER-2**
STRENGTH **STRENK-**
STREW **STER-2**
STRICT **STREIG-**
STRIKE **STREIG-**
STRING **STRENK-**
STROKE **STREIG-**
STRONG **STRENK-**

TRANQUIL **KWEIh-2**
TRANS- **TERh-2**
TRANSACTION **AG-**
TRANSCEND **SKAND-**
TRANSCRIBE **SKRIBH-**
TRANSFER **BHER-1**
TRANSFUSE **GHEU-**
TRANSGRESS **GHREDH-**
TRANSIENT **EI-1**
TRANSIT **EI-1**
TRANSITIVE **EI-1**
TRANSLATE **TELh-**
TRANSLUCENT **LEUK-**
TRANSMIT **(S)MEIT(h)-**
TRAP **DER-1**
TRAUMA **TERh-1**
TRAVEL **PAG-**
TRAVESTY **WES-4**
TRAY **DERU-**
TREAD **DER-1**
TREAT **TRAGH-**
TREATY **TRAGH-**
TREASON **DO-**
TREE **DERU-**
TREMBLE **TREM-**
TREMENDOUS **TREM-**
TREMOR **TREM-**
TRENCH **TERh-2**
TRIDENT **DENT-**
TRIM **DERU-**
TRINITY **TREI-**
TRIO **TREI-**
TRIP **DER-1**
TRIPLE **TREI-, PEL-3**
TRIPOD **PED-1**
TRITE **TERh-1**
TRIVIAL **WEGH-**
TROPIC **TREP-2**
TROT **DER-1**
TROUBLE **TWER-1**
TROUGH **DERU-**
TRUANT **TERh-1**

TRUCE **DERU-**
TRUE **DERU-**
TRUFFLE **TEU(h)-**
TRUNCATE **TERh-2**
TRUNK **TERh-2**
TRUST **DERU-**
TUBER **TEU(h)-**
TUESDAY **DEIW-**
TUFT **TAP-**
TUG **DEUK-**
TUITION **TEU-**
TUMOR **TEU(h)-**
TURBID **TWER-1**
TURBINE **TWER-1**
TURD **DER-2**
TURF **DERBH-**
TURN **TERh-1**
TUSK **DENT-**
TUTOR **TEU-**
TWEAK **TWIK-**
TWEED **DWO-**
TWELVE **DWO-**
TWENTY **DWO-, DEKM-**
TWICE **DWO-**
TWIG **DWO-**
TWILIGHT **DWO-**
TWILL **DWO-**
TWIN **DWO-**
TWINE **DWO-**
TWIST **DWO-**
TWITCH **TWIK-**
TWO **DWO-**
TYPE **(S)TEU-**

UDDER **EUhDH-**
ULCER **ELK-ES-**
ULTERIOR **AL-1**

VENUS **WEN-1**
VERB **WER-6**
VERDANT **VIRERE**
VERDICT **WERO-, DEIK-**
VERIFY **WERO-**
VERMICELLI **WER-3**
VERMIN **WER-3**
VERSATILE **WER-3**
VERSE **WER-3**
VERSION **WER-3**
VERSUS **WER-3**
VERTEBRA **WER-3**
VERY **WERO-**
VEST **WES-4**
VETERAN **WET-2**
VEX **WEGH-**
VIA **WEGH-**
VIADUCT **WEGH-**
VIBRATE **WEIP-**
VICE **WEI-4**
VICE- **WEIK-3**
VICINITY **WEIK-1**
VICIOUS **WEI-4**
VICTIM **WEIK-2**
VICTOR **WEIK-5**
VICTUAL **GWEI-**
VIEW **WEID-**
VIGILANT(E) **WEG-2**
VIGOR **WEG-2**
VILLAGE **WEIK-1**
VILLAIN **WEIK-1**
VINDICATE **DEIK-**
VINE **W(O)IN-**
VINEGAR **W(O)IN-, AK-**
VINTAGE **EM-**
VIOLATE **WEIh-**
VIOLENT **WEIh-**
VIRILE **WI-RO-**
VIRTUE **WI-RO-**
VIRUS **WEIS-**
VISCOUS **WEIS-**

VISE **WEI-1**
VISION **WEID-**
VISTA **WEID-**
VITAL **GWEI-**
VITAMIN **GWEI-**
VIVACIOUS **GWEI-**
VIVID **GWEI-**
VIXEN **PUK-**
VOCAL **WEKW-**
VOCATION **WEKW-**
VODKA **WED-1**
VOICE **WEKW-**
VOID **EU-**
VOLATILE **GWEL-2**
VOLITION **WEL-1**
VOLLEY **GWEL-2**
VOLUME **WEL-2**
VOLUNTARY **WEL-1**
VOMIT **WEMh-**
VOTE **WEGWH-**
VOW **WEGWH-**
VOWEL **WEKW-**
VOYAGE **WEGH-**
VOYEUR **WEID-**
VULNERABLE **WELh-2**
VULTURE **GWLTUR-**

WADE **WADH-2**
WOE **WAI-**
WAFER **WEBH-**
WAFFLE **WEBH-**
WAG **WEGH-**
WAGE (salary) **WADH-1**
WAGER **WADH-1**
WAGON **WEGH-**
WAIL **WAI**

WAIT **WEG-2**
WAKE **WEG-2**
WALK **WEL-2**
WALL **WALSO-**
WALLOW **WEL-2**
WALNUT **UOLCAE**
WALTZ **WEL-2**
WANDER **WENDH-**
WANE **EU-**
WANT **EU-**
WAR **WERS-1**
-WARD **WER-3**
WARDEN **WER-4**
WARDROBE **WER-4**
WARN **WER-4**
WARP **WER-3**
WARRANT **WER-5**
WART **WER-1**
WARY **WER-4**
WAS **WES-3**
WASH **WED-1**
WASP **WOPSO-**
WASTE **EU-**
WATCH **WEG-2**
WATER **WED-1**
WAVE **WEBH-**
WAX **WOKSO-**
WAY **WEGH-**
WAYFARER **WEGH-, PER-2**
WE **WE-1**
WEAK **WEIK-4**
WEALTH **WEL-1**
WEAPON **WEPNAM**
WEAR **WES-4**
WEASEL **WEIS-**
WEATHER **WE-2**
WEAVE **WEBH-**
WEB **WEBH-**
WED **WADH-1**
WEDGE **WOGWH-NI-**
WEDNESDAY **WET-1**

WEEP **WAB-**
WEEK **WEIK-3**
WEEVIL **WEBH-**
WEIGH **WEGH-**
WEIGHT **WEGH-**
WEIRD **WER-3**
WELCOME **GWA-**
WELFARE **PER-2**
WELL (healthy) **WEL-2**
WELL (water) **WEL-2**
WELSH **UOLCAE**
WERE **WES-3**
WEREWOLF **WI-RO-**
WEST **WES-PERO-**
WET **WED-1**
WHALE **(S)KW-AL-O-**
WHARF **KWERP-**
WHAT **KWO-**
WHEAT **KWEIT-**
WHEEL **KWEL-1**
WHEEZE **KWES-**
WHEN **KWO-**
WHERE **KWO-**
WHET **KWED-**
WHETHER **KWO-**
WHICH **KWO-**
WHILE **KWEIh-2**
WHINE **KWEI-**
WHIP **WEIP-**
WHIRL **KWERP-**
WHISKEY **WED-1**
WHISPER **KWEI-**
WHISTLE **KWEI-**
WHITE **KWEIT-**
WHITHER **KWO-**
WHO **KWO-**
WHOLE **KAILO-**
WHOLESOME **KAILO-**
WHOM **KWO-**
WHORE **KA-**
WHOSE **KWO-**

WICKER **WEIK-3**
WIDE **WI-**
WIDOW **WEIDH-**
WIELD **WAL-**
WIFE **WYF**
WIGGLE **WEGH-**
WILD **WELT-**
WILDERNESS **WELT-**
WILL **WEL-1**
WILLOW **WEL-2**
WIN **WEN-1**
WINCE **WENG-**
WINCH **WENG-**
WIND (air) **WE-2**
WIND (turn) **WENDH-**
WINDLASS **WENDH-**
WINDOW **WE-2, OKW-**
WINE **W(O)IN-**
WING **WE-2**
WINK **WENG-**
WINTER **WED-1**
WIPE **WEIP-**
WIRE **WEI-1**
WISDOM **WEID-**
WISE **WEID-**
-WISE **WEID-**
WISH **WEN-1**
WIT **WEID-**
WITCH **WEIK-2**
WITH **WI-**
WIZENED **WEI-3**
WOBBLE **WEBH-**
WOE **WAI**
WOLF **WLKWO-**
WOMAN **WYF, MAN-1**
WOOD **WIDHU-**
WOOL **WELh-1**
WORD **WER-6**
WORK **WERG-**
WORLD **WI-RO-**
WORM **WER-3**

WORRY **WER-3**
WORSE **WERS-1**
WORST **WERS-1**
WORTH **WER-3**
WOUND (injure) **WEN-2**
WRANGLE **WER-3**
WRAP **WER-3**
WRATH **WER-3**
WREATH **WER-3**
WRECK **WREG-**
WRENCH **WER-3**
WRESTLE **WER-3**
WRETCH **WREG-**
WRIGGLE **WER-3**
WRING **WER-3**
WRINKLE **WER-3**
WRIST **WER-3**
WRITHE **WER-3**
WRONG **WER-3**
WROUGHT **WERG-**
WURST **WERS-1**

XEROGRAPHY **KSERO-**
XEROX **KSERO-**

YARD (enclosure) **GHER-1**
YARD (three feet) **GHASTO-**
YARN **GHERh-**
YAWN **GHAI-**
YEAR **YER-**

YEARN **GHER-**
YEAST **YES-**
YELL **GHEL-1**
YELLOW **GHEL-2**
YELP **GHEL-1**
YES **I-, ES-**
YESTERDAY **DHGH(Y)ES-**
YET **I-**
YEW **EI-2**
YIELD **GHELDH-**
YOKE **YEUG-**
YONDER **I-**

YOU **YU-1**
YOUNG **YEU-**
YOUTH **YEU-**

ZEAL **YA-**
ZONE **YOS-**
ZOO(-) **GWEI-**